Film in African Literature Today 28

African Literature Today

1-14 were published from London by Heinemann Educational Books and from New York by Africana Publishing Company

Editor: Eldred Durosimi Jones

1, 2, 3, and 4 Omnibus Edition
5 The Novel in Africa
6 Poetry in Africa
7 Focus on Criticism
8 Drama in Africa
9 Africa, America & the Caribbean
10 Retrospect & Prospect
11 Myth & History

Editor: Eldred Durosimi Jones
Associate Editor: Eustace Palmer
Assistant Editor: Marjorie Jones

12 New Writing, New Approaches
13 Recent Trends in the Novel
14 Insiders & Outsiders

Backlist titles available in the US and Canada from Africa World Press and in the rest of the world from James Currey, an imprint of Boydell and Brewer

ALT 15 Women in African Literature Today
ALT 16 Oral & Written Poetry in African Literature Today
ALT 17 The Question of Language in African Literature Today
ALT 18 Orature in African Literature Today
ALT 19 Critical Theory & African Literature Today
ALT 20 New Trends & Generations in African Literature
ALT 21 Childhood in African Literature
ALT 22 Exile & African Literature
ALT 23 South & Southern African Literature
ALT 24 New Women's Writing in African Literature
ALT 25 New Directions in African Literature

Note from the publisher on new and forthcoming titles

James Currey Publishers have now joined Boydell & Brewer Ltd. *African Literature Today* will continue to be published as an annual volume under the James Currey imprint. North and South American distribution will be available from The University of Rochester Press, 68 Mount Hope Avenue, Rochester, NY 14620-2731, USA, while UK and International distribution will be handled by Boydell & Brewer Ltd., PO Box 9, Woodbridge IP12 3DF, UK.

ALT 26 War in African Literature Today
ALT 27 New Novels in African Literature Today
ALT 28 Film in African Literature Today

Call for papers

ALT 29 Teaching African Literature Today*

The issue will focus on experiences of teaching African Literature. Submissions can be on 1) Theoretical /pedagogical issues; 2) Productive teaching innovations; 3) Research reports on the teaching of African Literature; 4) Teaching African Literature across racial/cultural/national boundaries; 5) Problems of teaching African Literature in specific cultural/geographical areas; 6) Problems of teaching specific works/genres; 7) Student responses to African Literature
8) Teaching African Literature on-line – problems and prospects; 9) Teaching African Literature in an era of technology.

Guidelines for Submission of Articles

The Editor invites submission of articles or proposals for articles on the announced themes of forthcoming issues:

Ernest N. Emenyonu, *African Literature Today*
Department of Africana Studies, University of Michigan-Flint
303 East Kearsley Street, Flint MI 48502, USA
email: eernest@umflint.edu
Fax: 001 810 766 6719

Submissions will be acknowledged promptly and decisions communicated within six months of the receipt of the paper. Your name and institutional affiliation (with full mailing address and email) should appear on a separate sheet, plus a brief biographical profile of not more than six lines. The editor cannot undertake to return material submitted and contributors are advised to keep a copy of all material sent. Please note that all articles outside the announced themes cannot be considered or acknowledged and that articles should not be submitted via email. Articles should be submitted in the English language.

Length: articles should not exceed 5,000 words

Format: two hard copies plus disk of all articles should be submitted, double-spaced, on one side only of A4 paper, with pages numbered consecutively. Disks may be formatted for PC or AppleMac but please label all files and disks clearly, and save files as Word for Windows or Word for Macintosh.

Style: UK or US spellings, but be consistent. Direct quotations should retain the spelling used in the original source. Check the accuracy of your citations and always give the source, date, and page number in the text and a full reference in the Works Cited at the end of the article. Italicise titles of books or plays. Use single inverted commas throughout except for quotes within quotes which are double. Avoid subtitles or subsection headings within the text.

References: to follow series style (Surname date: page number) in brackets in text. All references/works cited should be listed in full at the end of each article, in the following style:
Surname, name/initial. *title of work.* place, publisher, date
Surname, name/initial. 'title of article'. In surname, name/initial (ed.) *title of work.* place of publication, publisher, date
or Surname, name/initial, 'title of article', *Journal*, vol. no.: page no.

Copyright: it is the responsibility of contributors to clear permissions

Reviewers should provide full bibliographic details, including the extent, ISBN and price, and submit to the reviews editor
James Gibbs, 8 Victoria Square, Bristol BS8 4ET, UK
jamesgibbs@btinternet.com

Film in
African Literature Today
28

A Review

JAMES CURREY
HEBN

James Currey
is an imprint of Boydell & Brewer Ltd
PO Box 9, Woodbridge, Suffolk, IP12 3DF, UK
and of Boydell & Brewer Inc.
668 Mt Hope Avenue, Rochester, NY 14620, USA
www.boydellandbrewer.com
www.jamescurrey.com

HEBN Publishers Plc
1 Ighodaro Rd, Jericho
P.M.B. 5205, Ibadan, Nigeria
www.hebnpublishers.com

First published 2010

1 2 3 4 5 13 12 11 10

British Library Cataloguing in Publication Data
Film and African literature today. — (African literature today ; v. 28)
1. African literature (English)—20th century—History and criticism. 2. African literature (English)—21st century—History and criticism. 3. Motion pictures and literature—Africa. 4. African literature—Film adaptations. 5. African literature (English)—Film adaptations.
I. Series II. Emenyonu, Ernest, 1939-
820.9'96'09045-dc22

ISBN: 978-1-84701-510-5 (James Currey paper)
ISBN 978-978-081-404-5 (HEBN paper)

Typeset in 9/11 pt Melior by Long House Publishing Services, Cumbria, UK
Printed and bound in Great Britain
by CPI Antony Rowe, Chippenham, Wiltshire

Contents

Notes on Contributors

Moradewun Adejunmobi teaches in the Department of African American and African Studies, University of California.

Africanus Aveh teaches in the School of Performing Arts, University of Ghana.

Aje-Ori Agbese teaches in the Department of Communication, University of Texas – Pan-African.

Raphael Obinna Amalaha teaches in the Department of Economics, University of Economics, University of Nigeria, Nsukka

Joyce Ashuntantang teaches English at Hillyer College, University of Hartford.

Ignatius Chukwumah teaches in the Department of English and Literary Studies, University of Nigeria, Nsukka.

MaryEllen (Ellie) Higgins is an Associate Professor of English at the Great Allegheny campus of Pennsylvania State University.

Timothy Johns is with the New York University.

David Riep is with the Department of Art and Art History, University of Iowa.

Kwawisi Tekpetey is a Professor of International Languages and Literatures at Central State University, Ohio.

Greg Thomas teaches in the Department of English, Syracuse University.

Editorial Article
The Interface Between Film & Literature in Contemporary African Writing & Imagination

Ernest N. Emenyonu

> In spite of the success Nigerian Literature has made over the years, Nollywood has till date, maintained a respectable distance from it. Very few works of Literature are made into films... Why has Nollywood not embraced this format in order to tap into the huge audience Nigerian Literature already has? (Ajeluorou 2010)

Anote Ajeluorou's article 'Literature ... resource still ignored by Nollywood' (*The Guardian,* Lagos, Nigeria, April 15, 2010), is a pertinent statement which underscores a critical issue of concern in contemporary African intellectual and cultural development. Although filmmaking and the film industry have evolved and made significant progress in varying degrees in some African countries, notably Algeria, Cameroon, Egypt, Ghana, Ivory Coast, Morocco, Nigeria, Senegal and South Africa, neither the industry nor the entrepreneurs have shown visible interest in the conventional 'romance' between films and literature, or an appreciation of the fact that African literary works could be a fertile source for the generation of African films, more so when works of creative imaginations by Africans have won worldwide acclaim and accolades dating back to the middle of the twentieth century. In particular, many African novels and plays have been distinguished for their complex, intriguing and edifying themes and plots which would make great and exciting movies if adapted into films. One reason proffered in Ajeluorou's article for the indifference shown by filmmakers to African literary works was that although 'films have a long romance with literature', in the case of Nigeria the non-tapping into creative works is because 'the origin of Nollywood is from the market and not from the literary, dramatic world ... and the financiers of the industry see it as commodity business and not a creative one.'

Elsewhere, under normal circumstances, film makers would go after authors or publishers of exceptional creative works for adaptations into motion pictures. There are many advantages – educational, cultural, intellectual, commercial – that would accrue from adapting popular works of fiction into films. In the African situation, in addition to all these advantages, the film versions would popularize the creative works, and also act as a catalyst for the improvement of the reading culture (which in some countries is either non-existent or abysmally low), as well as stimulate interest in literary studies, and afford teachers the opportunity to use technology to enhance or reinforce their classroom methodologies when they add films or power point presentations to their pedagogical resources. Yet the indifference remains unchanged and there is no sign that things will change in a foreseeable future.

It cannot be said that Africans are not excited by movies as a pastime. Nor is it correct that financial returns would not justify such ventures in the film industry. It is worth repeating that a large number of African literary works from all regions of the continent have achieved global fame and are used at various levels of educational systems inside and outside Africa. That fact alone saves an investor the task of feasibility studies about viability, supply and demand. The issue then shifts to a number of pertinent and salient questions: Are there African filmmakers talented and equipped enough to undertake the venture? What is the nature/status of the film industry today in Africa? What will be the incentives for foreign filmmakers and companies to come to Africa and undertake special filmmaking tasks? There are antecedents that may shed light on possible answers to these questions.

One of the most popular and widely discussed African novels of the twentieth century is Cyprian Ekwensi's *Jagua Nana* published by Hutchinson & Co., London in 1961, a year after Nigerian Independence on 1 October 1960. The global popularity of the novel was such that in the same year of its publication, a consortium of five international film companies – British Lion, Lux Film, Ultra Films, Delphia Film, and Jacob (international) of Germany – acquired the filming rights of the novel. In order that the film version should be Nigerian in background as in the novel itself, the representative company (Ultra Films of Italy) approached the Nigerian government for 'facilities' (mainly hospitality for the crew and technical services to be provided by the Film Unit of the Federal Ministry of Information). The government agreed that the company could be given permission to produce the film in Nigeria, 'provided the country would not be portrayed in an unfavourable light and provided also that the film, when produced, would be censored before the company left the country.' The government argued that those conditions were necessary because 'the film was not going to be a "prestige" film on Nigeria.'

Public opinion on the matter was sharply divided and the controversy was inflated out of proportion into an issue of national importance. Organized and mobilized opinions came out strongly against the filming of the novel. Women's groups and some church organizations maintained that the book reflected Nigerian womanhood unfavourably and would undermine the character and morals of Nigerian youth. On the other hand, there were members of the public and some intellectuals who fully supported the filming of the book, because 'with the whole of Africa becoming more art conscious, the making of this film could inspire writers and artists, producers and film directors to greater heights of creativity.' One of the strongest supporters, Coz Idapo, was unsparing in his sarcastic ridicule of both the Nigerian government and the general public. Writing in *Radio Times* (28 Oct. to 4 Nov. 1961), he said:

> If the volume of protest that Nigerians, both informed and uninformed, both literate and illiterate, have mounted against the filming of *Jagua Nana* is anything to go by in determining when God has spoken through the voice of the people, it can well be said that there must have been merrymaking in heaven in commemoration of the Federal Republic's firm stand against the filming of *Jagua Nana*. But I don't, for one moment, believe that God is so naïve and as unrealistic as we poor, pretentious and hypocritical humans. And I don't believe that it is because we are on the side of God that we are so vigorously opposed to the filming of *Jagua Nana*. On the other hand, I think we are opposed to the filming of *Jagua Nana* because we are, perhaps unconsciously, at war with art and its insistence on realism ...We Nigerians, as a hangover from our association with the immeasurably prudish British, are very prudish people and that prudery, because it prefers to walk with blinkers on, is never in love with art which insists on depicting nature – complete with its innocence and sinfulness, its saintliness and beastliness, and its beauty and ugliness – as it really is. (cited in Emenyonu, 1974)

Neither this nor other formidably aggressive views in defense of *Jagua Nana* as a work of great imaginative creativity and urged that it be filmed to open doors for tourism, inspire writers, artists, producers and film directors to greater heights of creativity, could persuade the government to change its stand. The filming was denied. This act of censorship was unprecedented in Nigerian history. *Jagua Nana* remains to date the only work of fiction in African literature to be debated on the floor of parliament, and by act of parliament, judged and condemned as pornographic.

Although there may not be any traceable connection, it is significant that no foreign filmmakers have to date shown real interest in the filming of Africa's classic novel, *Things Fall Apart* (1958), set in Nigeria, and written by one of the greatest storytellers of all time, Chinua Achebe. This novel, originally published by Heinemann of London, has become one of the most widely read works of fiction in the world today. Translated into 62 languages with sales over 12 million copies, *Things Fall Apart* tells the African side of the story of the coming of the early Europeans into Africa at the turn of the twentieth century. It is taught across disciplines as a ready tool for the deconstruction of the theory of *Social Darwinism* and dismantles the ethnocentric early Europeans' claim of their mission of salvation and civilization of the African continent. Its evocative prose, intriguing plot, intricate suspense, and fast-paced breath-taking actions, all ingredients of a classic movie, would make the case for enthusiastic adaptation into a motion picture. It is an African story, but it is also a story of all people who had in their history undergone bondage, dehumanization, colonization, with strange values imposed on them by alien people.

This may account for the widespread interest in *Things Fall Apart* from Africa to Latin America, from India to South Korea, from America to Australia and beyond. Achebe made a case for them all:

> Does the white man understand our customs about land? How can he, when he does not even speak our tongue? But he says that our customs are bad and our own brothers who have taken up his religion also say that our customs are bad. How do you think we can fight when our own brothers have turned against us? The white man is very clever. He came quietly and peaceably with his religion. We were amused at his foolishness and allowed him to stay. Now he has won our brothers and our clan can no longer act like one. He has put a knife on the things that held us together and we have fallen apart.(1958: 176)

Without doubt, *Things Fall Apart* is the catalyst of all that exists today in African literature without the sensationalism. So why has its local and global appeal and adoption beyond linguistic, racial, geographic and cultural boundaries not recommended it to filmmakers in Africa and outside? Many of the big names in the film industry in America have not shown interest – Spike Lee, Rasheed Bushareb, Forest Whitaker, Steven Daldry, Lawrence Fishburn, Denzel Washington, Morgan Freeman, Steven Spielberg – to mention but a few. With these turning their backs on the project, there is very little prospect that a solution is imminent from Hollywood. A film version produced in Britain starring John Sekka, Elizabeth Toro of Uganda, with John Pohland as director, turned out to be an absolute disaster. It lumped *Things Fall Apart* together with its sequel, *No Longer at Ease,* and rounded it up with scenes of the Nigerian civil war. The characters, strange to the setting of the novel could not even pronounce their Igbo names; place names were misspelt. The storyline and the plot were devoid of the cultural relevance with which Achebe richly endowed the novel. Scenes from both *Things Fall Apart* and *No Longer at Ease* were so raggedly juxtaposed and criss-crossed that the film was devoid of any tangible coherence. The muddle included the baptism of Obi's father – Isaac – where the *osu* are welcomed with open arms to the consternation of the congregation, back to back with Obi and Clara arriving straight from the Lagos airport to Joseph's apartment in Obalende suburb to be received by a Yoruba housekeeper, Bisi, whose quiet lunch they interrupted, then on to a train ride to Ibadan where Obi is a journalist, back to Clara's hospital in Lagos where Clara tells Obi that she got a letter from her father in Enugu telling her that he had promised her hand in marriage to a big businessman and, therefore, Clara tells Obi she cannot marry him because she is already spoken for! Then in Lagos we see Obi the journalist, scaling the fence (in the style of Eddie Murphy in *Beverly Hills Cop*) to gatecrash a party at a corrupt cabinet minister's residence! Nothing could be worse than that. The actors were quite seasoned but they were put in a situation where they had nothing in common with the setting, the events in the story, and the characters they were to represent.

Another failed attempt is a homemade film version scripted by a highly creative multi-talented Nigerian writer, Adiela Onyedibia. He adapted the novel to the screen in thirteen episodes with a total air time of thirteen hours. It is possible that this could have been the first stage of making a credible film of *Things Fall Apart* complete with authentic characterization, setting and cultural tone and flavor, by professionally editing the script to fit into a two- to three-hour movie. But the thirteen episodes have now been converted to a DVD marketed under the imprint of Nollywood. This confirms again that the Nollywood film makers are at variance in their mission, agenda and modalities with the lofty goals of an interface between film and literature in Africa at this point in time. No one has articulated this with viable ideas for the way forward better than Africa's ace dramatist, scholar and playwright, Femi Osofisan. In an interview (with Yinka Fabowale) published in the Nigerian newspaper, *Daily Sun*, May 20, 2010, Osofisan declared:

> Nollywood is sponsored mainly by (motor) spare parts dealers. They are the ones who finance it and they are not interested in the serious stuff for understandable reasons.They are simply business people and they want to make their money back as fast as possible.They are not interested in those higher considerations of culture. So, it's like selling fast foods, they just want to put the films there and make their money the following day... It is when we get foreign capital to invest in this that we are going to begin to get better quality simply because no other person is going to finance it. If you have a very good film script now and the Idumagbo marketers or so are not interested in that, you go to the bank, the bank will not give you loan, because they are not interested in sponsoring that and there is no national endowment for the arts that you can apply to for funding, so what happens?... If the government started by giving initial capital to support film making, it would spur on private ones. And what I meant by government support can be done in a number of ways. One, to create a bank to support a burgeoning (film) industry as we have Agriculture banks and so on, so that you can go and take a loan at a reasonable interest that will not kill you... Government can do that or put the money into a national endowment for arts, then a film maker can write proposal to that bank and get funding for his film... If we start with that, people who are willing to make films can now have access to fund, then we will have enough to counter the Nollywood market.

Against this background and scenario of film making and the film industry in Africa, the contributors to this issue of *African literature Today,* have examined the interface between film and literature in contemporary African writing and imagination, from a variety of perspectives including critiques of adaptations of African creative works into film, analysis of filmic structures in African dramatic literature, African writers as filmmakers, and the impact of the video film industry on literature and the reading culture in Africa. A major goal of this issue is to open the door for further discourse about new initiatives and new directions.

WORKS CITED

Achebe, Chinua. *Things Fall Apart*. New York: Anchor Books Edition, [1958] 1959.
Ajeluorou, Anote in *The Guardian*. Lagos, Nigeria, April 15, 2010.
Ekwensi, Cyprian. *Jagua Nana*. London: Hutchinson and Co. 1961.
Emenyonu, Ernest. *Cyprian Ekwensi*. London: Evans Brothers Limited, 1974.
Osofisan, Femi in *Daily Sun*. Lagos, Nigeria, May 20, 2010.

Strategies for Subverting Post-Colonial Oppression: Literature & Cinema in Early Sembene Ousmane

Kwawisi Tekpetey

A proponent of functional aesthetics, Sembene Ousmane embraced his vocation as a writer with a social and political agenda. In *What Is Literature?* Sartre defines the concept of literary commitment arguing that the writer is a speaker who reveals a situation to himself and to others with his very intention of changing it. According to the French philosopher, the writer is a person who has chosen a method of secondary action – action by disclosure. Addressing fellow exploited and oppressed people, Sembene, a committed artist, concentrates on liberation from various forms of oppression as the dominant theme in his work. However, any valid assessment of the effectiveness of commitment in literature must include the perception of the artistic message by the intended audience. Thus, a major concern for Sembene was whether his 'beautiful people'[1] were grasping the strategic undertones in his literary productions. He explained when he turned to cinema as a complementary medium of expression in these terms:

> Literature is a good thing, it is part of culture, but in a country where 80% of the inhabitants are illiterate, who is going to read what we write? As a man of letters I am better known in Europe than at home. Africans know me through the radio. Ask an African who can read what he knows. He will answer you that he does not have money for reading. And I understand him, instead of buying a book for five francs, he would rather buy rice. There is urgency about that. But everyone goes to the movies.[2]

When Sembene started writing in the 1950s, reading culture in Africa was quite underdeveloped because of the high levels of illiteracy in the population. Looking ahead in an article, Cyprian Ekwensi hoped the day was not far distant when the African would spend 'eight and six pence' on a book which would not enable him to pass an exam.[3] Indeed, above the level of popular magazines and daily newspapers, the only common reading at the time was of textbooks for the purpose of passing examinations. Parents had been known to refuse to allow their children to read fiction on the grounds that it was a waste of the precious time that ought to be spent on serious scholastic study. Apart from this concern with factual knowledge, the environment in many African homes often did little to stimulate reading. School children were expected to perform domestic chores in time that would otherwise be leisure, and if they were not in boarding schools, they usually had a long and tiring walk to and from school. Besides, books were rare in many African homes, and children seldom saw adults reading.

Cinema, on the other hand, played a more significant role. Throughout his travels in Africa, Sembene noted that an avid film public solidly existed. Cinema, then, could serve as an effective means of awakening consciousness and be used as a formidable weapon in the struggle against underdevelopment as well as against post-colonial oppression and injustice. Furthermore, it could constitute an important means of information, spreading ideas, and mass mobilization. The influence of cinema is reflected in some characters in Sembene's fiction. After watching a film on ancient Rome, Diagne in *O pays mon beau peuple* (O Country My Beautiful People) subsequently greets his friends: 'I salute you, People of Casamance,' and one of his friends remarks: 'Here comes the crazy one! Yesterday he went to watch a movie on ancient Rome, the whole week he will be a Roman, but after a cowboy film, he will be a cowboy and act tough…'[4] In *God's Bits of Wood*, Magatte and his apprentices are passionate about movies:

> Their discussions were invariably concerned with the same subject – the films they had seen in the days before the strike. They told the stories of every one of them, over and over again but never without feverish interruptions: 'You're forgetting the part where…' or 'No, that's not the way he killed the Indian.' Next to Western films, war films were their favorites. Sometimes as a change from their enforced activity, they played war games themselves.[5]

One learns about N'Dèye Touti that 'the reading she did, the films she saw, made her part of a universe in which her own people had no place.'[6] As for the photographer's apprentice in *The Money-Order*, 'his assiduous frequentation of cinemas where the cheapest kinds of French, American, English, Indian and Arab films were shown, had ripened his vocabulary.'[7]

However, films which appeared on colonial African screens spread a pernicious influence and promoted harmful acculturation for Africans. European film distributors flooded Africa with what one may describe as 'rubbish films' under the pretext that only such films were profitable. Worst of all, no constructive racial consciousness developed since African characters were called upon to project themselves in white heroes. Besides, they never played sophisticated or intellectual roles. In these films, a social myth was created with luxury and idleness presented as natural conditions of living. Sembene noted a commonly known fact when he stated:

> Since the birth of cinema … African countries have been subjected to Western image and its rhythmic movement. On the screens in Black Africa only stories of platitudinous stupidity foreign to our way of life are shown. And if perchance a Black person takes part in one of these films, most often he plays a token role, or that of a servant, or public comedian.[8]

Anthropological films set in Africa, for their part, also did very little to help Africans regain confidence and pride in themselves. In Francophone Africa, films like *Bozambo, Le roman d'un spahi (A Spahi's Novel), Bouboule 1er, roi nègre (Bouboule I, African King),* and *L'Homme du Niger (The Man from Niger)* served colonization as apologies for superiority of European culture. Most often, exotic aspects of Africa were given prominence with a deliberate distortion of the African image.

Just as an urgent task had been imposed on African writers through the misrepresentation of their people in literature by Westerners as found in Joseph Conrad's *Heart of Darkness*, a need for an authentic African cinema arose. The emergence of young African filmmakers in the sixties most of whom defined themselves as committed artists[9] could only be hailed as an opportune event, for one could reasonably expect that their objective would be to correct 'what has been done without us and against us,'[10] to borrow Ki-Zerbo's expression. Sembene, speaking on behalf of those African filmmakers, declared: 'We wanted, like our poets, our novelists, to bring to black-African heritage and to all mankind that aspect that was missing in the universal: the true image of Africa.'[11] Sembene was without doubt one of the best known pioneer African filmmakers, justifiably nick-named 'Pope of African cinema'[12] As a novelist, for a long time, he was overshadowed by more prestigious writers. However, with the camera, he quickly became an international figure. Only a period of four years intervened between his first short film *Borom sarret* and *Mandabi*, which confirmed his talent and incontestable authority as a filmmaker, after the popular success of *La Noire de … (Black Girl)*, the first full-length African film.[13]

In Sembene's early novels, cinematographic impulses could already be seen at work. *The Black Docker* opens with Diaw Falla's trial and then there is a long flashback to the circumstances that led to the assassination of Ginette Tontisane. The artist adopts a similar technique in the short story 'Black Girl,' where Diouana's suicide is first presented and then the facts relating to her tragic action are retraced. In *God's Bits of Wood*, instead of a linear progression of the narrative, the author follows the action of the railroad strike alternately in Dakar, Thiès, and Bamako. The same method is used in *L'Harmattan (The Harmattan)*. In both *God's Bits of Wood* and *L'Harmattan*, Sembene employs a polyphonic method in presenting and advancing the narrative. These novels are composed of a series of sequences, and time, as in cinematography, is reversible. Some Sembenian novels also depart from traditional techniques: they are less of narratives, descriptions, or psychological analyses; rather, they present series of tableaux rising in crescendo to a dénouement. In *God's Bits of Wood* and *L'Harmattan*, which involve a third-person narrator, no single character dominates the action. Rather, the novels provide panoramic visions through characterization of several individuals in various situations. The narratives alternate from one setting or character-cluster to another. But within any given 'character cluster,', one character may relatively stand out, for example, Bakayoko in *God's Bits of Wood* and Tangara in *L'Harmattan*. Furthermore, certain scenes in Sembene's novels would perfectly lend themselves to cinematographic presentation, for example, the women's march to Dakar in *God's Bits of Wood*. The artist displays the ability to direct large casts of characters. A cinematographic vocation is clearly discernable in Sembene's early novels, and it is not surprising that he adapted a number of his literary works for the screen: *Niaye* (*Véhi-Ciosane or White Genesis*), *La Noire de...* ('Black Girl'), *Mandabi* (*The Money-Order*), *Taaw*, and *Xala*.

It is always possible to make an imaginative use of literature in filmmaking. And filmmakers have been indebted to literature in a variety of ways especially when one considers *cinéma-écriture* (cinema-writing) and *caméra-stylo* (camera-pen), concepts which convey the idea of writing and reading a film. Literature and cinema may be viewed as one and the same art form expressed differently, and the difference is not simply that of 'word' on one hand and 'image' on the other. Robert Richardson wrote at the advent of what has been called the 'new literacy':

> the currently much belabored split between the word and the image, and the announcements of the end of the age of the print and the advent of the age of electronic image, and the diagnoses of post-literate man seems to me to vastly overrate the phenomena in question. The new literacy, the ability to 'read' streams of visual images, has indeed, at times, the chaotic, uncontrolled, unsophisticated and exuberant qualities that often accompany a significant innovation or advance, but I think it is beginning to be apparent that this new literacy is not a negation of the older sort of literacy, but an expansion or an enlargement of the idea of literacy itself.[14]

Sembene, for his part, regarded film as a branch of literature, and the theme of domination and a corollary of liberation in his literary works echoes in his films. Sembene's first film, *Borom Sarret* (1963), presents a day in the life of a cart driver in Dakar. 'Borom Sarret'[15] manifestly belongs to the group of 'have-nots'. The protagonist leaves for work on an empty stomach with only kola nuts for lunch. His wife's parting words to him are: 'Remember we have nothing to eat.' 'Borom Sarret' accomplishes his daily work diligently, accepting whatever task comes his way: he picks up a young man and a 'market mammy' and takes them to the market; he carries bricks, and later becomes an 'ambulance-man' helping to convey a pregnant woman to a maternity clinic. Subsequently, using his cart as a makeshift hearse, he comes to the rescue of a bereaved father and transports a deceased child to the cemetery. Finally, we find him assisting a public servant to move to the Plateau, the Westernized section of Dakar. It is during this last assignment that his cart will be confiscated and a fine imposed on him for straying into an area forbidden to cart-drivers.

Two scenes in the film reveal his state of mind, the consequence of the hard life that is his lot. At noon, when 'Borom Sarret' takes a break in his cart and is accosted by a crippled beggar for alms, he shows indifference. The protagonist exhibits the normal reaction of familiarity with poverty to the extent that he does not find anything pathetic about the beggar's condition, even though the beggar is a cripple and his only hope for survival in his society is to appeal for assistance. Even though the cart-driver is presented as a faithful Muslim, he remains unperturbed by the beggar's request in the name of Allah.

The scene with the crippled beggar contrasts with that of the griot which follows. The griot, who is in perfectly good health and visibly well-nourished, volunteers to sing the praises of 'Borom Sarret'. Even though he is not familiar with the latter's ancestry, the important thing is to flatter him, remove him from his immediate unsavoury reality, and plunge him into a world of fantasy. The griot recalls the fictitious glorious heritage of our hero when his ancestors were heroic and victorious conquerors. Impressed by the griot's performance, the protagonist parts with his entire morning's earnings. At the end of the scene with the griot, 'Borom Sarret' is left alone. The spectators disappear to pursue their various walks in life, and the protagonist has to start his existential struggle all over again alone. This theme of solitude is reinforced by the next scene in which we find a man going to bury his deceased child without the support of any sympathizers, a most unusual scenario in a communal society.

The protagonist's oppression stems from the insensitivity of a group, symbolized in the film by the public servant, who is relocating to the Plateau in accordance with his newly acquired status. The new elite exploit the masses for their own personal benefit, without any consideration for the welfare of those of deprived status. In the film, we have the impression that the protagonist is literally being oppressed under the weight of the elevated massive Plateau buildings. That new milieu has nothing in common with his own environment, and significantly, European classical music replaces the traditional African music in the background. It is not surprising that the public servant abandons the cart-driver when he is arrested, even though he had pledged protection. After his misfortune, 'Borom

Sarret' returns to his community with these words, 'We are at home here, there is no police,' words that suggest his misadventure occurred because he had 'wandered' where he did not belong. The rules of the game must be obeyed, a theme underscored by the griot's episode and the shoe-shine boy's 'unsolicited job' interwoven into it. While the griot is rewarded for operating according to the rules of the game, the shoe-shine boy receives no payment for his services for the opposite reason. Abiding by the rules for 'Borom Sarret' means acquiescence in his despicable condition without any aspiration towards social mobility.

'Borom Sarret' is a pathetic victim of circumstances that he only vaguely understands at the end of the film. The film is a reminder that social injustice is real in the society, a reality that those who are removed from 'Borom Sarret's' condition may conveniently ignore. For those who share the protagonist's lot, the film brings indignation that independence with its promise of work and happiness has only benefitted a few privileged people like the public servant. This indignation will be an important and necessary step towards the condemnation of the status quo and, possibly, revolt.

Sembene Ousmane's second film *Niaye* (1964) is an adaptation of his novella, *Véhi-Ciosane* or *White Genesis*. It is the filmmaker's first screen adaptation of a literary work. Regarding written works made into movies, Paulin Vieyra has observed:

> the difficulty of a film produced from a novel, whether known or not, but especially from a known novel is to succeed in bringing out the spirit of the novel. As it is not always possible to put the whole novel in a film, the producer and the adaptors must make a choice. And when we talk about choice we necessarily mean abandoning certain passages or shortening other passages to put the literary work in the film. It may happen that one would create other scenes for the film not found in the book.[16]

Véhi-Ciosane or *White Genesis* will require structural reorganization for an appropriate cinematographic form which will bring out the core of the novella. In *Véhi-Ciosane* or *White Genesis*, self-criticism is postulated as an indispensable path toward progress. The major themes in Sembene's work, we may recall, centre on oppression, humiliation, and the degradation of man with a counteracting theme of man's incessant struggle for liberation from these negative forces. In *Véhi-Ciosane* or *White Genesis*, an incestuous act engenders a critical situation causing a society to question its norms and values. From the ashes of degradation, to use the phoenix metaphor, a new society emerges turning its back on the tainted past, and looking forward to an optimistic future. Indeed, 'Santhiu Niaye', the setting of the story means 'new settlement' in Wolof.

The fundamental problem in the novella focuses on an infringement on traditional morality resulting in the disruption of communal harmony. The reasons for this disharmony, however, should not be sought solely in the incest, which only serves as a catalyst. Other forces have already started undermining the traditional structure. Many families have been driven up-country because of unbearable taxes. Conversely, there is a continuous exodus of young men to the cities, and Santhiu Niaye is progressively turning into an abandoned region. As a result, religion, tradition, customs, and communal life are all being systematically destroyed. The main theme of the novella revolves around decadence in the society and the society's inability to cope with the demands and needs of its members.

On the whole, Sembene preserves the 'spirit' of the novella in *Niaye*. However, with regard to form, there are significant reconstructions. It is the griot that narrates the story, presenting characters, and revealing motivations behind their actions. After the scandalous events in the village – a father commits incest with his daughter, and this leads to her mother's suicide, then parricide perpetrated by a demented son, and finally usurpation by an uncle – the village becomes polluted and flight appears as an attractive option for those who seek to preserve 'purity'. At the end of the story, the griot announces his departure from the village declaring he is going where he hopes 'truth will be the work of honest minds and not a birth privilege.'[17] However, in the film, the griot returns to the village to attest that lies will always be contested. Sembene breaks down the moral which the griot's return implies:

> If you cannot tell the truth where you are born, where your friends and your relatives are, where you are part of your surrounding, where will you tell the truth? Elsewhere? Elsewhere you will be a stranger. Whoever leaves a little truth without denouncing it will not stand up for the truth which endangers his life.[18]

Charity should, indeed, begin at home.

Another noteworthy modification in the film is that the villagers do not rally behind the rejected *iman* as we find in the novella. The *iman* seems to be part of the degraded past which must be forsaken for the new promise of the future, symbolized by Khary's new-born baby, Madiagua Diob.

The film, *Niaye*, unsurprisingly received more attention than the novella, *Véhi-Ciosane or White Genesis*. However, early viewers felt the film, like the novella, was a disgrace for Senegal and that their dirty linen was being washed in public. Senegalese audiences argued it should not even be shown to other Africans. Of course, many conceded that the problem exposed in the film was not peculiar to Senegal; but nationalists still considered it was improper to show ugly aspects of Senegalese reality to the outside world. However, as Ama

Ata Aidoo points out writing about Ayi Kwei Armah's *The Beautyful Ones Are Not Yet Born,* 'if the only way to get one's linen clean is to wash it in public, then one does exactly that'.[19]

The major complaint about the film was its didacticism. The griot narrates the story with running commentary, in the manner of an African oral narrative performer. Viewers reacted: 'Tell us the story without telling us your position. We will judge for ourselves.' It must be observed that although African oral narratives are didactic, the moral is never stated; it is revealed through images. It appears, however, that Sembene listened and did not reproduce this *Niaye* technique subsequently.

Many innovations are found in *La Noire de ...* (1966), the cinematographic adaptation of the short story with the same title ('Black Girl'). The film introduces new themes not found in the short story. In addition to the racial theme and the oppression of the domestic servant which are given prominence in the short story, the film stands as a satire on post-independent Senegal marked by failure.

The plot in both the short story and the film is based on an authentic news item. But, the social context is very precise: Senegal some years after independence, where colonial structures still persist. In explaining his film Sembene affirmed: 'The dialectics of history: neocolonialism still exists under the guise of cooperation.'[20] After independence, shanty-towns around modern Dakar did not disappear, and unemployment remained the lot of many. Young girls and women continued to hire themselves out or prostitute themselves to eke out a living. At 'La Place des bonnes' (Maidservants' Square): girls aspiring to be become domestic servants wait endlessly for employers to come and choose prospective workers just as one may find at a cattle or sheep market.

Though Africans are now running the government, the living conditions have not improved. The pre-independence idealism professed by the representatives of the people clashed with opportunism; elected deputies seemed to be guided only by their own selfish, material interests. They are in politics not because they want to make the lives of the people better but rather to enrich themselves. Sembene suggests this in the film through the snatches of a conversation between three deputies who briefly cross Diouana's path. The deputies are outrageously parading in tailcoats, and it is evident they are far removed from the people who voted them into office. As representatives of the people, they should seek their welfare, but in their conversation, they are apparently not prepared to engage in any action likely to jeopardize their newly acquired advantages. Thus, the modern buildings in the film as well as the beautiful items at the supermarkets, in short, the 'good things' in Senegal are there for the enjoyment of the new African elite and the white minority. For the average Senegalese, perhaps, the only gain of independence is 'Place de l'Indépendance,'[21] where Diouana and her lover pose for a picture.

In spite of independence, the French still held comfortable key positions, with considerable benefits that allowed them to go on vacation in France accompanied by their Senegalese servants. The French nationals felt very secure in Senegal, and as one of them hints in a rejoinder in the film, a coup d'état is out of the question 'so long as Senghor is there.' The French came to Senegal mainly as technical assistants and were motivated less by any real 'cooperation' than by the huge incomes they could transfer to banks in France. A conversation between Diouana's employers and their friends in France reveals the mercenary attitude of the French technical assistants, who were not always free from racism even if it is subconscious. Unwary Africans like Diouana could fall victim.

Diouana's fascination for France, and her irresistible attraction towards the so-called 'metropolis', may be construed as flight from oneself, and there is only one step separating flight from oneself and alienation. The theme of alienation is first revealed through a visual sign at the beginning of the film in the white ancestral African mask, which Diouana presents to Monsieur P. on her first day of work in Dakar, and which she recuperates in France before committing suicide.[22] At the end of the film, Diouana's little brother seizes the mask when her employer returns the personal belongings of his deceased sister. There is a long sequence through Medina, the indigenous district of Dakar, with syncopated African music, rising to a crescendo, while Diouana's brother wearing the mask, pursues the white man and removes the mask at the end of the film to reveal his black face. This symbolism recalls Frantz Fanon's *Black, Skin White Masks* and points to the need for the Senegalese to remove any white masks that they may be wearing. But Sembene also seems to be suggesting the image of a continent which through its culture is searching for authenticity.[23]

Apart from this visual image representing complex alienation and possible liberation, one could read a more subtle and profound symbolism in the film. Diouana is caught in a quasi-exile, deprived of means of communication, and even of her own voice. She has to rely on half-hearted interpretations or indifferent commentaries of her employers when they read letters from home to her. Diouana is confined to a linguistic prison within the walls of the apartment where she lives. Throughout the film she remains silent, only presenting a passive appearance. Even though the soliloquy in the film translates her inner thoughts in a lyrical manner, it is spoken in a Europeanized voice. It seems this contrast is deliberate since in *Borom Sarret*, one hears the protagonist's own voice, albeit in approximate French. On the contrary, in *La Noire de...*, the artificiality of the soliloquy is marked by the tone as well as by its lyrical excess. Another noteworthy hint of alienation in the film is Diouana's clothing. In spite of her European wig and high heels, she remains an alien in France. Before committing suicide, however, she divests herself of her European accoutrements, and resorts to African cloth and hair-do. This symbolizes her final spiritual return to authenticity.

Diouana's employers refuse to recognize that she has similar needs and desires. Madame does not understand why a servant should be allowed to go out occasionally: 'Why should she go out? She does not need it,' she remarks. No wonder her husband is surprised after Diouana's suicide to discover in her suitcase a photograph of her with her boy-friend in Dakar. He is astonished to learn that, after all, Diouana was capable of feeling, loving, and suffering. The protagonist's suicide registers a protest against her condition as a domestic servant as well as against the lack of human relations between herself and her employers. Although the racial, colonial and neo-colonial aspects of the film are important, equally significant is the interpretation of the oppression inherent in a domestic servant's condition.

The film *La Noire de...* throws new meaning on the short story. Formal independence did not modify or eliminate that relationship of domination and dependence between neo-colonizers and neo-colonized. However, a note of optimism runs in the final scenes of the film, and the sequence may be viewed as a manifesto. With vigilance Africa would one day achieve its real liberation. In a roadside classroom, mass education is laying the foundations for future Senegal. The symbol of the African child pursuing the white man with the mask represents a desire to promote a state free from European tutelage, and drawing from the sources of African civilization.

After *La Noire de...*, Sembene sought to promote African languages in his films. The screen adaptation of the artist's novella *The Money Order* was produced in two versions: *Le Mandat* in French, and *Mandabi* in Wolof. As Sembene comments on his use of African languages in his films: 'For me, cinema is the best night school. It allows me not only to do what literature does not allow me to do but also to make people speak in their own language, namely Wolof.'[24]

Producing films about Africans in African languages rings more true to life. When Ibrahima Dieng shows up at the Post Office to cash his money order in the French version of the film, both the postal agent and Ibrahima speak in French. The gap between them comes out more clearly in *Mandabi*, the Wolof version of the film, through a communication barrier: the postal agent addresses the protagonist in the official French language, but the illiterate protagonist does not understand him. Sembene's use of Wolof in his films also gives Senegalese audiences a sense of direct participation. Besides, the actors feel more at ease and are therefore able to render their best performance. In *Mandabi* the actors express themselves naturally, acting their roles more appropriately, whereas in *Le Mandat* they appear awkwardly artificial.

Mandabi (1968), the screen adaptation of the *The Money Order*, is the first African film with dialogue entirely in an African language, except for the ones involving civil servants. The film follows the novella very closely, and the most notable new scenes are: Ibrahima Dieng having his hair shaved at the beginning of the film; Ibrahima catching a glimpse of one of his wives in an outdoor bathroom; the Paris scene as the letter-writer reads Ibrahima's letter; Ibrahima's daughter's obsession with the white doll; and finally, a hawker of second-hand brassieres.

The scene with the barber is clever. The novella begins with the postman, delivering the letter from Paris to Ibrahima's wives. Their husband is not home, and in the film we have an explanation: he is with his barber. The sequence depicts the protagonist as a simple, good-natured man, an important trait of his character which will account for some of his misfortunes. This aspect of Ibrahima Dieng also forms part of his traditional make-up. When the protagonist's eyes unintentionally fall on the partial nakedness of one of his wives in the outdoor bathroom, he averts his eyes immediately because the sight shocks his traditional sense of decency.

The sequence about Abdou's life in Paris provides an insight into African life in France. Abdou, a street cleaner, is cold and hungry and he can no longer count on traditional African solidarity. Sembene no doubt included this scene to disabuse the minds of his fellow countrymen as well as other Africans about Europe viewed as an Eldorado of 'greener pastures'. Abdou belongs to the group Albert Memmi refers to as 'the new slaves' in *Dominated Man*:

> There are 35,000 new black slaves in Paris … It's even worse than that. The slave used to belong to someone, to a man in any case. Of necessity, there entered into this relationship, beyond its basic iniquity, something fundamentally human … Now, these new black slaves, our slaves are not the slaves of anyone in particular. That is to say, no one believes he is responsible for them.[25]

A fascination with France forms part of the African's alienation, and it leads to an imitation of Western way of life which is sometimes quite ridiculous. When Ibrahima goes to seek assistance in cashing in his money order from his distant cousin, the latter fetches his jacket before leaving for work in the unforgiving African sun. The conversation of the clerks at the City Hall is interlarded with modern slang expressions delivered in Parisian accent. But perhaps the most striking image of alienation is found in Ibrahima's little daughter playing with a white doll, an image which runs through the film like a *leitmotif.*

Sembene observes post-independent Senegal as a moralist. He describes this reality on the level of day-to-day existence and reveals modern Senegalese society in moral and economic crisis. Ibrahima falls into the category of nationals who have remained in the margin of the independent country's development, those who are left out and left behind. All he has is his very modest house on the outskirts of Dakar, his two wives and nine children, numerous mouths waiting to be fed by an unemployed man. Sembene traces the various stages of Ibrahima's dramatic mishaps and adventures which finally lead the protagonist to his disillusionment, accompanied by a painful awareness of the reality of the new African environment after independence.

Independence hardly brought the anticipated progress to the country: many streets in the city are not tarred and unemployment still remains a serious problem. Abdou notes in his letter to his uncle: '*There is no work in Dakar. I could not spend my time all day, year in year out, sitting doing nothing.*' Because of lack of employment, begging has become a profession. Witness the woman beggar who accosts Ibrahima twice to ask for alms: she has found the trick for making several begging rounds in a day by changing her clothes and her 'lines'. People have contrived devious ways to face their existential problem. Gorgui Maïssa, for example, does not hesitate to become a griot, and receives 50 francs for singing the praises of a complete stranger; a fake photographer pretends to be taking photographs of his customers.

But the new middle class does not share the post-independence frustrations. Sembene never hid his aversion for the new elite who remain oblivious of the promises made to the masses during the liberation struggle. Independence became a betrayal of the people, and the new elite show indifference to the human concerns of the suffering masses. The new class represented by Dieng's distant cousin, live in modern houses and their way of living shamefully contrasts with that of the broad masses. Social change has produced a growing gap between the masses and this small Westernized elite. Besides, the post-colonial administration is plagued by many imperfections. Throughout both the novella and the film, Sembene provides instances of corruption, bribery and dishonesty. Ibrahima comes to know with each encounter with the divisions of the bureaucracy how the pay-off is the fastest way to obtain a service.

Indirect colonial oppression, neo-colonialism, has replaced direct colonial oppression. The new privileged class, agents of neo-colonialism, oppresses the masses in a number of ways, and Ibrahima is presented as one of their victims. The protagonist's woes begin at the post office when he is asked for his identity card, a prerequisite for cashing a money-order. He has never heard of the document in question; before colonial time, one did not need an identity card to move about. Instead of explaining the necessity of the document, the civil servant insults the venerable old man, humiliating him publicly. At the police station, Ibrahima suffers a similar humiliation. He is handled roughly, pushed around and insulted only to be told rudely that he must produce an identity card. In an attempt to obtain a birth certificate at the City Hall, the civil servant insists on his exact date and place of birth when he is pertinently aware that in the 1900s when Ibrahima was born, rigorous birth registers were not maintained in Africa.

With the unwinding of events, Ibrahima realizes that honesty, this time-honored value, one of the foundations of his religion, has been twisted and turned into a criminal act: it is only lying, cheating and stealing that now pay. His experiences with the money order allow him to understand how deeply shaken the moral structures of his society have become: money has become the only recognized moral value. There is lucidity mingled with irony in the way in which the author portrays the little opportunistic crowd gathering around Ibrahima after he receives the money order. Various individuals illustrate, in diverse ways, the malicious aspect of people who seek to take advantage of a situation, a friendship or a relationship. Mutual support and solidarity, recognized as positive traditional African attributes, have degenerated into the abuse of the goodness of people and cunning calculations. In *Mandabi*, Sembene is also protesting against the absurdity of the new independent society in which honest people appear ill-adapted.

In the novella, Ibrahima Dieng, educated in the fatalistic tradition of Islam, attributes his misfortunes to Allah; he seems to accept situations without seeking to modify them. This fatalistic aspect of Ibrahima Dieng's character is not suggested in the film. But if Ibrahima does not revolt it is partly because he does not fully understand the new dispensation. Sembene underscores the necessity to understand the forces and mechanisms operating in the new society as a prerequisite for transforming society. The awareness and insights Ibrahima has gained by the end of his misadventures will be vital experience to be shared with the rest of his countrymen.

The major interest of both the novella *The Money Order* and the film *Mandabi* lies in their social and political message. Independence has not brought the end of oppression nor injustice, and the society appears to have sunken into a deep moral abyss. But the artist does not resign himself to the unacceptable conditions. After his tragicomic adventures, Ibrahima undergoes a metamorphosis and declares he will also put on the skin of a hyena since honesty has become a crime. However, this individual revolt in the jungle is not a solution. Indeed, Sembene offers a more effective way out.

At the end of the story the postman brings another letter from Paris. The contents of the letter remain unknown. But that is not important. What is important is the lesson the postman gives the protagonist in simple words fraught with revolutionary connotations. He assures Ibrahima 'Tomorrow, we will change all that.' Astonished, Ibrahima asks 'Who is we?' and he is told the 'we' includes him, his wives and, indeed, all the oppressed. Although the protagonist seems perplexed by the postman's words, there is no doubt that he will be on the side of the postman when the day of awakening dawns.

The social conditions may grow worse with corruption, begging and profiteering, all of which Sembene denounces vigorously. But all hope is not lost. It can be said that Bah, the postman, brings false hope with the money-order advice slip at the beginning of the story. However, he thereby affords the protagonist an opportunity to gain an understanding of the realities in the new society. Rather than enfranchising the oppressed and marginalized in African society, those without power or influence, African independence has led to the social domination as well as the repressive hegemony of the elite class.

In conclusion, Sembene's early films appeal to a hunger for characters and situations to which Senegalese audiences can easily relate. They serve his social and political aim of critically investigating post-independent Senegal while affirming his belief in the revolutionary potential of the down-trodden in African society to revolt against neo-colonial oppression and create a just society. The filmmaker views the struggle against post-colonial injustice as a first step to a radical restructuring of society in Africa. There may be disenchantment in the new African city after independence. But as our elders say, to be disappointed with the first harvest of one's plot of land is not necessarily the end of one's love for the land or for one's future. Embedded in Sembene's films from *Borom Sarret* to *Mandabi* are strategies for subverting post-colonial wrongs with a view to awaken consciousness in order to effect change and bring about real post-colonial liberation. Sembene truly shows an optimistic faith in African social and political development.

NOTES

1 cf. title of Sembene Ousmane's second novel, *O pays mon beau peuple*.
2 English translations of quotations where there are no published English versions are mine. Interview with Ousmane Sembene in *Pas à pas* reproduced

in *Culture et Développement* – fiche de lecture: *Les bouts de bois de Dieu*, déc. 1964.

3 Cyprian Ekwensi, 'Outlook for African Writers,' *West African Review,* Vol. 21, No. 268, January 1950, p.19. 'Eight and six pence' at that time is approximately 50 US cents today.

4 Ousmane Sembene, *O pays mon beau people*, pp. 115–16.

5 Ousmane Sembene, *God's Bits of Wood*, p.154. First published by Doubleday, 1962.

6 Ibid, p. 57.

7 Ousmane Sembene, *The Money Order with White Genesis*, p. 116.

8 Ousmane Sembene, 'L'image cinématographique et la poésie en Afrique' in Paulin Soumanou Vieyra, *Ousmane Sembene: Cinéaste,* p. 165.

9 Bernard Chansou, 'S.O.S. de nos cinéastes,' *Le Soleil*, 23 mai 1970, p. 8.

10 Joseph Ki-Zerbo, 'Histoire et conscience nègre' in *Présence africaine* No. XVI, p. 53.

11 Ousmane Sembene, op. cit., p.173.

12 Ferid Boughedir dixit quoted in *Jeune Afrique* No. 488, mai 1970.

13 *La Noire de…* has been described by Georges Sadoul as 'le premier long métrage nègre' in *Dictionnaire des films,* p. 173.

14 Robert Richardson, *Literature and Film*, p. 13.

15 In Wolof, 'borom sarret' means cart-owner. The cart is a popular means of cheap transportation of goods in Senegal.

16 Paulin Vieyra, op. cit., p. 49.

17 Ibid.

18 Ibid., p. 54

19 Ama Ata Aidoo, Introduction to Ayi Kwei Armah, *The Beautyful Ones Are Not Yet Born,* p. vii.

20 Louis Marcorelles, 'Ousmane Sembene, romancier, cinéaste, poète,' p. 24.

21 It is at the 'Place de l'Indépendance' (Independence Square) that we have the scene of Diouana walking on the War Memorial while her lover frantically urges her to come down. Paulin Vieyra interprets the image in these terms: 'I think that it is a significant scene of some concern for the author. One can assert that Ousmane Sembene is contesting this symbol of human sacrifice, endured by the Senegalese people, as a national patrimony to be revered. The men died, Sembene seems to be saying, for a cause which does not concern Senegal, even less Africa, since the people who should be aware of this symbolism, represented by this monument do not know the respect due to a War Memorial. Diouana quite naturally, without any shade of a sense of guilt, walks on the monument while her boy-friend, brought up precisely in the socio-cultural context of the colonizer, reacts as the colonizer would himself to the extent of talking of sacrilege.' (Paulin Vieyra, op. cit., p. 80).

22 There is a striking correlation between Diouana and the mask. In France, she is exhibited as an exotic object just like the mask, which is proudly hung in the sitting room of her employers as their colonial trophy. The mask is Diouana's only link with her native land in France, and this is why she reclaims it before committing suicide.

23 Marie-Claire Wuilleumer, op. cit., p. 140.

24 Siradiou Diallo, 'Document: Sembene Ousmane,' in *Jeune Afrique* No. 629, le 27 janvier 1973, p.45.

25 Albert Memmi, *Dominated Man*, pp. 127-8.

WORKS CITED

Works by Sembene Ousmane

Novels

The Black Docker, London: Heinemann, 1987. English translation of *Le docker noir*, Paris: *Présence africaine*, 1973. First published by Nouvelles Editions Debresse, 1956.

O pays mon beau peuple, Paris: Le livre contemporain, 1957.

God's Bits of Wood, London: Heinemann, 1976. English translation of original French publication, *Les bouts de bois de Dieu*, Paris: Le livre contemporain, 1960.

'La Noire de…' in *Voltaïque*, Paris: *Présence africaine*, 1962. Published in English as 'Black Girl' in *Tribal Scars*, Washington: Inscape, 1975.

L'Harmattan, Paris: *Présence africaine*, 1964

The Money Order with White Génesis, London: Heinemann, 1987. English translation of the original French publication *Véhi-Ciosane ou Blanche Génese suivi du Mandat*, Paris: *Présence africaine*, 1966.

Xala, Paris: *Présence africaine*, 1974. Published in English as *Xala* by Lawrence Hill Books, 1997.

Niiwam suivi de Taaw, Paris: *Présence africaine*, 1987. Published in English as *Niiwam and Taaw* by Heinemann, 1992.

Films

Borom Sarret, 1962 [In French]

Niaye, 1964 [In French]

La Noire de…, 1966 [In French with English subtitles]

Mandabi/Le mandat, 1968 [In Wolof and French with English subtitles]

Taaw, 1970 [In Wolof with English subtitles]

Xala, 1974 [In Wolof and French with English subtitles]

Other Works Cited

Armah, Ayi Kwei, *The Beautyful Ones Are Not Yet Born*, Collier Books Edition, 1969.

Memmi, Albert, *Dominated Man*, New York: Orion Press, 1968. English translation of original French publication *L'homme dominé*, Paris: Gallimard, 1968.

Richardson, Robert, *Literature and Film*, Bloomington: Indiana University Press, 1969.

Sadoul, Georges, *Dictionnaire des films*, Paris: Seuil, 1976.

Sartre, Jean-Paul, *What Is Literature*, Methuen, 1967. English translation of *Qu'est-ce que la litérature?* Paris: Gallimard, 1948.

Vieyra, Paulin Soumanou, *Ousmane Sembene: Cinéaste*, Paris: Présence Africaine, 1972.

Other Films Cited

Bernhein, Michel, *Le roman d'un spahi*, 1940

Crichton, Charles Ainslie, *Bozambo*, 1935

De Baroncelli, Jacques, *L'Homme du Niger*, 1939

Milton, George, *Bouboule 1er, roi nègre*, 1933

From Negritude to Migritude? Moussa Sene Absa's *Ainsi meurent les anges* (And so Angels Die)

MaryEllen Higgins

In a 2004 essay for *Notre Librarie,* Jacques Chevrier celebrates diasporic African writers in Paris who shift countries, languages and cultures 'sans complex,' who position their art within the realm of 'world literature à la française,' and who have long relinquished Negritude in favor of migritude (13-17). The study of Paris-based writers of African descent is not new; Bennetta Jules-Rosette's *Black Paris: The African Writers' Landscape* introduced Parisianism, an identity discourse constructed by francophone authors who have abandoned, in her view, Senegalese poet and former president Léopold Sédar Senghor's philosophy of Africanité, or 'reclaimed Africanness' (9). The writers Calixthe Beyala and Simon Njami – the latter penned the introduction to *Black Paris* – are hailed as representatives of both movements. In a section of a special issue of *Modern Fiction Studies* titled 'From Négritude to Migritude,' Pius Adesanmi argues (in his article, 'Redefining Paris') that while first-generation Negritude writers traveling to Paris were often 'transient exiles and/or deracinated, alienated intellectuals' who returned to the continent, a second generation of migritude writers, often Paris-born, 'refuses to construct Africa as a site of salutary return' (2005: 965-7). The migritude writers, like the Parisianists, relocate the local: they envision a wider, more global belonging, one centered in Paris but ultimately part of a cosmopolitan community of multiple rooted artists.

Before continuing, one might ask how far one must venture to become cosmopolitan, or in what direction one must travel. In Chevrier's description of world literature, there seems to be a lingering assumption that the author situated in Africa remains fixed in the 'local,' while the African writer who appropriates Paris as his or her own 'goes global.' Artists such as Moussa Sene Absa have reversed this scenario, so that the site of international exchange is transposed to the cosmopolitan South. While migritude authors may position themselves – or be positioned by critics – as world writers à la française, Absa participates in world cinema à la Sénégalaise.

Absa's 2001 film *Ainsi meurent les anges* (And so Angels Die) demonstrates the flaws in the version of migritude that imagines an African local in order to define itself. To conceive of Parisian migritude as world literature à la française, and Senegalese literature or cinema as 'local' art is to miss the point that Dakar – a city that is home to migrants from areas as diverse as Guinea, Mali, Mauritania, Morocco, Lebanon, China, and France – is also quite global.

Absa, like Ousmane Sembene before him, challenges the assumption that for postcolonial cinema to go global, it must pack up and head North. Although not necessarily in direct dialogue with theories of migritude or cosmopolitanism, Absa's *Ainsi meurent les anges* raises interesting questions about cosmopolitan identity and cosmopolitan art. Absa's aesthetics are cosmopolitan; they draw particularly on the legacy of Black internationalism seen in the Negritude poets. At the same time, Absa's use of video technology in *Ainsi meurent les anges* can be viewed as an attempt to ground Senegalese cinema locally, away from the its dependence on international funding, and away from its inequitable marriage with European centers of production.

In the spirit of Harney's *In Senghor's Shadow*, I do not want to replicate studies 'more preoccupied with debating the validity and relevance of proposed categories than with dealing with the artworks and artists at hand' (2004: 7). In trying to piece together possibilities for interpretation that Negritude and migritude offer, one may begin to unravel some of the mysteries of Absa's film. Migritude, or the dynamics between migration and Negritude, has an alternate articulation in *Ainsi meurent les anges*. Unlike the migritude writers, Absa's poet-protagonist Mory (played by Absa) revisits the return narrative of earlier generations of African writers, although it is unclear at the film's conclusion whether Mory's homecoming marks a transitory journey or an attempt to reclaim Senegal as his home. Like the Negritude writers, Mory turns to poetry to lament his losses; he recites celebrated Negritude poems with an even younger generation in Senegal and France. Mory's migration to Paris does not follow the trajectory of earlier writers who traveled as students as part of French colonial assimilation projects, however. Rather, Mory is a struggling expatriate and failed post-Negritude artist who has just been thrown out of his house by his French wife; he appears to be more connected to the generations of African migrants whom conservative French politicians persistently threaten to deport. These stories, the tales of non-elites, Mory asserts, are stories that no one seems to want to hear. As if disrupting the relative success stories of the Parisianist and migritude writers of 'world literature à la française,' Mory, while listening to a musician play the kora in a Paris bar, cries out, 'Je suis pas la. M'excusez messieurs. Je ne fais rien. Je raconte une histoire qui me fait chier de la raconter!' [I'm not here. Excuse me, gentlemen, I'm not doing anything. I'm telling a story that pisses me off when I tell it].

Absa's depiction of one poet's migrant experience in *Ainsi meurent les anges* recalls the internationalism of the Negritude poets and the cosmopolitan artistry of migritude writers. The film's musical score, which includes the kora, jazz, reggae, and the djembe, draws its inspiration from Africa and the transnational African diaspora, as did Senghor's poetry. Mory uses transnational cultural references: he appropriates Parisian monuments (the Bastille angel) as effortlessly as African diasporic sites of memory (Gorée Island). Like the Negritude poets, Absa participates in a transnational refusal to accept racist and colonialist assumptions that Europe is the earth's promised land. However, from the beginnings of his directorial career, Absa, like Chevrier's migritude artist, did not entertain romantic notions of a celebratory return to the agrarian African sources found in Léopold Sédar Senghor's poetry, nor did he reconstruct Negritude's cinematic counterpart: what Manthia Diawara calls 'return to the source' films (1992: 159).

In a 1997 interview titled 'Conflit des générations? 'Y'en a marre du cinéma-calebasse!'' [Conflict of Generations? Enough of Calabash Cinema!] Absa speaks of an emerging African cinema 'qui est urbain, qui pose des problèmes contemporaines et qui a l'adhésion d'un publique' [that is urban, that poses contemporary problems and that has a connection to a public audience].[1] Absa does not critique the employment of pre-colonial settings in cinema, but rather argues that film critics and festival juries should give equal consideration to 'une nouvelle generation qui n'a pas connu le village, qui a des préoccupations contemporaines et qui les pose avec beaucoup de maîtrise technique' [a new generation that did not grow up in the village, that poses contemporary concerns with a lot of technical mastery] (qtd. in Faye, 9). It appears that Absa, like the migritude writers, rejects Senghor's Africanité, yet there is an echo Senghorian nostalgia for a *royaume d'enfance* – kingdom of childhood – in *Ainsi meurent les anges*. Absa does not dismiss the notion of rootedness, then, but the assertion of an essentialized agrarian rootedness. Indeed, the city has increasingly become the territory of Senegalese childhoods. Senghor's interpretations of his Senegalese childhood and his rootedness were, after all, distinctly personal and not global.[2]

Despite the classification of Negritude as an historic art of resistance inspired by an outdated philosophy of essentialized origins, Negritude and its legacy are continually being re-evaluated. As Belinda Jack has argued, Negritude is not a monolithic doctrine with a single origin, but rather a philosophy with multiple versions and a complicated history. Perhaps in a move to recognize those diverse versions of Negritude, the protagonist of *Ainsi meurent les anges* quotes from the less canonical Negritude poets Birago Diop and David Diop. As Mory leaves Paris for Senegal, his son Waali, who has never been to Africa, recites David Diop's poem 'Afrique.' Absa's focus on David Diop, who was born in Bordeaux to Senegalese and Cameroonian parents, reminds the viewer that writers of African descent born in France – those who are the focus of contemporary studies of migritude and Parisianism – were also part of the Negritude movement. Diop's second manuscript perished with him as his plane crashed between Dakar and Paris, rendering him forever positioned between two continents, suspended in the paths of migration. In the film, Mory's manuscripts are cast about the streets of Paris before he leaves for Senegal.

It is interesting that David Diop's poetry, and not Senghor's, haunts Absa's film. And it is an even younger generation – Mory's son and then his nephew – who recite Diop's 'Afrique,' a poem that laments the author's exile from Africa. The celebrated poem begins, 'Afrique, mon Afrique/Afrique des fiers guerriers dans les savanes ancestrales/ Afrique que chante ma grand-mère/ Au bord de son fleuve lointain/ Je ne t'ai jamais connue' [Africa, my Africa/Africa of proud warriors in the ancestral savanas/Africa of whom my grandmother sings/ Beside her distant river/ I have never known you]. Although Mory has indeed 'known,' or lived in Africa, he never arguably 'knew' the proud warriors on ancestral savannahs. The viewer could take this to mean that the urban artist's memory, or perhaps his *royaume d'enfance*, is no longer connected to ancestral savannahs, or that the proud warriors who fought against colonization have transformed in the contemporary context into national leaders who are complicit in neocolonial enterprises. Or perhaps Mory sings for those in the diaspora like the character Alain, his friend who has never been to Africa, and says that he is not ready to return, or Mory's France-born son Waali, whose *enfance* in Paris will likewise diverge from Mory's. At the conclusion of Diop's poem, Africa responds to the disparaging speaker, drawing parallels between the continent and a tree 'Qui repousse patiement obstinément/Et dont les fruits ont peu-à-peu/ L'amère saveur de la liberté' [That grows back patiently obstinately/And little by little whose fruit possesses/the bitter taste of freedom]. Throughout the narrative, Mory, like the tree, re-asserts his roots, a move that contrasts sharply with his stepfather's severing of his own body. Mory's 'roots' here are not planted in a monolithic source, or single space: he claims the cosmopolitan aesthetics of Negritude, the globalized space of contemporary urban Senegal, and the legends of Gorée's Maam Kumba Castel.

Mory's severed connection to his childhood sweetheart Kumba, the princess of his *royaume d'enfance*, is the result of both paternal manipulation of masculinist versions of tradition and economic disparities between Senegal and France that prompt migration. Mory's stepfather, Djaji, refuses to accept Kumba as his daughter-in-law under the pretext that she is of a lower caste. Mory insinuates that the ulterior motive for the rejection is that Djaji desired her for himself. The name Kumba recalls the legend of Maam Kumba Castel, the guardian spirit of Gorée (Diouf 2000: 571). And as Carmela Garritano writes, 'Kumba's character functions as absence, the lack within [Mory] that he searches to fill, and for the film audience, she is a mystery to be unraveled' (162). Another mysterious absence – one that is more prominent than Kumba's – is Senghor's. It is tempting to see Kumba in terms of the Senghorian trope that depicts Africa as a beautiful woman, yet Kumba is not Senghor's 'femme nue, femme noire' [nude woman, black woman] or the 'terre promise' [promised land] of the famous poem. She is not romanticized mother Africa, but a tragic figure who longs to escape from her fathers, and who ultimately marries a wealthier man and then dies while giving birth. Mory's friend in Senegal tells him 'Kumba is *your* Kumba,' not the woman defined by his stepfather. Absa's version of Kumba suggests a rejection of Senghor's version of Africa as the idealized 'femme nue, femme noire'. Yet it is doubtful that the corrupt father figure in the film is supposed to be an embodiment of Senghor – one of the fathers of Negritude and the former head of the newly independent nation of Senegal – given Absa's suggestion that the significance of the stepfather-son relationship has a Pan-African reach:

> This film presented me with the question of how to approach the problem of the father in a society where he occupies an untouchable place. African man has not looked his father in the eyes. How else can we explain the violent, fratricidal rage which spreads across this continent? It is a matter of understanding the Oedipal complex in the African context through the experience of an intellectual who has missed his calling.[3]

If Mory's Oedipal battle entails ousting his stepfather, or narrating his own version of Kumba, the larger conflict is generational. The trope of Africa as mother experiences a gendered reversal; here the staging of postcolonial Africa is played through stepfathers and sons. In the scene where Mory recites the title poem as he looks over the graveyard where Kumba is buried, he asks the ancestors not to open their eyes, perhaps so they do not see that elders in Gorée have ordered him to go back to where he came from – meaning France – or because Djaji has cut off his own toes in order to fit into a new pair of European shoes. This climactic scene posits assimilation as self-mutiliation; here assimilation seems less motivated by Francophilia and more so by economic ambition and the quest for status through displays of material wealth. Mory's biological father is deceased and his stepfather has disappointed him, yet he finds some consolation in his alternate artistic fathers. Mory is reminded of Birago Diop's poem, 'Spirits,' which reads, 'Les morts ne sont pas morts' – The dead are not gone – 'Ecoutes plus souvents les choses que les êtres' – listen to things more often than beings. When Mory's mother has his future prophesied in cowrie shells, she is told that he is possessed by spirits. Perhaps he is possessed by the spirits that inhabit Birago Diop's poem, one that calls upon the listener to attend to the breathing of the ancestors and not the prescriptions of the living.

It is also possible to read the film as homage to Absa's cinematic father-figures. Absa's film is not the first to engage with issues surrounding Senegalese migration to Paris. After the Negritude poets' historic transnational gatherings in Paris, and decades before Absa, Beyala and Njami became internally known, the 1955 short film *Afrique sur Seine* was directed by sub-Saharan migrant artists in Paris: Robert Carristan, Jacques Mélo Kane, Mamadou Sarr, and Paulin Soumanou Vieyra. *Ainsi meurent les anges* pays particular homage to the cinéaste Djibril Diop Mambety, whom Absa assisted on *Hyenas* (1992). The protagonist of *Ainsi meurent les anges* recalls Mambety's protagonist of the same name in his 1973 film, *Touki Bouki* (*The Journey of the Hyena*).[4] The Mory in Mambety's oeuvre is a young man who dreams of migrating to France with his girlfriend Anta, dreams that are mirrored by the escapist desires of Absa's Mory and Kumba. The legendary figure in cosmopolitan Paris, Josephine Baker, sings a refrain about Paris as a slice of paradise on Earth that rings ironically throughout Mambety's ouevre. In Absa's film, the viewer is left with Aminata Naar Fall's lyrics, 'Tu ne sais où tu vas' [You don't know where you're going]. At the conclusion of *Ainsi meurent les anges*, Mory seems to be prepared to return to France, yet like his cinematic predecessor Mory, he remains on the docks as the ferry (here, the Gorée-Dakar ferry) pulls away. The title of Absa's film, 'And so Angels Die', is similar to the title of the third feature film in the trilogy that Mambety did not have time to complete before his death, *Malaika*. *Malaika* means angel in Swahili, and *malaaka* denotes angel in Wolof, a trans-lingual choice of words consistent with Mambety's trans-continental aspirations. Mambety was an ultimate creator of world cinema à la Sénégalaise. In *Hyenas,* Mambety fused a Swiss play, tropes of the American Western, and political commentaries on the World Bank's role in Africa.[5] In *Badou Boy* (1966) and *Le franc* (1994), Mambety appropriated the comic antics of silent film luminaries such as Charlie Chaplin and Buster Keaton. Throughout, as Anny Wynchank notes, Mambety inserted African oral tales of tricksters such as *Bouki la hyène* and *Ananzé l'araignée*. For Mambety, cinema making was not merely an eclectic appropriation, but reinvention; his aesthetics were an attempt to recreate his dreams (Ukadike 1998: 147). Mambety's influence can be discerned in Absa's reconfiguration of a cosmopolitan narrative (the Oedipal conflict) in an African context, and in his visual representations of Mory's memories and lost dreams.

Absa's film recalls Mambety's narrations of 'ordinary people' who face a series of choices in a world that is fraught with consumerism. Mory's poem echoes the rebellions against European assimilation by the Negritude poets, yet the story positions the Senegalese Djaji as the new agent of identity control. Just as the betrayal of the fathers of the new Senegalese nation is underscored at the conclusion of Sembene's film, *Faat Kine* (2001), Mory accuses his Djaji of ruining his opportunities for happiness. The fathers of both Mory and Kumba – and later the father of Yacine, who arranges her marriage to Mory for a sum – choose material possessions and the elevation of their own status over the aspirations of their children. The title poem reads, 'Ainsi meurent les anges/les voil s'émmerveiller sur la rivière d'argent' [and so angels die/ see them marveling over the river of silver/money].' In French, Djaji tells Mory that he has cast a blanket of shame over him, because he left Senegal in rags, and returned the same. Djaji is convinced that Mory's return narrative should conclude with the fulfillment of economic promises during his marriage negotiations, even though Mory did not consent to a second marriage. Yacine, the expected second wife, is then married off to a German suitor who brings expensive gifts for her family. Senghor's vision of the authentic convergence of cultures – cultures that could celebrate their own heritages and engage in mutual appropriation on equitable grounds – has remained unrealized here because decolonization – both economic and psychological – is not yet complete.

Through the motif of corrupt arranged marriages – of fathers who greedily promise their daughters to those who offer the greatest sums – and through the depiction of stepfathers who are willing to sever their own roots to fit into small European shoes, Absa issues a thinly veiled critique of national leaders who have succumbed to the lure of consumerism. Much has been said about the economic growth inspired by transnational workers 'from below'; Absa's protagonist rebels against a community that views the migrant solely as a vehicle for economic growth, one that equates fulfillment and promise with economic prosperity gained elsewhere. Mory is seen by that community not as a poet but as a shameful failure, a migrant who loses his job as a supermarket cleaner, one defeated by unemployment and debt. Although Absa is a successful director, he inspires viewers to contemplate the fates of migrants who leave a situation of high unemployment in Senegal only to face unemployment in France. Mory's subsequent departure from Paris is not depicted as a retreat into an idealized version of African traditions, à la Senghor, however. Instead, he returns to Gorée to explain to his stepfather that he cannot pay his debts. The arranged marriage plot serves to question, not romanticize, how 'tradition' is practised by his elders, and to critique Senegal's badly arranged economic liaisons with Europe.

Ainsi meurent les anges interrogates the 'great expectations' associated with international journeying and expatriation, expectations caught in a wave of *ex-patriatism*, or mass migration to places of work abroad. One cause of migration, and the source of Mory's troubles, is the badly arranged economic marriage (or divorce settlement) between France and Senegal. This arrangement is also at the heart of the production troubles of Senegalese artists who, wishing to make their films locally, resort to video technology. The old French colonial cannons that sit atop Gorée Island are a prominent image in the film. The viewer sees the French gun barrels pointed inward at the islanders, rather than out to sea, suggesting neocolonial sabotage. The angels of 'And so Angels Die' appear several times: on the individual level, the angels are the innocent dreamers, Mory and Kumba, whose dreams are crushed under the weight of their fathers' greed. The dream of independence, too, has been shrouded in the politics of debt, the politics of a continued forced marriage between Africa and the North. Before he leaves France, Mory visits the Bastille angel in Paris: that winged, gold statue on the Colonne de Juillet commemorating liberty and post-Bastille revolutions. If the first artistic revolution was Negritude; African cinema, perhaps, is the next. It is possible that the angels are also references to Absa's spiritual guides: Maam Kumba Castel, the Negritude poets, and filmmakers like Djibril Diop Mambety. In the final scene of Mambety's last film, *La petite vendeuse de soleil* (1999), a voiceover announces that the story is now cast into the ocean, a return to a source with fluid national boundaries. The poet Mory sits by the ocean in contemplation at the conclusion of *Ainsi meurent les anges*; Absa's film can be read as a continuation of Mambety's commitment to decolonization, and his groundless, cosmopolitan legacy.

Though narratives of migration are heterogeneous, there are several common motifs that have emerged: the interrogation of the idealization of spaces abroad as economic havens; the painful dislocation that emigrants experience as they live removed from home in a place that treats them as 'others'; the creation of diasporic communities abroad that retain, recover, or reject their bonds with the hearth; and the migrant writer's ability to choose from multiple cultures. In Absa's film, Senegalese poetry's cosmopolitan routes, as well as its personal African roots, are the sources returned to. While the physical, geographic position of the artist may be beyond his or her control, the aesthetics of the art itself need not be bound by the national. To claim access to global art, regardless of one's location, is to refuse the idea that culture is static and nationally owned. What both migritude and

Absa's film share is a redefinition of rootedness. Mory remains on the dock in Gorée, despite the pressure to seek economic prosperity elsewhere; Parisianists refuse to leave their space by the Seine, despite reactionary French politicians. At the same time, Absa's employment of video technology, which could render his film more accessible to Senegalese audiences accustomed to imported cinemas, is a statement that Senegal's technology should be locally owned. I would not describe film production grounded in Senegal as 'Senegallywood,' given Senegalese directors' resistance to Hollywood's commercialism. In any case, although the migrant artist may be 'sans complexe' when confronted with cultural ownership or cultural borrowing, that is not to say that one has to accept lingering, often debilitating economic ties between Senegal and Europe.

NOTES

1. All translations from the French in the text are mine, unless otherwise noted.
2. During the October 2006 Colloque Senghor at the University of the West Indies in Cave Hill, Barbados, the Senegalese scholar Souleymane Bachir Diagne discussed Senghor's deconstruction of his own essentialism within his highly personalized descriptions of his atypical childhood in Senegal. Senghor was brought up a Christian by Serer parents in a nation that is predominantly Muslim and Wolof. Diagne's lecture was titled 'L. S. Senghor's Philosophy of Dialogue Between Cultures and Religions.'
3. The quote from Absa here is taken from the introduction to *Ainsi meurent les anges* located on the website of its distributor, California Newsreel. The essay is available at http://www.newsreel.org.
4. The possible link between the character Mory in Mambety's *Touki Bouki* and Absa's Mory is suggested briefly in the introduction to *Ainsi meurent les anges* by California Newsreel. Kindly see endnote 3 above for the URL.
5. For an elaboration on Mambety's appropriation of the Western, see Dayna Oscherwitz's 'Of Cowboys and Elephants: Africa, Globalization, and the Nouveau Western in Djibril Diop Mambety's *Hyenas*,' forthcoming in *Research in African Literatures*.

WORKS CITED

Absa, Moussa Sene. *Ainsi meurent les anges*. Senegal: California Newsreel, 2001.

Adesanmi, Pius. 'Redefining Paris: Trans-Modernity and Francophone African Migritude Fiction.' *Modern Fiction Studies* 51.4 (2005): 958-75.

Chevrier, Jacques. 'Afrique(s)-sur-Seine: Autour de la notion de "Migritude"'. *Notre Librarie* 155-156 (2004): 13-17.

Diawara, Manthia. *African Cinema: Politics and Culture*. Bloomington: Indiana University Press, 1992.

Diop, David. 'Afrique.' In *Coup de pilon*. Paris: *Présence africaine*, 1956.

Diouf, Mamadou. 'Assimilation coloniale et identités religieuses de la civilité des originaires des Quatre Communes (Sénégal).' *Canadian Journal of African Studies/Revue Canadienne des Études africaines* 34.3 (2000): 565-87.

Faye, Modou Mamoune. 'Conflit des générations? "Y'en a marre du cinéma-calebasse!"' *Le Soleil* (Dakar) 21 March 1997: 9.

Garritano, Carmela. 'Troubled Men and the Women Who Create Havoc: Four Recent Films by West African Filmmakers.' *Research in African Literatures* 34.3 (2003): 159-65.

Harney, Elizabeth. *In Senghor's Shadow: Art, Politics, and the Avant-Garde in Senegal, 1960-1995*. Durham: Duke University Press, 2004.

Jack, Belinda Elizabeth. *Negritude and Literary Criticism: The History and Theory of 'Negro-African' Literature in French*. Westport, CT: Greenwood Press, 1996.

Jules-Rosette, Benetta. *Black Paris: The African Writer's Landscape*. Urbana and Chicago: University of Illinois Press, 1998.

Senghor, Léopold Sédar. 'Femme nue, femme noire' in *Chants d'ombre*. Paris: Éditions du Seuil, 1945.

Ukadike, N. Frank 'The Hyena's Last Laugh: A Conversation with Djibril Diop Mambety.' *Transition 78* (1998): 136-53.

Wynchank, Anny. *Djibril Diop Mambety ou le voyage du voyant*. Paris: Éditions A3, 2003.

Laughing Off Apartheid: *Drum* Magazine & the Political Economy of Laughter in Late Apartheid Film

Timothy Johns

During the last days of apartheid, something funny happened: comedy began to fuel the official ideology, the National Party's cultural script. Over the course of the 1980s, two popular film comedies sanctioned by the apartheid state – *The Gods Must Be Crazy* and *The Cosby Show* – catered, in odd ways, to the state's shaken cultural orthodoxy. While *The Gods Must Be Crazy* offered the patronizing example of a primitive African caught up unawares in the violence of modern life, *The Cosby Show* projected feeling for a non-threatening bourgeois family of African descent, symbolically out of touch with the mass movement which greeted apartheid's final decade. This article explores the way these two comedy programs – one an immensely popular South African export, released as a feature film abroad; the other an immensely popular American television show imported into South African living rooms – sanctioned not only official narratives of apartheid, but also provided a space for these narratives to continue within the post-apartheid political settlement. Against a tradition of criticism celebrating comedy for anti-statist ideological authority, here I argue comedy served to restore the official talking points of the regime just as it was signing off. Through its cathartic manifestation, comedy allowed audiences to 'laugh off' insidious elements of apartheid's economic structure while, at the same time, marginalizing the image of the black worker, the property owner of the city, from center stage.

To convey this unlikely idea of comedy – the farcical, the ludicrous, the ridiculous – as an instrument of state power, this essay contrasts the cathartic dimensions of these late apartheid comedies with the tragic realism honed, several decades earlier, by the Sophiatown-based *Drum* generation. Beginning in the 1920s and reaching critical mass with the monthly publication of *Drum* magazine in the 1950s, black intellectuals, especially from the Sophiatown 'location' of Johannesburg, began to challenge the official apartheid vision of the African in the city. Whereas *The Gods Must Be Crazy* and *The Cosby*

Show highlighted, in different ways, a sense of African arrival in the city through comic turns, gritty urban material from *Drum* magazine – at least until the eviction of residents from Sophiatown in 1960 – emphasized a tragic dramatic model. Anticipating the dark human comedy of this generation, R.R.R. Dhlomo's 1928 novella about the black experience in the city would simply be called *An African Tragedy*. How then was the standard *Drum* tale of the African worker arriving in the city, a theme traditionally riven with stark realism and tragic implications, reformed, during apartheid's last days, into something comic? Drawing on the cross-fertilization between film and fiction in *Drum* material, as well as research on African film spectatorship, I suggest that, for apartheid ideologues, a transformation from tragedy to comedy could only develop against a contested backdrop of moving labor – labor moving into urban spaces where the official arbiters of comedy did not want labor to be.

I

Stereotypes of black film spectatorship in South Africa developed hand-in-hand with the making of a modern labor force. Indeed, many studies of film in the region inevitably become, almost surreptitiously, studies of labor and labor recruitment. Early in the twentieth century, films screened to potential workers in rural areas – with the assistance of mobile vans owned by mining companies, equipped with generators – exposed black audiences, often for the first time, to moving pictures. Thus, in an effort to procure an industrial work force, film spectatorship grew alongside a massive labor recruitment scheme. Put another way, attention to moving pictures developed in concert with a program of moving bodies. As Glenn Reynolds notes in a recent dissertation, 'It was this movement of bodies, the steady displacement of recruits from the countryside to mining center, that led to the expansion of film-viewing opportunities for indigenous spectators after World War I' (2005: 4).

Movement emerges, then, as a key hermeneutic, a method or theory of interpretation linking patterns of film and labor. In the way of diamond and gold discoveries, the region reoriented its economy from a predominantly agrarian model to one based on industrial capitalism, particularly in the mining sector. Invariably, radically, this economic remodeling transformed demands on African labor. As Mahmood Mamdani notes in *Citizen and Subject: Contemporary Africa and the Legacy of Late Colonialism* (1996), within the nineteenth-century model, 'white farmers called for the breaking up of tribes to release labor that could be absorbed and controlled on settler farms' (68). However, under the design of industrial mining which followed, an entirely different arrangement took hold: internationally-financed corporations 'restructured the industrial workforce into one composed principally of migrant labour' (102). Partly by coincidence, by the dawn of the twentieth century, at the very moment that silent cinema began to inform popular consciousness, industrial mining 'required the retention of tribal reserves from which labor would be released when required and to which it could be returned when not needed' (68):

> In other words, while the official demand had once insisted on a static South African worker set in place, now the model required that black labor remained itinerant – a body continually journeying from the mines to the townships and back, and, in the greater seasonal trajectory, from the mines to the provincial 'homelands'.

A comfortable, settled domestic life in the city remained off limits.

But rather than reinforce one another, the new medium of entertainment and the new model for labor had to coexist – at least in this official discourse – as separate, irresolvable entities, entities perpetually in contradiction. The state could, with passes and police harassment, move the worker at will, like a chess piece. Yet a philosophy of cultural *permanence* continued to guide the white supremacist agenda – as if the African worker never moved at all. In *Homelands, Harlem, and Hollywood: South African Culture and the World Beyond* (1994), Rob Nixon notes how 'Apartheid became, across the world, popularly associated with fixity – with a refusal to 'move with the times' and, more precisely, with attempts to petrify racial and ethnic identities in a condition of timeless purity and physical isolation' (4). Paradoxically, then, under the logic of apartheid, a theory of cultural fixity would correspond to the practice of physical movement. Indeed, this was precisely the contradiction which apartheid-era accounts about black film spectatorship preserve. For if the African did not appear comfortably fixed before film, if she appeared to move away in fear and terror, the story of this reaction could add fresh credence to the argument that this same type of personality was not fully capable of permanent settlement in the city.

Thelma Gutsche's *History and Social Significance of Motion Pictures in South Africa 1895-1940* (1972) provides an interesting peek into this yellowing variety of film criticism. Since stereotypes in Gutsche lend themselves to the same ideas about provincial Africans that, a decade later, *The Gods Must Be Crazy* exploited, her monograph requires brief discussion here. Toward the end of *History and Social Significance*, in a modest section of about provincial African movie audiences ('*Natives: Entertainment*'), Gutsche observes that, before 1940, films shown in the 'remotest parts [of South Africa] at first terrified native inhabitants' (Gutsche 380). After a movie sponsored by the Native Recruiting Company would end, 'assembled audiences not infrequently rose as a body and inspected the back of the screen to [figure out] what had happened to the people they had just seen' (379). Terror reigned. For Gutsche notes that 'early audiences in some [rural] areas became hysterical when they saw their first *Felix the Cat* cartoon and rushed screaming into the night declaring the drawings to be 'ghosts'' (379).

And what of the urban film spectator? Although Gutsche admits black audiences in the cities became 'sophisticated,' reaction to cinema remained, in many cases, 'unexpected' – though there did exist evidence, according to Gutsche, that cinema 'kept otherwise idle natives off the street and occupied their leisure time' (378-9). But for proponents of white minority rule, the benefits of black film spectatorship went beyond simply 'sublimating potential criminal tendencies' (378). The Reverend Ray E. Phillips, an American missionary stationed in Johannesburg, would maintain that cinema could cool the worst outbreaks of worker grievance. In *The Bantu are Coming* (1930), Tim Couzens (1985) notes how 'Phillips' greatest boast was his use of movies as a peacemaker during the Great Strike of 1922' (97). 'When the strike was declared,' writes Phillips, 'we were asked by the Chamber of Mines to speed up the showing of films' (Phillips 1930: 149). The grievances of African workers appeared at a boiling point ('hot as a wasp's nest' are Phillips' words). Yet when the sun had faded and films were screened, workers laughed off the grievance. In this often cited passage, Phillips comments:

> Soon all the 4000 [workers in the compound] were shouting themselves sick with laughter as they watched Charlie [Chaplin], Larry Sermon, Buster Keaton, and others do their funny stuff. Never was there such a treat; so many laughs. At the end of two hours the compound was limp and weak from shouting, the vengeful spirit had long since vanished, and the great crowd bade us good night in the usual joyous way – many still laughing. There was no murder that night at the New Primrose [compound]. (Phillips 149)

In the missionary's intervention, comic films proffer the requisite Hollywood ending. Once a seething 'swarm,' 'hot as a wasp's nest,' the African spectator had suddenly laughed himself 'limp.' In Phillips' account, then, the 'vengeful spirit' of labor resistance could be iced by the comic genre. Alternative ways of understanding film spectatorship would certainly emerge. Yet, as we will see, it was this belief in the pacifying power of comedy, in the catharsis of laughter, which would often recur in South African history.

Although these 'very primitive' characterizations of the African spectator, these questionable accounts from earlier decades, may seem tediously anachronistic; and though a number of recent film critics, including Manthia Diawara, have heroically challenged the notion of any kind of 'backward' reception to cinema in sub-Saharan

Africa whatsoever; what remains striking about the passages cited above are the alternating portraits – first in Gutsche, then in Phillips – of terror and comedy. First let's take terror. For years, even in the very heart of Europe, from the birth of cinema studies, a myth has persisted about 'terror in the aisles': a belief that crowds, watching moving pictures for the first time, experienced collective panic (Gunning 1999: 818-32). According to Tom Gunning, 'in traditional accounts of the cinema's first audiences, one image stands out: the terrified reaction of spectators to [Louis Lumière's] *Arrival of a Train* (818). *Arrival of a Train*, a film first screened in Paris in 1895, depicted a locomotive heading into a train station, straight for the screen. 'According to a variety of historians, spectators reared back in their seats, or screamed, or got up and ran from the auditorium (or all three in succession)' as the imaginary train approached (818). Looking back at this early infancy for movie spectatorship, at an audience which naively mistakes a filmed locomotive for the real thing, the tendency has been to assume a certain aloofness: '*We* don't believe in the screen image in the manner that *they* did' (819). Which is to say, a discrimination is made between a contemporary audience, 'us' (people who effortlessly digest modern entertainment) and 'them' (the crowd stuck in the past, one step behind; an audience with no sense of scientific advancement, spectators who sense something terrifyingly anthropomorphic and primordial in cinematic projection). This discrimination between spectators at the movies was invested, from the very outset of film studies, with a clearly delineated imperial subtext. Indeed, the 'absolute novelty of the moving image' was said to reduce the first audience in Paris 'to a state usually attributed to savages in their primal encounter with the advanced technology of Western colonialists, howling and fleeing in impotent terror before the power of the machine' (819).

What was innovative about *The Gods Must Be Crazy* was the seamless web it constructed between this mythology of terror and a Chaplinesque brand of comedy – a hybrid aesthetic which served to police the imaginary boundary between metropolitan and non-metropolitan space. In the movie's notorious opening scene, a metropolitan man sitting in a plane high above the Kalahari drops a Coca-Cola bottle through a window. The bottle hits !Xi, a San man (or 'bushman' according to the old rhetoric) sitting peacefully below. Here, in this violent accidental exchange, a lesson about commodity relations emerges. As the African's 'virgin' experience with commodities, as his initial confrontation with modern objects, the film's opening sequence relates modernity as painful experience. However, the experience of pain on-screen permits a feeling of pleasure to ripple through the audience. For though the official poster for the movie would promise identification with all human subjects ('At last, a comedy everyone can laugh with!'), the point remained that the audience was, in fact, laughing *at* – and decidedly not *with* – the San actor on-screen. The intended audience is meant to gently humor !Xi's naiveté, but he must experience pain for the audience to laugh. Tragedy translates as comedy, as counterpoint.

Here, then, lies the 'comic' lesson of apartheid: the closer the ordinary African subject attaches himself to the things of the city (Harare is cited, but the model is clearly Johannesburg), the more pain he will endure. But to plot this perverse mix of comedy and tragedy, the movie must reemploy, within an age of sound and color, a figure from the silent black-and-white past: Charlie Chaplin. The silence of !Xi ('Only in a few instances are [his] thoughts or words translated') recalls Chaplin's early genius (Gugler 2009: 73).

Chaplin, as we know, first produced movies in an age before 'talkies'; that is, before the advent of sound film. Without these sonic textures at his command, Chaplin had to develop a thoroughly physical brand of humor. This brand of physical comedy – essentially a comedy of the moving body – would correspond, in the hands of apartheid logic, to the requisite narrative about moving labor, the story of the laborer's permanent discomfort beside urban belongings. !Xi's rapid gestures, his violent physical movements on-screen, appear – like the speed of urban life and urban work – frantic and overheated. Moving toward the orbit of the city, the dominant African subject, the provincial bumpkin, can never feel 'at home' in town, even in his own skin. His 'natural' tendency, especially when faced with urban stability, is violent movement – movement so excessive the audience is prompted to laugh, as the movement outfits the body meant to release it.

Despite superficial similarities, however, Chaplin and apartheid's bushman remain quite distinct creatures. In Chaplin, the myth of provincial stupidity dies on the vine. After entering town, the tramp continually learns and improves. Indeed, much like black South Africans attracted to the pace of Johannesburg, Chaplin's tramp never returns to the simpler life and its provincial pathology – nor does he wish to. By the end of *The Gold Rush* (1925), the tramp finds himself bathing in riches, a millionaire. Thus the figure on-screen appears to have undergone a complete economic and psychological overhaul. In this altered state, the tramp – a figure representing, in Chaplin's own time, the lumpenproletariat of the European city – assumes a place within the immediate orbit of capital and, more importantly, a feeling of comfort in modern metropolitan space, amidst metropolitan entertainment and commodities. Although Chaplin's hero does not entirely shed the old garb, he no longer retains the petrified consciousness of the provinces. So while apartheid's !Xi remains constantly puzzled and tragically exposed when surrounded by the accoutrements of modernity, Chaplin's engagement with these same objects becomes increasingly progressive and instructive – for both actor and audience. Chaplin's theater transforms objects of daily life 'from something ordinary, familiar, [and] immediately accessible, into something peculiar, striking and unexpected' (Brecht 1964: 143). 'Suddenly, [Chaplin] disorientates us,' Henri Lefebvre observes, 'but only to show us what we are when faced with [modern] objects; and these objects become suddenly alien, the familiar is no longer familiar' (Lefebvre 1991: 11). A common commodity – an item like a Coke bottle – thus becomes suddenly arresting in the tramp's hands. In this way, the joke lies not on the shoulders of the tramp alone: the audience also has pie on its face. A comic division between 'us,' the sophisticated spectators, and 'them,' the country bumpkins on-screen, undergoes constant inversion in Chaplin – a comic flirtation between on-screen material and audience reception which would remain, in apartheid cinema, completely off limits.

In contrast to the comedy of Chaplin, then, *The Gods Must Be Crazy* offers a parable about the African provincial's continual short-comings before the doorstep of urban enlightenment. Pained and confused by the commodity; driven on a wild goose chase to discover the commodity's secret, godlike powers, the film develops its traction, its laughs, around relentless semiotic confusion. Mistaking secular goods for legitimate gods (or in Quixotic terms, windmills for dragons), the hero is prevented from ever finding true comfort in the city. When the 'crazy' engagement with modern life is over, only then can !Xi return to something like normal life and his provincial cocoon. By the movie's final credits, we find our hero back in the Kalahari, near his quaint kraal, far from the anxieties of urban life. Peaceful tribal continuity has been restored – a coda which suggests an act of ethnographic grace, the helping hand of civilization as it rights the spiraling gloom of the endangered primitive's brush with modern things and modern times.

Mirroring the hand of the regime, Andrew Steyn, the Afrikaner zoologist in the movie (whose voice was dubbed into English for international release), shadows and protects the African country bumpkin's volatile ride. Yet he never punctures the 'bushman's innocent 'immaturity'. What Hegel once called Africa's 'childhood of history' is left intact. Indeed, the zoologist's guidance shelters !Xi not only from the confusion of urban entertainment, but, more pointedly, from the advances of a black liberation movement: insurgents who, in Keystone Kops fashion, literally slip on the movie's banana peels. Once the guerilla threat is exorcised, after the act of ethnographic restoration has finally been performed, the beauty of tribal stupidity can once again reflower. Rolling back the curtain to the origins of film and a fossilized ethnographic history, the encounter with the Coca-

Cola bottle can now finally heal. Yet by stressing, through various contradictions, ethnographic *fixity* in a film about 'native' *movement,* the real stand-in for Charlie Chaplin, the modern black migrant arriving for work in the mines of Johannesburg, becomes marginalized, lost from view. In other words, the romantically 'simple' San stands in for the real worker of the mines, the 'New African' divorced from modes of tribal life. In a film which broke box office records and spawned numerous sequels, the official apartheid narrative would bypass a serious study of the African worker – the very energy behind a modern, moving Johannesburg – and replace him with with a comic foil.

II

In *Drum* literature and film about the black experience in the city, surprising overlap often exists with this pro-apartheid plot – at least on the surface, in the broad outlines. For instance, in 'The Suitcase,' a short story by Ezekiel Mphahlele published in *Drum* in February 1955 (under the pseudonym 'Bruno Esekie'), we find a number of the same exigencies which would later greet the 'bushman' of apartheid. Like !Xi, Timi, the hero of Mphahlele's tale, finds himself 'led on something of a wild goose chase' (Mphahlele 1989: 73). While, in *The Gods Must Be Crazy,* the hero fruitlessly seeks deeper spiritual meaning in a Coke bottle, the hero of this *Drum* tale fruitlessly pounds the pavement for a decent wage (73). But the connections run deeper. Like !Xi, Timi must also solve the puzzle of a mysterious object – in this case, a suitcase. During a bus ride from central Johannesburg to the Sophiatown slum, the titular object is left behind by a pair of passengers. Desperately in need of money ('Now his wife was ill. She was about to have a baby; a third baby.'), Timi assumes unlawful ownership over the abandoned item (74). Like the Coke bottle, the contents inside the suitcase – its deeper 'meaning,' if you will – remain a mystery to the protagonist, at least until the very end, when the suitcase if finally opened. But where the apartheid film mines this uncertainty for laughs, Mphahlele's short story takes a decidedly tragic turn. Ensnared by the police, forced to directly confront the contents of the suitcase, the story ends in a nightmarish blur:

> It was a ghastly sight. A dead baby that could not have been born more than twelve hours before. A naked, white, curly-haired image of death. Timi gasped and felt sick and faint. They had to support him to the counter to make a statement. He told the truth. He knew he had gambled with chance; the chance that was to cost him eighteen months' hard labour. (Mphahlele 78)

Tragedy, at least as Aristotle defines the term, depends on people falling from high places: kings, prime ministers, tycoons, vice chancellors. But in 'The Suitcase' and other *Drum*-era fiction, tragedy is endured – again and again in this kind of lurid fashion – by the lower orders: informal laborers, *tsotsis*, black miners, queens of the local *shebeen*, urchins on the street. Nevertheless, behind the surface of *Drum*'s deliberately sensational, humorless portraits of dead babies and the city's lower depths, one can still glean the fall from up high. What prompts this tragic design, in my view, is anxiety about owning a home – and losing it, falling from grace. Ordinary Africans, the black lumpenproletariat entrenched on the Johannesburg Reef, desired a piece of the gold city to call their own. Sophiatown, despite its rough and tumble atmosphere and reputation, provided this opportunity – at least for select home owners. 'The persistence of Sophia rankled with the [apartheid] regime,' observes Rob Nixon, 'because it was one of the last areas where city blacks could legitimately own property' (36). Therefore, loss of working class designs on property – especially after Sophiatown began to be bulldozed in February 1955, the same month Mphahlele's story was published – channels something of this tragic quality. '[T]he regime insisted that blacks would only be tolerated in the city as renters and temporary sojourners with no permanent claim on urban residence. The face of Sophia mocked apartheid, so it had to be destroyed' (Nixon 37). Hence Mphahlele's suitcase: the emblem of the sojourner; of the family man in flux; of the African without a place for his own wife or children; of the figure moving, in harried fashion, from one 'location' and impulse to the next; of the man who, looking inside the interior, can only find a face – 'A naked, white, curly-haired image of death' – destroyed. At the end of Sophiatown's renaissance, the suitcase of the story might be said to represent the raw, itinerant future; the grinding feeling of homelessness under the official state apparatus; while the dead African child, so young the skin remains white, registers a feeling for the aborted present.

What gets lost in this analysis of urban property is the fact that, as much as writers of the *Drum* generation hoped to remain in Sophiatown, they also desired to escape it. And this is where the escapism of American cinema fit in, the novel cross-fertilization of Hollywood film and black South African literature of the times. 'There was a sanctuary in the cinema,' *Drum* writer Bloke Modisane remarks in his autobiography, *Blame Me on History* (1963). 'I was a cinema fan, the cinema being the only cultural recreation for the Africans, [the only place] I could take a date...for a two-hour escape from the physical reality of South Africa' (133). So while the bricks and mortar of the city, concrete property in Sophiatown, was greatly desired, so too was an 'escape' from the 'physical reality' of the state and the slum – deliverance offered at the local bioscope. Any cursory perusal of *Drum* reveals the influence of the B-grade Hollywood scripts, the sensational 'pulp' literature and film of the 1950s. *Drum* literally wore Hollywood on its sleeve: the 'Palm Beach suits, straw hats and white shoes' described, for instance, in Henry Nxumalo's 'The Birth of a Tsotsi' (1951) confirm the extent to which fancy fashion, observed on-screen, mixed in with Sophiatown's daily grime (Nxumalo 1989: 19). But if film influenced fiction, the opposite held true as well. Co-written by members of the *Drum* generation, Lionel Rogosin's remarkable low-budget movie, *Come Back, Africa* (1959), featured appearances by *Drum* regulars Can Themba, Lewis Nkosi, and Bloke Modisane, as well as a show-stealing cameo by Miriam Makeba. Here chatter and critique – and the place of the African in the city – came to be redeemed across mediums, in film and fiction at once. Compared to the comic barbs which would later greet an African actor hopelessly hovering at the periphery of urban space, *Come Back, Africa* presented black urbanism from an embedded – if still embattled and precariously unsettled – point of view.

III

Come Back, Africa is now receiving modest scholarly attention. Indeed, after apartheid, a number of critics began to restore the image of the African in the city through this particular film – an image tarnished by apartheid history and grim offerings like *The Gods Must Be Crazy*. But we should never mistake academic scholarship for popularity, peer-reviewed articles for an immensely successful film's lasting influence. *The Gods Must Be Crazy* jump-started a hysterical legacy that, in many ways, still haunts us. 'The film had its greatest success in Japan, where it was the highest-grossing movie in 1982. In France, it won the Grand Prize at the Chamrousse Festival...and became the top box office success in 1983. In the US, after a false start in 1982, it was released afresh in 1984, moved from art houses to commercial theaters and became the biggest foreign box-office hit in movie history' (Gugler 2003: 71). Although occasional protests greeted screenings of the movie – on college campuses in America, for instance, where divestment movements were taking shape – *Gods* became a cultural coup for the faltering regime. As an example of the film's lasting international influence, as late as a decade later, around the time of South Africa's 1994 presidential election, Hong Kong reproduced three loosely based copies: *Crazy Safari* (1991), *Crazy Hong Kong* (1993), and *The Gods Must Be Funny in China* (1994) (Gugler 78-9). International audiences, then and now, may not have fully realized that absorption in this template underscored tacit approval for the apartheid imagination. But as Siegfried Kracauer noted in *From Caligari to Hitler: A Psychological History of German Film* (1947), 'The international reception of any achievement depends upon its capacity for arousing fertile misunderstandings everywhere' (Kracauer 51). Apparently 'fertile misunderstandings' bloomed!

Many decided that comedy simply could not reinforce the logic of oppression. When *The Gods Must Be Crazy* was taken to task for its mean-spirited construction of black life, critics tripped over one another to defend the film. Vincent Canby, then a *New York Times* movie critic, wrote: 'I think it's safe to guess that Mr Uys [the director] is certainly neither a racist nor an apologist. Nobody with the sense of humor that he displays in *The Gods Must Be Crazy* could be... [N]arrowness of vision is antithetical to the creation of laughter' (Davis 93).

But one wonders: Is 'narrowness of vision' really 'antithetical to the creation of laughter'? Mikhail Bakhtin, whose *Rabelais and His World* characterized comedy as carnivalesque and anti-authoritarian, paved the way for much of today's critical response to the genre. Bertolt Brecht, however, noting the enjoyment of moviegoers during a screening of Chaplin's *The Face on the Bar Room Floor* (1914), cynically observed that comic film 'owes at least part of its effectiveness to the brutality of the audience' (Lynn 1997: 131).

> Under apartheid, Brecht's paradigm for comedy makes a better fit than Bakhtin's. The act of laughing during a comedy could help purge the savage truth of the reality outside the theater – or, in the case of *The Cosby Show*, outside the comfort of one's own living room.

In conclusion, I examine how the late apartheid media doubled up their bets with this second comedy, *The Cosby Show*. The top-rated television program during apartheid's dying days, *The Cosby Show,* glued South Africans to their living room seats with the same ferocity *The Gods Must Be Crazy* captured abroad, during the same era, in movie theaters. 'First broadcast on TV4 at 10:30 pm Mondays, a typically late night entertainment channel geared toward whites and broadcast in English, the program ... caused ripples through society,' writes Linda Fuller in *The Cosby Show: Audiences, Impact, and Implications* (1992: 110).

To be sure, *The Gods Must Be Crazy* and Bill Cosby's 'sit-com' (situation comedy) appear, at first glance, a strange alliance, an odd couple – and not simply because of the different film mediums (feature 35 mm and a television broadcast). An upwardly mobile pair of African-American professionals, a gynecologist and a lawyer happily married and comfortably settled in a Brooklyn brownstone – the Huxtables were hardly the exploited San of Uys' film. In a sense, the African-American family broke with the old stereotype: black terror when confronted with modern things and modern places. A retired South African teacher is said to have responded: 'The whole [Cosby] series shows that people of other colours are very much alike mentally, and it should break down South Africans' unfortunate way of condescending to "lesser intelligence"' (Fuller 1992: 112-13).

Much of the scholarship about *The Cosby Show*'s South African stint has emphasized this positive reception, the program's progressive representation of black characters. Many felt the image of educated, middle class African subjects appeared at odds with apartheid discourse. Yet observers might also notice that the two comedies – *The Gods Must Be Crazy* and *The Cosby Show* – became compatible during an unusual historical transition: the movement out of apartheid proper into an ameliorated (some would say 'neo-liberal' or 'neo-colonial') version of it. My own contention is that, just before Nelson Mandela took power, a Cosby-like vision of bourgeois blackness became desperately needed by the proponents of the old white minority rule.

We should not underestimate the fact that, in a nation fanatical about censorship, P. W. Botha, the head of the National Party, gave the green light to *The Cosby Show*'s weekly screening. Remarkably, until 1976, television had been completely banned in South Africa. Any program shown on national television, especially in the 1980s, had to pass rigid ideological muster. Years earlier, 'Apartheid's chief architect, Prime Minister Hendrik Verwoerd, urged that TV be regarded with the same circumspection as poison gas and the atom bomb' (Nixon 1994: 45). Many therefore saw the endearing laughter that greeted *The Cosby Show* as a trojan horse, a weapon that could be used, within the bowels of the apartheid media apparatus, to undo it. Used as a carrot to put pressure on the regime, Bishop Desmond Tutu convinced Bill Cosby to withdraw the show from circulation in South Africa in 1987 (Nixon 160).

Then why was Botha interested in popularizing this type of material in South Africa? As Sut Jhally and Justin Lewis note in their American study of the Cosby phenomenon – *Enlightened Racism: The Cosby Show, Audiences, and the Myth of the American Dream* (1992) – the breaking down of barriers and racial prejudice in the sitcom became a hollow gesture without a more thorough exploration of property relations and class. Huxtable family comfort, the easy humor of the American family, appears underwritten by the economic security of a social elite. Although the family supposedly lives in Brooklyn, a major urban borough of New York City, their milieu is distinctly *sub*-urban, divided from the gritty inner city trials projected, decades earlier, in *Drum*.

To some observers in South Africa, Cosby elitism, the nuclear family's cozy isolation from radical causes and progressive urban action, stood out. As one respondent to a survey wrote: 'I feel that *The Cosby Show* is a very good show but it is a bit hard to believe because I don't think that families can be as happy like that ALL THE TIME.'

Another critical respondent noted that South African blacks 'do not see any humour in seeing other black people finding it "so easy" and most probably even feel a little resentful' (Fuller 112-13). All South Africans were not impressed by smiling, laughing Huxtables. Indeed, no Stokely Carmichael or Amiri Baraka, much less a Paul Robeson or Angela Davis, paraded among the comedy's cast. A legacy of African-American struggle, closely monitored throughout the twentieth century by black South Africans, would remain deeply sublimated by the show, flattened by the Reaganesque glow of Cosby's genteel calculus. In fact, the black family's suburban make up would have been impossible to transfer to the 'new South Africa,' as only thin foundations for a substantial black middle class existed. But since *The Cosby Show* celebrated private property and bourgeois decorum, as well as a possible antidote to militant disobedience, guardians of apartheid welcomed it with open arms. As Botha himself once remarked: 'If a man has possessions and is able to build his family life around these possessions, then one already has laid the foundations for resisting communism' (Norval 233-4). Bill Cosby's Cliff Huxtable, family patriarch in a household brimming with possessions, thus helped buttress 'resistance' to apartheid's ever-present menace.

As Aletta Norval points out in *Deconstructing Apartheid Discourse* (1996), the final years of the state 'necessitated the construction of a black middle class with a stake in the system.' The regime 'facilitated the delimitation of a space in which an "acceptable" blackness could exist legitimately within the boundaries of "white" South Africa.' Moreover, the projection of this 'black middle class was understood as the urban corollary of the "good tribal" African' (Norval 233). For these reasons, in the popular imagination, the two comedies fit apartheid ideology to the core. Under the two-tiered scheme, a civilized, post-apartheid black elite (black middle class citizens like the Cosbys) could be constructed in relief of the uncivilized tribal subject (!Xi, the San 'bushman'). In the late apartheid imagination, these two seemingly disjointed comic vehicles could thus operate in tandem, joined at the hip. And the cathartic laughter which greeted these spectacles could sap something of the *Drum* generation's serious portrait of the African in the city.

WORKS CITED

Bakhtin, M. M. *Rabelais and His World.* Trans. Michael Holquist. Cambridge: Cambridge University Press, 1968.

Brecht, Bertolt. 'Short Description of a New Technique of Acting which Produces an Alienation Effect.' 136-47. From *Brecht on Theatre.* Trans. John Willett. New

York: Hill and Wang, 1964.

Couzens, Tim. *The New African: A Study of the Life and Work of H. I. E. Dhlomo.* Johannesburg: Ravan Press, 1985.

Davis, Peter. *In Darkest Hollywood: Exploring the Jungles of Cinema's South Africa.* Randburg, South Africa: Ravan Press; Athens, Ohio: Ohio University Press, 1996.

Diawara, Manthia. *African Cinema: Politics and Culture.* Bloomington: Indiana University Press, 1992.

Fuller, Linda K.. *The Cosby Show: Audiences, Impacts, and Implications.* Westport, Connecticut: Greenwood Press 1992.

Gugler, Josef. *African Film: Re-Imagining a Continent.* Bloomington, IN; Cape Town; Oxford: Indiana University Press, David Philip and James Currey, 2003.

Gunning, Tom. 'An Aesthetic of Astonishment: Early Film and the (In)credulous Spectator.' From *Film Theory and Criticism: Introductory Readings. Fifth Edition.* Eds Leo Braudy and Marshall Cohen. Oxford University Press, 1999.

Gutsche, Thelma. *The History and Social Significance of Motion Pictures in South Africa, 1895-1940.* Cape Town: Howard Timmins, 1972.

Jhally, Sut and Justin Lewis. *Enlightened Racism: The Cosby Show, Audiences, and the Myth of the American Dream.* Boulder: Westview Press, 1992.

Kracauer, Siegfried. *From Caligari to Hitler: A Psychological History of German Film.* Princeton, NJ: Princeton University Press, 1974.

Lefebvre, Henri. *Critique of Everyday Life. Volume One.* Trans. John Moore. New York and London: Verso Press, 1991.

Lynn, Kenneth S. *Charlie Chaplin and His Times.* New York: Simon & Schuster, 1997.

Mamdani, Mahmood. *Citizen and Subject: Contemporary Africa and the Legacy of Late Colonialism.* Princeton NJ: Princeton University Press; Oxford: James Currey, 1996

Modisane, Bloke. *Blame Me on History.* New York: E. P. Dutton & Co, 1963.

Mphahlele, Ezekiel. 'The Suitcase,' 73-8. From *The 'Drum' Decade: Stories from the 1950s.* Ed. Michael Chapman. Pietermaritzburg: University of Natal Press, 1989.

Nixon, Rob. *Homelands, Harlem and Hollywood: South African Culture and the World Beyond.* New York and London: Routledge, 1994.

Norval, Aletta J.. *Deconstructing Apartheid Discourse.* New York and London: Verso Press, 1996.

Nxumalo, Henry. 'The Birth of a Tsotsi,' 18-23. From *The 'Drum' Decade: Stories from the 1950s.* Ed. Michael Chapman. Pietermaritzburg: University of Natal Press, 1989.

Phillips, Ray E.. *The Bantu are Coming: Phases of South Africa's Race Problem.* London: Student Christian Movement Press, 1930.

Reynolds, Glen. 'Image and Empire: Cinema, Race and the Rise of Mass Black Spectatorship in Southern Africa, 1920-1940.' Unpublished dissertation in History, State University of New York at Stony Brook, 2005.

The Works of Jean-Marie Teno & Raoul Peck: Restoring Life to a Fleeced Continent

David M.M. Riep

'Someone said at independence "The principle victory of colonization was also to have perpetuated a real cultural genocide." '[1] The issues of cultural genocide and assimilation both play a major role in the history of the African continent. Although each specific region experienced diverse effects from the unforgiving colonial process, the shared devastation left in its wake cannot go unnoticed. In the films *Afrique, je te plumerai* (*Africa, I will fleece you*), by Jean-Marie Teno, and *Lumumba: Death of a Prophet,* by Raoul Peck, these issues are explored within the guise of two specific West African countries. Although both directors explore the lasting effects of colonialism on multiple layers, they each dedicate specific scenes to the visual arts of Africa, both of which confront the appropriation and reassignment of meaning in regards to such objects. By examining the use of the visual arts in the fleecing of African culture, both filmmakers provide powerful statements regarding colonialism and the resulting histories that unfolded, and use their respective media to resist and respond to the contemporary colonial continuum.

When addressing such a broad topic as the visual arts and its ability to express meaning, a logical starting point centers on the idea of context. It can be argued that once something has been taken out of its original context, it can take on any assigned meaning. The act of appropriation therefore becomes a tool by which individuals or cultures are placed in a position of power, and assume the ability to assign or reassign meaning. This idea of appropriation is explored in an unassuming scene from Peck's film on Patrice Lumumba. Under the vocals of *Independence Cha Cha Cha,* Peck leads the viewer through Belgium's Royal Museum for Central Africa.[2] The viewer is taken through an expansive hall, lined with cabinets full of 'curiosities' from the Belgian Congo. While Peck takes us through the exhibit space, a chilling voiceover subtly alerts us to the essence of the visual imagery, 'There are many ways of killing someone.'[3] Throughout the scene, we wander through the space, which is filmed from a low angle, limiting the viewer's access to the contents of the cabinets themselves. One notices the groups of white Belgians browsing the hall, which is supplemented by exotic plants and various examples of wildlife from Central Africa. Alongside the 'stuffed' animals on display, which are examples of various 'types' of species, we are also presented with a sculptural group representing the indigenous human culture of Leopold's Congo. The sculptures seem quite appropriate, in that they also represent species 'types,' playing into European stereotypes of 'savage Africa.'[4] Peck gives us various views of a muscular Congolese man, who appears to be engaged in a physical struggle. One can contrast this to a well known figure-type of the Western canon, Michelangelo's *David*.[5] While this Western 'type' embodies the fullness of man's potential, highlighting the disciplined mental and physical capacity of civilized culture, the Congolese example seems to emphasize the polar opposite. Clearly, the position of the figures and the focus of their respective gazes give rise to fundamental divisions of power. While *David* stands erect, alert and composed, his gaze looking confidently toward the future, his African counterpart's focus is much more immediate, as he engages in a physical struggle and maintains a crazed facial expression. His primitive mind is given visual representation in a savage form, which is frantically engaged in an uncivilized activity.

Peck also includes several views of a Congolese female sculpture in this scene, further expanding this notion of savagery, as she is presented as an exotic, sensual specimen. This full-figured nude offers the viewer a glimpse of erotic Africa, where primal desires are made manifest in her reclining form. One is quickly reminded of the many Western examples of the reclining nude in the arts, such as Titian's *Venus of Urbino* .[6] However, in contrast to Titian's representation of beauty, which is virtually elevated to an expression of spirituality, we are presented with a naked female whose passive yet seductive pose flirts with the vulgar. She is presented both visually immediate, and immediate as a decorative object of use. Through the emphasis on her sexuality, she is reduced to an object of consumption, along with the various examples of material culture found among the display cabinets.

The figures not only serve to define boundaries between the humane and the savage, but open up the possibility for further post-colonial discourse through which African cultures are positioned in terms of lack and absence, in both a physical and mental capacity. While the myth of Africa as the 'Dark Continent' was conditioned by internal European concerns, this constructed identity served numerous ends, supported by the sciences, to show how Africans were biologically different and lower than human.[7] Race thus became an evolutionary development, where the African was positioned as below the proper starting point for social development, and thus in need of imperial guardianship. This belief in racial superiority and inferiority soon translated itself in a physical manner, where physical characteristics were equated with one's social development in human society.[8] Interestingly enough, the development of ethnology as a legitimate science further proved helpful in justifying the colonial activities of the West within the African continent.[9] Thus, a hierarchy was created wherein cultural beliefs and constructions of identity were the basis of social, and to a greater extent human, stratification. While the methods of ethnology are no longer regarded as scientifically legitimate, one can see in Peck's film sequence how its early developments still play a relevant role in the formation of identity between the West and the 'Other.'

In addition to confronting the constructed notions of identity, the inclusion of the film's museum sequence goes hand in hand with Peck's aforementioned statement about death. Colonial Belgium truly did find various ways of killing the indigenous Congolese cultures. The civilized people of Belgium were surely presented with a false view of Congolese cultural 'types,' which served to re-emphasize their lower status as human beings, and therefore justify the colonial activities that took place over the past century. Aside from the sculptural representations of Congolese 'types' found among the exhibition space, further attention should be directed toward the display cabinets, and their contents. As the viewer is guided through the museum space, one can notice the enormous quantity of objects arranged behind the glass. Glimpses of carved figural sculpture are seen among weapons, textiles and other objects of cultural significance. This display itself, although unassuming, adds another dimension to the Belgian narrative of the Congo.

When it comes to museums and display techniques, the viewer is often unaware of the role of the curator and his or her interpretation. In a display such as the one shown by Peck, one is reminded of Susan Vogel's 1988 exhibition Art/artifact, which focused on display politics and African art.[10] In this exhibition, Vogel reminds us that the physical setting of an object adds to its overall meaning and reception by its viewing audience. Regarding Peck's film, one may apply several ideas from Vogel's work that further identify the cultural appropriation that is taking place in this seemingly harmless scene. To begin, one immediately notices the overall look of the Central African Ethnography gallery. Although the very name itself serves to strip away any individuality from these various cultures, the organization furthers the notion of conqueror and conquered. Neat and orderly, the great hall is lined on either side with expansive wood and glass cases, nearly overflowing with objects grouped under the title of 'Central Africa.' The style of this presentation alludes to the idea that the objects on display are void of any complex meaning.[11] This is accomplished by the grouping of objects within the cases, suggesting that each individual object is equal in value and meaning to any other. Not only does this downplay the existence and importance of diverse cultures within the region, but places the viewer in a position of power through the viewing of the region's 'collective spoils.' One must not overlook the fact that these objects represent 'Central Africa' to the Belgian viewing audience, who simply browse through an environment that has been contained through the civilizing force of colonialism. As Peck advances through the gallery space, one notices how this display technique begins to further reinforce ideas of worth and value, regarding the objects themselves, and the cultures that produced them. The casual display not only glosses over the cultural significance of the objects, but suggests that they are not very valuable. Unlike the highly regarded artistic masters of the West, whose works are displayed individually and demand private space within their environment, the grouped display of the Congolese objects advocates that they should not be viewed as valuable works of art, but rather 'specimens,' as would be found among the entomology cases of a natural history museum. Rather than highlighting the inherent qualities of the specific objects, the presentation creates a generalized display of 'exotic African culture' to quench the curiosity of the civilized viewer.

In addition to the display politics evident in this scene, Peck may have been expressing further ideas through his use of museum footage. While one can identify the overt problems found in the Central African Ethnography gallery, there are several underlying themes that further the presence of a 'cultural genocide' enacted through Belgian colonial rule. One of the major understatements in this scene revolves around the collection itself. Although rather unassuming, one should note that the very presence of these objects in the gallery suggests a story in itself. Throughout the scene, Peck shows casual Belgian citizens browsing the 'native curiosities' within the safe confines of their social environment. Yet, there is no evidence of how these objects arrived in their current location. I would suggest that Peck further alludes to the stripping away of culture on a tangible level through this scene. Although many major points in his film regarding the loss of culture are visualized through colonial-era propaganda film, the physical presence of these art objects in a Belgian institution is a powerful way to physically express these ideas. The continued exhibition of these objects, which lack any Congolese intervention, bolsters a continuum of colonial power relations into the post-colonial period. By their very presence, one may assume that the politics of travel, display and consumption have remained untouched, even while the political grip of colonialism was loosed. By removing the objects from their cultural context through appropriation, the conquered take on new meaning as assigned to them by the conqueror. However, this negotiation of meaning comes full circle in the films of both Peck and Teno, who expose the neo-colonial presence in their respective countries, and reappropriate meaning through their own work.

Peck's emphasis on meaning and context can be further explored through Vogel's work on a broader level. Regarding the art of Africa, she explains that 'Western culture has appropriated [it] and attributed to it meanings that are overwhelmingly Western.'[12] This idea is articulated in such displays as the one provided by Peck. These display politics highlight the fact that the viewing (Western) audience is unclear about the original status of the objects, and too quick to accept the impossibility of viewing them through the eyes of the original audience.[13] Furthermore, as Peck observes throughout his film, the original audience itself has been stripped of its own 'original status,' which in essence kills its very existence.

Peck highlights a final point of interest regarding the appropriation of both object and culture by emphasizing what has been removed. Throughout the scene, the viewer sees image upon image of Congolese objects, yet no indication is made which points to the fact that millions of Congolese people died unnatural deaths while these cultural 'specimens' were brought back to Belgium. I would suggest that Peck avoids any type of specific attribution to the displayed objects in order to allow the viewer access to the collection through a 'Belgian lens.' By allowing the objects to remain in their anonymity, one gains the perspective of the viewing audience, gazing upon the exotic 'other.' This emphasis on the gaze as a signifier of power and status can equally be applied to the activities of the 1897 World Fair, upon which Peck also highlights in regards to issues of exile and identity. While the Fair, much like the museum exhibit, served as a site for Western entertainment and consumption, the lifeless objects that one finds on display today were replaced by living beings from the Belgian Congo, equally objectified and exiled from their home. Chilling parallels may be drawn as Peck wanders through the countless display cases in this scene. As we are taken through the museum, one may relate this act of wandering and displacement to the Congolese who were placed on living display at the World Fair, as well as the restless soul of Patrice Lumumba, Peck's prophet, whose exiled spirit shared a similar fate.[14]

Likewise, Jean-Marie Teno also uses the visual arts to emphasize the idea of cultural genocide and appropriation. During a scene relating a story told to him by his grandfather, Teno provides the viewer with images of artists creating various works of art in a remote settlement. His voiceover states the following:

> Once upon a time, in a country where abundance and prosperity reigned. The country of the larks. One day, some hunters of another color arrived from abroad. The larks offered them all the good things they had in their village. Delighted, the hunters decided to remain in this country where they found an abundance of things lacking in their country.
>
> They said to the larks, 'We are brothers, your place is my place, you are going to work for me, for presently I am in great need,' The hunters arrived in ever greater number, and settled in. Everyday, sometimes without eating and drinking, the larks had to work. The entire village had to work, even women and children. Their song become a lament that often could be heard late into the night. One day the hunters departed. Before parting they installed a new chief. The new chief was to their liking. Some say, that he was a hunter-sorcerer, who, very old and fearing death, found the force to shed his earthly body and slipped into the first hut he found. There he entered the body of a newborn lark. From that day on, the village witnessed a strange breed of larks with no respect for their brothers, whom they treated like slaves, they even agreed to stock in their villages toxic wastes refused by other villages.[15]

Although one could equate the juxtaposition of word and image in this scene to a comment made by Teno expressing his regret for not paying closer attention to village culture during his school years, and the onslaught of colonialism throughout Cameroon, the true significance goes much deeper. The art objects shown throughout this scene are not cultural 'types,' as is shown in Peck's Royal Museum, but specific objects of royalty linked with the Bamum kingdom of western Cameroon. Throughout the Cameroon Grasslands, rulers and kings used the arts to bolster their prestige and authority.[16] Not only did the arts serve as a visual symbol of power and status, but art objects were often exchanged upon the creation of political alliances, between both indigenous and foreign cultures.[17] The kings who were represented by these art objects were viewed as divine religious leaders, and oversaw the structure of society through their cultural seat of authority. Although the encroachment of colonial forces greatly reduced this authority, the arts were still used exclusively by kings and his nobles through the early twentieth century.[18] Because many of the Cameroon Grassland kingdoms attributed all art objects to their kings, the objects served a very specific purpose in relating conceptual ideas of power and authority in a visual manner.

Through the audio and visual aspects of this scene, Teno links the arts with the cultural genocide that occurred through colonialism. While we see these royal artists creating visual objects of kingship, Teno's narration outlines the colonial process by which the authority of these kings was stripped away by the 'hunters,' namely the European powers that consumed Cameroon in the nineteenth and twentieth centuries. As we watch these artists at work, we are reminded of those whose rightful position of power was taken away, and rendered a useless thing of the past. By overthrowing local authority, the colonial forces dealt a death blow to the Cameroon Grassland cultures, relegating the memory of such histories to the outskirts of developed society.

After this juxtaposition, Teno skillfully transitions to a closer examination of local rule and authority by presenting the viewer with an image of former Bamum king Njoya's (ruled 1885-1931) palace. This scene serves as a response to the colonial myths which, for the case of Cameroon, justified the assimilation of indigenous populations into French cultural systems. Teno presents the viewer with a local historian who outlines a brief history of King Njoya, and his innovations as a 'king/inventor.'[19] Njoya, aside from his use of the visual arts to bolster his authority, developed a complex written language that was used throughout his kingdom as a unifying cultural force. His development of Shu-Mon as an official language served to eradicate the language system of his enemies, thus creating cultural solidarity. This action by Njoya creates a fascinating predicament regarding intercultural relations and assimilation, which ties in well with the French colonial process. Through establishing Shu-Mon as an 'official language,' the king created an outlet through which to dissolve the cultural heterogeneity of his enemies. Likewise, upon the arrival of the French in 1919, the very same action would occur through the establishment of an official western language throughout Cameroon, and the closing of all indigenous schools that were previously established by Njoya. Similar in their motives, both cultures viewed culture-specific language systems as an obstacle to complete assimilation and the promotion of new social aspects from an outside entity.

I find it interesting that Teno chooses to focus on Njoya at this point of the film, following the hint at 'cultural genocide' regarding the marginalization of the arts and, by extension, indigenous rule. Although Njoya was driven from power and exiled by French colonial forces in 1930, his expert use of the visual arts through assimilation rivals that of the colonizing factions. One can gain a quick understanding of this by viewing two images of Njoya taken in the early twentieth century. The first image shows Njoya being presented with a painting of Kaiser Wilhelm in 1906.[20] In this photo, Njoya skillfully positions himself as the central figure, garnering the greatest visual and symbolic importance. One may note the presence of Cameroonian soldiers dressed in western-style military uniforms flanking Njoya on both sides. Njoya himself appears dressed in indigenous fashion, setting himself apart from both the soldiers, and the colonial officials. Through this image, we see Njoya as a well-respected ruler who, in spite of colonial occupation, maintains his status as king, and maintains his cultural ideals within this framework. Not only are the various individuals, both Cameroonian and German, arranged in a manner that brings the focus of attention on him, but Njoya assimilates the western-style military uniforms as a visual indicator of his military power, while maintaining his ties to indigenous beliefs and ideals through his own garments. In contrast, another image of Njoya taken in 1908 shows us an added aspect of his exploitation of the visual arts.[21] In this image, we see Njoya preparing for the *nja* festival, where he is backed by an official wearing the traditional garment.[22] However, Njoya himself wears a colonial uniform, again drawing attention to himself through contrast. By assimilating this western garment into an indigenous celebration, Njoya not only calls attention to his ability to effectively rule in opposing frames of reference, but takes on the connotations of power linked to the colonial uniform, thus assimilating the ideas into his own culture.

Although these are but two examples of Njoya's exploitation of outside influences, they serve to counter the colonial myths built up by the French as justification for their presence in Cameroon. As Teno highlights the role that Njoya played in the indigenous development of the country, he continues to pair the images of royal art objects with his telling voiceover. Again, the viewer is presented with images that serve as an index for Cameroonian culture itself. While Teno's historian explains the history of writing in Cameroon, which was developed prior to the arrival of any colonial forces, he flashes images of Njoya's beaded throne. As he dubs this leader as a 'king/inventor,' Teno cuts to a royal art object bearing a spider, which is a sign of wisdom in the Cameroon Grassland kingdoms.[23] Following this visual exchange, Teno's featured historian expounds on the history of the kingdom, which is recorded in a text dating from 1911, which traces the royal Bamum lineage back for hundreds of years. It is at this point that Teno abruptly confronts his audience with a stark mental question: Why isn't this history published or taught?

These various scenes regarding Bamum royalty are further used to highlight the cultural genocide that took place in Cameroon through comparisons to French colonial-era films. After the viewer is presented with the arts and intellectual developments of local rulers, such as Njoya, Teno compares this with the visual imagery that was emerging from the French colony in the early twentieth century. While we are bombarded with black and white images of young Cameroonian students, dressed in uniforms and marching in order, a French voiceover proclaims the fact that European schools are necessary in order to provide the natives with 'practical training.'[24] This training would 'orient their minds to needs of a normal life,' which centered on the development of 'trained peasants.'[25] The film further informs the viewer of the need for French cultural intervention, which would effectively save the Cameroonians from their primitive culture. This training would instill a 'love of France', and develop 'moral character,' which was surely missing from their current state of being.[26] The film also explains that native intelligence is 'superior to European children up to puberty,' which expands on the idea that African cultures are expert in childlike naiveté.[27] Teno supplements this scene with his own voiceover, explaining that the colonial authorities replaced local kings and rulers with individuals who could simply read and write French, thus recalling a quote from earlier in the film which states, 'To become someone, you must study as a white person. The color of success is white. Black is still the color of despair.'[28] By promoting individuals who have taken on the colonial language, rather than individuals who show outstanding abilities, the French identified yet another way of usurping indigenous culture and ideals. The French language thus becomes a sign of surrender, where individuals are forced to rend themselves of their cultural heritage in exchange for self-preservation. This proves yet another angle by which a colonizing force can effectively 'kill' a culture, without physically harming its population.

A third and final example of the role of the visual arts in regards to cultural primacy can be found in Peck's visual introduction of Patrice Lumumba. While Peck presents the viewer with a photograph taken during a press conference on the cusp of Congo independence, he describes the scene with the following voiceover:

> 'A strange Flemish painting: The Press Conference. I can't help wondering what these people were doing here? Some appear bored. Some are there by coincidence, others against their will. A farewell scene perhaps, without the participants' knowledge.'[29]

Again, I find it interesting that Peck chooses to directly reference the visual arts, although from a Western perspective in this case. Although one may simply pass this off as lyricism, I would suggest a deeper significance with his choice of words. As modern Belgium comprises three relatively autonomous regions, including Flanders, Peck directly relates the image to colonial Belgium, giving the western culture ownership over the scene by labeling it a 'Flemish painting.' This statement takes on further meaning when one examines the historical aspects of painting in the region. Throughout the seventeenth century, regional painters such as Frans Hals began to emerge as preeminent portrait artists. From an art historical standpoint, one can link his work with a general shift in painted subject matter from aristocratic portraiture to the ordinary middle class.[30] Artists like Hals specialized in group portraits, which included a variety of individuals, depicted together on a single canvas. When relating Peck's dialogue to the art history of the region, several connotations emerge. First, one may note the fact that Baroque portrait artists focused on men and women who did not belong to the upper reaches of society.

Examples like his 1633 work *Archers of St. Hadrian*, and *The Women Regents of the Old Men's Home at Haarlem*, from 1664, provide a glimpse of this. The emphasis of these portraits was to express the pride of the ordinary, seemingly unimportant members of society. Although this can be linked with a Puritan system of beliefs, I would suggest that Peck uses this comparison to express the false pretenses through which Belgian remits control of the Congo at independence. Rather than reflecting a scene of grandeur and excitement, the Congolese individuals seem tired and weary, while the colonial members appear aloof and unconcerned, hinting at the true nature of the event. The individuals appear as ordinary, just like in Hals' images, possibly expressing the event's lack of importance from a Belgian perspective. As one views Peck's film in its entirety, the realization sets in regarding the presence of colonial control after Congo independence, suggesting that the political shift in power was completed only in word, rather than deed. This is further addressed through Peck's voiceover, which mentions that this photograph may represent 'a farewell scene perhaps, without the participants knowledge.'[31] This is true on many levels, not only in regards to Patrice Lumumba's political role in an independent Congo, but regarding his very life itself. The image also provides a chilling foreshadowing regarding the Belgian presence in the Congo, which would continue 'without the participant's knowledge.'

While both directors utilize the visual arts to express certain ideas regarding cultural genocide and appropriation, their films also serve as a response to the atrocities of the past. Through a reevaluation and revision of past events, Teno and Peck create a dialogue of exchange with colonial history, where culture becomes a commodity. In the struggle for the control of meaning, both directors use their films as a response to the colonial past of their respective countries, appropriating the colonial images and ideas for their own use.

Although the idea of resistance is mentioned by Teno near the end of his work, regarding a scene featuring a father educating his children, the film *Afrique, je te plumerai* is an act of resistance in itself on many levels. One major way that Teno accomplishes this is through his filming style. Throughout the production, the viewer is presented with contemporary views of Cameroonian society, along with colonial-era propaganda footage. This visual disruption of old and new functions as a form of revisionism, provides new commentary from a populous that was formerly silenced. While this juxtaposition identifies the staged presentation used to express colonial ideology in the historical clips, Teno utilizes this very same style in his contemporary scenes, offering an equally staged, yet effective message for the viewer. He creates obvious theatrical exchanges, such as his interview with the local television director, that are written in such a manner as to highlight the overt subjugation of Cameroonian culture in the major media outlets, in favor of Western ideals. Through his technique, Teno reverses the role of appropriator and appropriated, by creating an opposing piece of propaganda. Not only does it highlight the overt presence and influence of Western culture in Cameroon, but provides the viewer with a contemporary example of 'propaganda film,' thus shedding light on the veracity, or lack thereof, found in the colonial-era footage.

Teno also relies on visual juxtaposition to buttress his message of neo-colonialism in contemporary Cameroon. Time and again, Teno provides the viewer with scenes taken from these early films, and positions them against his contemporary scenes in order to support his ideas. For example, one can reference the relationship between the local Cameroonian historian, and the French film clip featuring neatly dressed Cameroonian children. Although the older film was used to persuade its audience of the progress that was taking place in the colony, as well as the need for 'civilizing development,' Teno proves its subjective nature by aligning it with tangible evidence of indigenous scholarship and education, thus nullifying the French colonial justification.

Finally, Teno confronts the negotiation of meaning through his own statements, heard throughout the film. A great example of this can be seen in his stating that he 'want[ed] to make a film from the point of view of the native.'[32] Teno identifies himself as a 'native,' which is ironic, given the connotations that one links with this term through Western frames of reference. However, by placing such a label upon him, Teno expropriates this term, filling it with new meaning, through the layered messages of resistance that he develops throughout his production.

Likewise, Peck uses several aspects in his film *Lumumba, Death of a Prophet*, to reassert a Congolese point of view through acts of appropriation. For example, in the opening scenes of his film, Peck captures Belgian citizens wandering the streets, oblivious of the fact that they are being filmed. Although his voiceover references the memory of Patrice Lumumba, who is forever tied with this Western nation, his very act of 'capturing' Belgian citizens within his film serves as an act of appropriation. Through this, Peck shows them exposed to the elements – rain, wind and snow – and stages their restless appearance alongside the idea of Lumumba's restless spirit that wanders the streets of this colonial nation, 'tickling the feet of the guilty.'[33] Through this scene, Peck constructs a version of Belgium that pleases him, and serves his ideas of presenting a particular aspect of this nation in regards to the tragic story of Lumumba. Just as King Leopold constructed a Congolese version that served his ends at the 1897 World Fair in Brussels, Peck appropriates the colonizers, and exhibits them within his own frame of reference.[34]

This idea of appropriating an image and constructing its meaning is repeated throughout the film, especially through the aforementioned scene at the Royal Museum for Central Africa. Throughout the displayed collection of Congolese objects, one is presented with a series of captured objects without meaning. However, Peck uses his film to reassert a new signification upon the very institute that removed the presence of Congolese culture from the art objects. Throughout this scene, Peck creates a dichotomy between viewer and viewed, both of whom share the attribution of anonymity. While the Belgian visitors approach the various display cases that contain traces of an anonymous other, Peck positions the visitors themselves as equally anonymous, stripped of any specific identity. Through the act of filming, he reverses the gaze and places the Belgian populous on display for his own viewing audience. Not only does this re-emphasize the notions of wandering and exile, but it allows Peck, and by extent the viewer, to create and assign meaning to the anonymous subjects. This notion comes to fruition near the end of the film, when Peck literally generates identities for the various Belgian subjects, giving them names and developing storylines for each. Through this realization, one begins to see not only how Peck constructs a Belgium that fits into his narrative, but how the colonial era films likewise constructed particular views in order to express their messages and ideals. Just as Peck uses his footage of contemporary Belgium in order to express a specific point of view, so the colonial filmmakers staged specific scenes to fit their frame of reference. Through this, both of the film types enact a brand of 'cultural genocide' through appropriation of form and meaning, constructing a reality that fits its framework.

Although the use and meaning of visual art objects offer a complex dialogue within the colonial history of the African continent, their use in the films by Peck and Teno present an opportunity to both revisit and reenact the colonial agenda. While the investment of power by the two directors may be situated differently in the appropriation of form and meaning, both Peck and Teno present a reaction to a highly systematic colonial discourse. Not only do the objects function as effective tools in readdressing the ideas and methods of colonialism, but they operate as a visual index for the cultures that created them. By including scenes which center on the visual arts of Cameroon and the Congo, both Teno and Peck explore the limits of cultural genocide through such ideas as assimilation, negotiation of meaning, and context. Furthermore, both directors employ the medium of film, another visual art, to readdress and renegotiate the troubled histories of their respective countries. Through their work, one can grasp the importance of the visual arts in regards to the past, and can begin to understand the revised dialogues that the visual arts generate for the future.

NOTES

1 *Africa, I will fleece you (Afrique, je te plumerai)*, dir. Jean-Marie Teno, California Newsreel, 1992.

2 *PRI's The World*, 20 July, 2006, Public Radio International, 20 October 2006 <http://www.theworld.org/?q=node/2499%20July%205,%202006>. The song *Independence Cha Cha Cha* was written and performed by Congolese musician Joseph Kabasele, who was later known as Grand Kalle, and his musical group African Jazz. The song, which was recorded in 1960, served as an anthem for the newly independent Congo, and emphasized the importance of a unified consensus in the governing of the country. Established in 1897 following the World Fair, the Royal Museum of Central Africa now holds almost the entire archives of Congo explorer Henry Morton Stanley.

3 *Lumumba: Death of a Prophet*, dir. Raoul Peck, California Newsreel, 1992.

4 For further reading on the development of African stereotypes in the West, see Jan Nederveen Pieterse, 'Savages, Animals, Heathens, Races,' *White on Black: Images of Africa and Blacks in Western Popular Culture*, (New Haven: Yale University Press, 1992) 30-51.

5 Michelangelo completed this work in 1504 for the city of Florence, as a visual symbol of civic pride.

6 Titian's work, which dates from 1538, established the standard for paintings of the reclining nude.

7 For more on this topic, see Patrick Brantlinger, 'Victorians and Africans: The Genealogy of the Myth of the Dark Continent,' *'Race,' Writing and Difference*, eds Henry Louis Gates, Jr. and Kwame Anthony Appiah (Chicago: University of Chicago Press Journals, 1992) 166-203.

8 Pieterse, 45-51. Pieterse presents the various studies by Pieter Camper (1722-89) and his development of the 'Camper's facial angle,' which served as a scale for measuring physiognomic proportions. His method was one of the first which employed scientific instruments to measure racial differences.

9 Nicholas Mirzoeff, 'In and Out of Slavery,' *Unesco Courier* July-August (2001): 27-28. Mirzoeff notes that the development of these race-based sciences stemmed from the abolition of the Atlantic slave trade. This is due to the idea that humans were no longer legally different, and these disciplines brought about a new form of distinguishing between races by classifying people according to physical features.

10 Vogel's book *Art/artifact: African Art in Anthropology Collections* accompanied this exhibition, and includes several essays on culture and its relationship to exhibition politics.

11 Susan Vogel, 'Always True to the Object, in Our Fashion,' *Exhibiting Cultures*, ed. Ivan Karp and Steven D. Lavine (Washington: Smithsonian Institution Press, 1991) 198. In her essay, Vogel gives several examples of display styles, and outlines the connotations found within each.

12 Vogel, 192.

13 Vogel, 199.

14 Peck is careful to note that the 'participation' of the Congolese individuals at the World Fair eventually led to their deaths from illness and over-exposure. He explains that these individuals were interred in Tervuren, Belgium, where they remain to this day.

15 Teno.

16 Monica Blackmun Visona, Robin Poynor, Herbert M, Cole and Michael Harris, *A History of Art in Africa* (New York: Harry N. Abrams, 2001) 338.
17 Visona, 338; 345. One may also note that Njoya gave a beaded throne to German colonial officials in the early twentieth century.
18 Visona, 342.
19 Teno.
20 For a view of this image, see Visona's *A History of Art in Africa.*
21 Ibid.
22 Visona, 348-9.
23 Visona, 347. Among the Bamum, spider divination is widely practiced, which links this symbol of divinatory knowledge with the idea of wisdom and far-sightedness. Furthermore, as a result of this divination process, the spider is often tied with ancestral power and insight from the afterlife.
24 Teno.
25 Teno.
26 Teno.
27 Teno.
28 Teno.
29 Peck.
30 For more on the general trends found among regional Baroque art of the 17th century, see chapter 19 of Fred S. Kleiner and Christin J. Mamiya, *Gardner's Art Through the Ages: The Western Perspective, vol. II* (Belmont, CA: Thomson Wadsworth, 2006).
31 Peck.
32 Teno.
33 Peck.
34 Adam Hochschild, *King Leopold's Ghost* (New York: Houghton Mifflin, 1998) 176-7.

WORKS CITED

Africa, I will fleece you (Afrique, je te plumerai). Documentary directed by Jean-Marie Teno. Distributed in the US by California Newsreel, 1992.

Hochschild, Adam. *King Leopold's Ghost.* New York: Houghton Mifflin, 1998.

Lumumba: Death of a Prophet. Documentary directed by Raoul Peck. Distributed in the US by California Newsreel, 1992.

Mirzoeff, Nicholas. 'In and Out of Slavery.' *Unesco Courier* July–August (2001): 27-8.

Pieterse, Jan Nederveen. 'Savages, Animals, Heathens, Races.' *White on Black: Images of Africa and Blacks in Western Popular Culture.* New Haven: Yale University Press, 1992. 30-51.

PRI's The World. 20 July, 2006. Public Radio International. Accessed 20 October 2006 <http://www.theworld.org/?q=node/2499%20July%205,%202006>.

Visona, Monica, Robin Poynor, Herbert M. Cole and Michael Harris. *A History of Art in Africa.* New York: Harry N. Abrams, 2001.

Vogel, Susan. 'Always True to the Object, in Our Fashion.' In *Exhibiting Cultures,* ed. Ivan Karp and Steven D. Lavine. Washington: Smithsonian Institution Press, 1991. 191-204.

Haile Gerima's Pan-African 'Message to the Grassroots': Hearing Malcolm X in Amharic – or *Harvest 3000 Years*

Greg Thomas

Former Black Panther Party militant and current intellectual powerhouse, Elaine Brown examines 'New Age Racism' in *The Condemnation of Little B* (2002), an absolutely crucial work which continues to take El-Hajj Malik El-Shabazz as a central political and intellectual guide:

> During the height of his popularity in the early sixties, Malcolm X broadly explored and explained how a culture of slavery had indeed survived and was still wedded to the socioeconomic structure in America at that time. Malcolm's raw and powerful imagery related to the two primary roles blacks served in the slave structure: the Field Slave and the House Slave. Noting that blacks in either capacity were slaves, Malcolm cited how critical differences in their roles and relationship to their Masters affected the institution of slavery and its continuation. (Brown 2002: 211)

It could easily be argued that Brown wrote one of the most important books in Black Studies in particular, in the period after the movement for Black Power and its destabilization by COINTELPRO, the FBI or US state's so-called 'counter-intelligence program' designed to neutralize or liquidate all liberation struggle and dissent or dissidence.[1] While many others continue to move further and further away from original Black Studies and Black Power objectives, she is committed and bold in her scrupulous analysis of what she calls 'New Age House Negroes' and 'New Age House Negresses' as well as 'New Age Massahs' and 'New Age Miss Anns' in a chapter entitled 'The Abandonment' (207-60).[2] Malcolm X resounds in her words throughout *The Condemnation of Little B: New Age Racism in America*, where she concludes:

> Still owning nothing of significance, blacks as a people have little significance in postindustrial America except as unskilled labor and a potential consumer market. Beaten down in the losing battle for equality, in employment, education, and social standing, forty acres forgotten, the black masses languish underemployed and unemployed, undereducated and uneducated, and poor in the nation's ghettos ... If they cannot assume this cheap labor/consumer role, blacks have no real value or place in the New World Order. (ibid. 212)

Since the eightieth birthday commemoration of Malcolm X on May 19th 2005, his name continues to be heard in Hip-Hop lyricism, even if non-radical (Black and white) traditions continue to ignore him and canonize a pacifist Martin Luther King, Jr. instead. The artist Common is pictured under a portrait of him in the artwork on the back cover of his most recent album, *Be* (2005), the title song of which begins: '*I wanna be as free as the spirits of those who left / I'm talkin Malcolm, Coltrane, my man Yusef.*' A rap super-group of sorts, Black Market Militia samples a speech of his on a track aptly listed as 'Audubon Ballroom' (*Black Market Militia*, 2005); in which he sounds serious as he rejects applause as an appropriate response to his onslaught against white racist violence in favor of Black self-defense: 'Please, I don't want to hear this. 'Cause handclapping's been done long enough.' Lastly, the lyricist now most notoriously identified with what has come to be called 'Rap COINTELPRO,'[3] Lil' Kim mic-checks his revolutionary spirit on *The Naked Truth* (2005); 'Whoa!' hears her declare: '*I stand behind Martin Luther King / But I'm more like Malcolm X / Guerillas beatin on they chest / Git it right, I'm Malcolm X!*' Contemporary Black radical traditions insist on invoking his name and praxis in a chronically counter-revolutionary age.[4]

The cinema of Haile Gerima must be counted among the traditions that remember and reinscribe the spirit of Malcolm X and his monumental Pan-Africanist significance. For example, *Ashes and Embers* (1981) is the tale of a Vietnam War veteran who has nightmarish flashbacks from which he awakens at one point to a vision of Patrice Lumumba and Malcolm. Are they photographic splices, posters on the wall or perhaps memories from his mind's eye? In *Child of Resistance* (1972), a meditation on Angela Davis, political struggle and imprisonment, he appears (along with King) in the image of a martyr, when a surreal science of assassination threatens to liquidate another Black revolutionary figure.[5] *Bush Mama* (1976) stages a heated exchange which takes place in a Watts bar between the heroine, Dorothy, and her cynical neighbor, Molly, who claims that violence merely begat violence in the murder of Malcolm X. Dorothy responds that preachers of non-violence meet the very same demise at the hands of white America and its violence, historically; she storms out, enraged and forever changed. Then, there is a montage-tribute which includes Malcolm in *After Winter: Sterling Brown* (1985), a documentary on the legendary poet and scholar. One could argue that his presence is writ large in the resistance text of *Sankofa* (1993), too.[6] But none of these sightings are as powerful as the ones in another Haile Gerima film, which is where some would least expect to find him, all alleged Pan-Africanism evidently aside: *Harvest 3000 Years* (1975).[7]

Mirt Sost Shi Ami*: Or, Haile Gerima's 'Message to the Grassroots'*

> Most Africans, if they read and critically think and study and want to make history, will come around to a Pan-Africanist position, not in its classic context but as it evolved to be whatever the new Pan-Africanism would be.

Thus spoke the filmmaker in 'The Mis-Education of Haile Gerima: The Ethioguide Interview' (Gerima 2005: 5). More than anyone, it seems, he gives serious trouble to the classifying schemas of 'African Film Studies' or at least certain academic studies of African film which may lay claim to a theory or practise of Pan-Africanism at some level, while they undermine it at the very same time or in the very same voice. These studies appear to almost always preceed continental 'nation-state' by 'nation-state' in a fashion that frequently or conceptually disconnects the continent of Africa from the African diaspora, and the countries of the continent from each other – *despite* the far-reaching Pan-Africanism of the founding theoreticians and practitioners of an African cinema of liberation: Ousmane Sembene, Med Hondo and Gerima himself. Thus, under the entry 'Haile Gerima (Ethiopia)' in N. Frank Ukadike's *Questioning African Cinema: Conversations with Filmmakers*, the critic says of the filmmaker: 'All of Gerima's features mentioned above, except of *Harvest 3000 Years*, focus on the African-American experience, raising the issue of whether this filmmaker should be considered an African filmmaker or an African-American filmmaker' (Ukadike 2002: 254).[8] Why is the boundary-crossing of the Pan-Africanist so troubling, categorically, in its defiance of 'either-or' logics that would be imposed at the level of criticism? A quite similar dynamic is found in Françoise Pfaff's *Focus on African Film* or 'From Africa to the Americas: Interviews with Haile Gerima' (2004).[9] Ntongela Masilela's 'The Los Angeles School' (2002) would codify Gerima as 'the African member of the Los Angeles School' and then underscore 'the specificity of Ethiopia in African history' (6). Is this not all too casual a move given conventional colonial geopolitics on and off the continent which claim that neither Africans in the diaspora nor Ethiopians in Africa itself are 'really' and 'truly' African? Where is the radical Pan-Africanism of the critic that would compliment the radical Pan-Africanism of the artist-as-filmmaker? Why it is so troubling that Gerima makes *Child of Resistance* and *Ashes and Embers* ... then *Harvest 3000 Years* ... then *Sankofa* and *After Winter* ... then *Adwa: An African Victory* (2000), and so on? This trouble must be overcome in order to read, critically think and study; to come around and make history, in his words, as Pan-Africanists – against colonial (and neo-colonial) mis-education.[10]

Most observers tend to agree that it was *Harvest 3000 Years* (*Mirt Sost Shi Ami* in Amharic) which first 'established Gerima as a director of international standing' (Pfaff 1988: 149). A restored version of the film would be presented as a 'classic' in May 2006 at the festival in Cannes, France.[11] Previously, it had won the Black Filmmakers Hall of Fame's Oscar Micheaux Award for Best Feature Film, in 1976, along with the French Critic Association's Georges Sadoul Prize; the London Film Festival's Outstanding Film Award; and the Grand Prizes at the Locarno International Film Festival in Switzerland and the Figueira da Foz International Film Festival in Portugal. Yet it has garnered relatively little sustained critical attention since the period of its initial release. This fact may very well be changed by its restoration and representation as a 'classic' at Cannes.

To synopsize the narrative of *Harvest 3000 Years* is no simple task. Tony Safford and William Triplett described it as a 'quasi-documentary on the rhythms of peasant life caught up in a struggle for liberation' in 'Haile Gerima: Radical Departures to a New Black Cinema' (1983, 59). Teshome Gabriel wrote in *Third Cinema in the Third World* (1982) that it concerns 'an honest peasant family working on a plot of land,' a 'greedy landlord' and 'the life of an insane man.' 'On a deeper level,' he continues, 'the film is truly about Ethiopia and about systems of oppression that enslave individuals and thereby create a repressive ideology of total submission.' The 'need for revolutionary action' is therefore paramount (90). The filmmaker himself once said that 'it's about a peasant family, their hard work, their dignity in relationship to a symbolic landlord' (Pfaff 1977: 28). If many other commentators were to use the categories of feudalism rather exclusively to discuss the film, even though these categories have very specific European meanings, historically, Mbye Cham concludes in 'Art and Ideology in the Work of Sembene Ousmane and Haile Gerima' (1984): 'The principle objective of the primary set in the films of these directors is to analyze and expose the real nature and dynamics of oppressive and exploitative systems which are capitalism, neo-colonialism, feudalism or a combination of these' (84).[12]

This combination is key for both Malcolm and Gerima: X's 'Message to the Grassroots' (from 1963) is all-important here. Its famous examination of things feudal and non-feudal remains unacknowledged, or neglected, at least among academics. The distinction it drew between the Black revolution and the so-called 'Negro revolution' was neither a strictly national nor contemporary distinction (X 1989: 7). While civil rights ideologues refer to the Brown vs. Board of Education decision of the US Supreme Court as their benchmark for politics in the early 1950's, Minister Malcolm would stress the significance of the Bandung Conference on Afro-Asian unity to make his point about independence and self-determination (5). He makes it plain that the Black revolution is worldwide in scope as he walks us through a history of *bona fide* revolutions; and this revolutionary history of his is as anti-feudalist as it is anti-racist and anti-imperialist. He instructs us to look at the 'American,' French, Russian, Chinese, Cuban and Algerian revolutions and, of course, the Mau Mau in Kenya (7–9). To the reformists who throw around the language of 'revolution' in ignorance, he highlights the battle of the landless against the landlord. He systematically examines the historic characteristics, motives, objectives, results and methods of revolution in this classic speech: '[R]evolution is for what? For land. Why did they want land? For independence. How was it carried out? Bloodshed' (7). 'Land is the basis of freedom, justice and equality,' globally (not 'love,' colonial integration, etc.). This is the Malcolm deemed by John Henrik Clarke 'the finest revolutionary theoretician and activist produced by America's black working class in [the twentieth] century' (Clarke 1991: 146); and, ideologically, this is what only begins to tie X to Gerima's 'drama of the unbridgeable contrasts between peasants and landowners: between indifference and a grim, backbreaking existence as little more than beasts' (Gerima 1995: 32).

The 'madman' of *Harvest 3000 Years* cited in Gabriel's *Third Cinema in the Third World* is named Kebebe; he is 'mad-*angry*,' but is he 'mad-*insane*' in truth? His land was stolen by the lash-wielding landlord while he was away fighting for freedom, national freedom. Having lost his wife and family as well, he is literally homeless in his dispossession as the film opens, living outdoors under a bridge built by the Italians ('before they left'): 'I fought for those who bragged liberation. They robbed my land I bled for and dumped me here.' Day by day, every morning, he marches to the edge of the property that was once his to denounce the evil of the landlord who is the picture of a colonial master in Black face. He does not denounce him out of self-interest. He shouts him down by calling him a pig, a swindler, an exploiter, a tricknologist trained by the Italians no less. When the landlord calls Kebebe 'insane,' in turn, his interlocutor is doubtful: 'I don't think he's insane. He chooses his words too carefully.' When Kebebe is later arrested by policemen who accuse him of being a swindler, simply because he is on the street as a man who owns nothing, Kebebe protests: 'When you're criticized, you call me mad. That's all you know.' Madness is anger, its insights, and the audacity to deliver them in the face of power. Everything Kebebe stands for on screen is what Malcolm X stood for off screen; he echoes him marvelously throughout *Harvest 3000 Years*, sometimes *verbatim* in his tongue-lashing of the system of oppression.

In *Bush Mama*, the heroine's cynical neighbor refers to 'that crazy nigger X, Malcolm X,' as she justifies his murder by the state and her fatalistic accommodation to state repression and oppression in North America. The 'bad nigger' is a 'crazy nigger' according to this mentality. He or she is 'crazy' for confronting the state or society's irrational logic and authority, judged 'crazy' for not conforming to the insanity that rules. This matter sets the tone for much of *The Autobiography of Malcolm X as Told to Alex Haley* (1965), a terribly mediated text where the 'mad' man himself maintains, 'I *believe* in anger' (Haley 1965: 421).[13] Malcolm's mother, Louise Little is diagnosed if not rendered 'insane' by the state in its efforts to dismantle their Garveyite family in the wake of what they know to be the Ku Klux Klan murder of his father, Earl Little. When he left the Nation of Islam many years later, his brother Philbert would read a statement in support of Elijah Muhammad at a press conference that exploited this same propaganda to stigmatize Malcolm's practice of independence – an independence which was personal and political, social and organizational in its practice.[14] He is branded as 'crazy' because of the truth of his criticism of the establishment; and it is this heroic bravery or fearlessness that is resurrected cinematically in *Harvest 3000 Years* – via Kebebe.

Kebebe's supreme verbal confidence is familiar to Pan-African audiences as he leans casually on the fence of the landlord, confidently castigating him in black-and-white footage that visually framed our media images and memories of Malcolm X – Malcolm on the screen, at the microphone, mad or angry but far from insane. It is crucial for us to listen carefully to a particular scene when Kebebe explains to Berihun, the oldest male child of his honest peasant family, how losing his land and status simply 'opened [his] eyes.' Kebebe recalls a time in Addis Ababa when thousands of poor people were 'herded into concentration camps like cattle' in preparation for a visit from Queen Elizabeth of England, as if their poverty were their own fault as well as a cause for imprisonment: 'If you'd witnessed that, you'd have lost your sanity like me,' he informs young Berihun. But this loss of 'sanity' is viewed as a welcomed loss of the arrogant status of privilege. Such 'sanity' is decoded as blind complacency, corruption and conformity, a condition from which Kebebe awakens. He comes to symbolize a 'class suicide' not of his own making, embracing the loss of status confused with 'sanity,' moving from blindness to clarity and consciousness at last. An invocation of Amilcar Cabral (1969) here could just as well be an invocation of Malcolm X, who spoke at length of the Black pseudo-bourgeoisie in Haley's 'autobiography' (Haley 1965: 46; 48-53; 252; 364) and elsewhere. His anti-elite consciousness is a central part of what he saw as the need for Black people to come together as a whole and see each other with 'new eyes' (X 1989: 40). Such a vision is common to Malcolm and Kebebe, the character through whom Gerima has said that he 'knew [he] could put [his] message across,' according to *Ouaga: African Cinema Now!* (Nee-Owoo and Owusu 1988).

More or less unmediated, Malcolm's most lasting insight in 'Message to the Grassroots' must be on 'the house Negro and the field Negro,' a socio-cultural and politico-economic statement reiterated by both Brown's *The Condemnation of Little B* and *Harvest 3000 Years.* For whenever Kebebe assaults the landlord with his mind and his mouth, there is another character, Kentu, who is sent to chase him away with the prospect of physical violence. On a typical occasion, Kebebe states: 'Call your puppets. The fat dog is always protected by puppets. Kentu, stay out of this. You don't understand the cause. I pity the slavery you endure.... Don't be on that pig's side. He keeps you alive with an empty stomach. A slave for a piece of bread.... Ignorance has blinded your eyes, kept you subservient.' The 'blind' Kentu responds by running back to his lord and master, reporting loyal and proud: 'What a rebellious guy he is. I drove him away. I, your servant, would break his head. But it might cause you trouble.' The script of Gerima does not refer to Kentu (and the like) as a serf, significantly, or a servant. They are *slaves* – of a master, who is slurred as a *pig* with *puppets* in tow.[15] Does Malcolm X even need to be quoted on this subject, still? His comments are world-renowned. The 'house Negro' is the slave who fights harder than the master to put out his house on fire; who identifies with his master when 'we sick,' etc., etc., etc. He or she responds to the urge to run away, escape or separate by calling the 'field Negro,' of course, 'crazy' (X 1989:, 10). And when he or she claims that they have left nothing in Africa, the answer in 'Message to the Grassroots' is: 'Why, you left your mind in Africa' (11). Explicitly and expressly, Malcolm proclaims himself a 'field Negro' to rebel against slavery in the present and the past, that is, the feudal arrangement of European slavery in the Americas and the 'neo-slavery' of contemporary white racist capitalism in these and other spaces.[16] It is uncanny how *Harvest 3000 Years* recasts his immortal criticism of masters, puppets and slavery, continentally at one with the diaspora in its depiction of complicity and Pan-African revolt (nearly two decades before *Sankofa*, to boot).

The cinematic theme of exploitation is sonic and visual as well as narrative, so to speak. The exploited are not shot from on high to signify and simultaneously reinforce their subjugation. The exploiter is shot with high, wide angles 'to achieve a distorted, dwarfed' posture, by contrast (Gerima 1995: 32). His image is not glorified. It is redrawn to contest and denaturalize or pathologize his position of power and privilege. Neither the exploiter nor the exploited are left faceless. The constant close-up view of those who toil is at all times humanizing (no matter how extreme the abuse which it *is* crucial to capture on film). It is never objectifying, for they are not the trucks of the oppressive state and economy that drive across the screen, from beginning to end, as a virtual character onto themselves. Literally, they drive by like symbols of the 'Third Worldist' thesis of Eduardo Galeano's *Open Veins of Latin America* (1973), not to mention Walter Rodney's *How Europe Underdeveloped Africa* (1972). In one scene, Berihun is told by the mad militant of the wretched European exploitation of their country's resources. When the subject comes back to the Queen of England's Ethiopian vacation, for which the poor are jailed in droves, the sound of the trucks will silence his outrage from the background, deafeningly off-screen. The visual then appears after they overpower his voice. In another scene, the trucks 'full of goods' are explained by Kebebe at last. They carry off the products of exploitation to 'Mekele, Asmara, Masawa' and then 'ABROAD.' The politics of exploitation in Gerima's cinema are not strictly 'feudal' (or '*pre*-colonial'), *per se*, consequently; while elitist, without question, they are 'quasi-feudalist' and capitalist, colonialist and neo-colonialist.

Beyond the critical handling of all these modes of domination that are the hallmark of Malcolm X, his decoding of dreams and nightmares resonates in this context also. Hardly the stereotypical 'social realist,' Gerima mixes dream sequences (or 'fantasy') and realism as a rule. So Dorothy in *Bush Mama* dreams of clubbing the social worker of the state upside her head with a bottle, a fantasy transformed into reality for a second when illustrated on film. Gerima was at work on this feature when he stopped production temporarily to go to Ethiopia to work on *Harvest 3000 Years*, in which even the trusty Kentu dreams of replacing his lord and master – or sitting in his 'big house' chair. His seems to be the colonized fantasy analyzed by Frantz Fanon in *Peau noir, masques blancs* (1952) (*Black Skins, White Masks* (1967)), since he wants to become the master, not eliminate him. He cannot think of harming or killing his master. That would be the fantasy of the colonized analyzed by Fanon in *Les damnés de la terre* (1961) (*The Wretched of the Earth* (1963)). This dream replicates the nightmare had here on camera by the nameless landlord himself. But his sexism makes him arrogantly ignorant of the third, most dangerous dreamer of the film, Beletech (Berihun's sister), the girl child who has a militant Fanonian fantasy that could be a picture of revolutionary struggle. On this matter of gender, or sexual politics, *Bush Mama* and *Harvest 3000 Years* reconnect, symbolically, as Beletech insists on the political content of her dream when nightmare and dream are confused in the absence of a proper political analysis. This insistent distinction is no less a hallmark of Malcolm X, who aggressively decoded the 'American dream' as a tragically ignorant nightmare of massive imperialist proportions: 'I had a dream,' Beletech intones several times (in the past tense), if this dream is in fact a nightmare until her fantasy of revolt is realized explosively at the end of her dream of violence (*à la* X and Fanon) as opposed to 'non-violence' (*à la* King et al).

It was on December 20, 1964 that Malcolm remarked, famously, at the Audubon Ballroom: 'You don't have to be a man to fight for freedom' (35). This represents a radical departure from Nation of Islam doctrines, which were reflected (or, rather, refracted) in *The Autobiography of Malcolm X as Told to Alex Haley*. He began to institutionalize his sexual ideological shift in the Organization of Afro-American Unity (OAAU) before his assassination. To her dream, many critics seem to prefer Beletech's disruption of male chauvinism in the realm of children's games, an undeniably important sequence in *Harvest 3000 Years*; and although her violent intelligence in Ethiopia is not the focus of Manthia Diawara's understanding of her vis-à-vis 'the emancipated girl' motif in African cinema (Diawara 1989: 204), it certainly compliments this interpretation nonetheless. Fully awake, at night, Beletech is still anxious to share her dream of rebellion with her mother and grandmother. Dreams are supposed to be shared in the morning, she is told, but their mornings are monopolized by hard labor. So she is given a special permission to speak this reverie whose images substitute for the film, almost, at key points. In this nightmare-turned-dream or fantasy, she and her family are in the field. The landlord sits in his chair with Kentu standing nearby. The landlord and his son Tenku are dressed in festive white. Tenku ties Beletech's mother and father to an oxbow and whips them, forcing them to pull the plow. Her father is dressed in work clothes. When the parents cannot continue pulling, making 'cattle' and 'chattel' one cinematically, their son (Berihun) and daughter (Beletech) are tied to the plow along with them. We had seen a very Hollywood version of this specific image in 1974 in *The Autobiography of Miss Jane Pittman*, starring Cicely Tyson. 'We couldn't hear it,' says Beletech: 'We united and began to free ourselves.' They break the oxbow and the breaking free sounds 'like lightning.' This is when Beletech 'woke up,' a double-entendre to be sure. Her mother attributes the lightening to a storm. Beletech counters that it was the oxbow breaking – sounds of resistance. Her grandmother agrees, deeming this 'a *real* dream' and a miracle. Following Malcolm X, whose politics of gender have been suggested in much more liberal, US national terms by bell hooks (1992) as well as Angela Davis (1992), Gerima maintains: 'I don't see one gender as privileged in the struggle for liberation. I look at the system that victimizes us all' (Safford and Triplett 1983, 64); and, 'I am not in the gender-dichotomy world that this society has' (Woolford 1994, 95).[17]

Beletech's later drowning while searching for the landlord's cattle out of fear is as symbolic for *Harvest 3000 Years* as, the Birmingham, Alabama church-bombing of 'four little girls' (Addie Mae Collins, Carole Denise Miller, Carole Rosamond Robertson and Cynthia Wesley) was for the orature praxis of Malcolm X in 1963 and beyond. Politically, moreover, Beletech is the bearer of the call for unity that consumed 'Message to the Grassroots.' 'What you and need to do is learn to forget our differences. ... You don't catch hell because you're a Baptist ... a Methodist ... a Democrat or a Republican ... a Mason or an Elk, and you sure don't catch hell because you're an American; because if you were an American, you wouldn't catch hell. ... You catch hell, all of us catch hell, for the same reason' (X 1989, 4). Black people catch hell as a whole because of the reduction to chattel socially interchangeable with cattle by 'a common oppressor, a common exploiter and a common discriminator' (5). Paradoxically, Beletech proves to be precisely that kind of shepherd of whom Malcolm spoke in his historic 'Appeal to African Heads of State,' his letter to delegates of the second conference of the Organization of African Unity (OAU) convened in 1964 in Cairo:

> We also believe that as heads of the Independent African states you are shepherds of *all* African peoples everywhere, whether they are still at home on the mother continent or have been scattered abroad.
>
> Some African leaders at this conference have implied that they have enough problems here on the mother continent without adding the Afro-American problem.
>
> With all due respect to your esteemed positions, I must remind all of you that the good shepherd will leave ninety-nine sheep, who are safe at home, to go to the aid of the one who is lost and has fallen into the clutches of the imperialist wolf. (X 1989: 73)

The landlord of *Harvest 3000 Years* had threatened Beletech at the outset of the film: 'Tend the cattle. See that none gets lost. ... If just one is missing, you'll pay with your life.' She is afraid that she can't afford not to risk her life for the recapture of his cattle whose social status she virtually shares. She, her mother who has to cut *grass* and carry it to market for sale, and the now landless Kebebe who protests that he 'can't even live by selling' *grass*, they are all symbolic of Malcolm X's '*grass*roots' message about 'freedom, justice and equality' to be secured by means of Black revolution. The 'need for revolutionary action' is paramount, indeed.

This is how Gerima's classic closes – with an 'ending' that is not 'happy,' or 'tragic,' but provocative and instructive. It is very much in line with the political philosophy of life and death and self-defense promoted by X: 'Don't lay down a life all by itself. No, preserve your life, it's [the] best thing you've got. And if you've got to give it up, let it be even steven' (X 1965, 12). An ex-prisoner and nationalist freedom fighter himself, Kebebe approaches the landlord and confronts him with analogous thoughts in mind: 'Today, I'll deal with you even if it takes my life.' It is the first and last time that they occupy the four corners of the screen together, as veritable ciphers of social-class contradiction. The people ('peasants') are noticeably disgruntled by extreme degeneration and exploitation. When the landlord comes to collect all the fruits of their blood, sweat and tears, they cry: 'My lord, what's my family to live on' and 'He doesn't even greet us anymore.' It is not they who act, however; it is Kebebe. He climaxes *Harvest 3000 Years*'s extended diatribe against exploitation by dubbing the landlord a 'bloodsucker.' This was the unforgettable description of capitalism documented by *Malcolm X Speaks: Selected Speeches and Statements* in 1965, for starters.

> It is impossible for the system of capitalism to survive, primarily because the system of capitalism needs some blood to suck. Capitalism used to be like an eagle, but now it's more like a vulture. It used to be strong enough to go and suck anybody's blood whether they were strong or not. But now it has become more cowardly, like the vulture, and it can only suck the blood of the helpless. As the nations of the world free themselves, then capitalism has less victims, less to suck, and it becomes weaker and weaker. It's only a time in my opinion before it will collapse completely. (X 1989: 199)

This is certainly a 'racist capitalism,' a capitalist imperialism of 'white-supremacy' under attack. There is no European capitalism versus European communism dichotomy in this anti-capitalist and anti-colonialist Pan-Africanism. Outside the more narrow economic historical schemas of the West and its unexamined application in film analysis, African film analysis in particular, Kebebe literally assaults the landlord who is seen as a bloodsucker *and* the agent of a bloodsucking state – in an international system: 'It's not your fault,' he explains: 'The state is on your side.' Kebebe beats him to death with his own stick, in any event. The landlord pays for his arrogant disdain and his dismissal of Kebebe as 'insanity itself.' The people don't join him, or rejoice. Kebebe has to flee. 'He killed the lord,' they yell. No spontaneous uprising ensues in the absence of mass education and organization, a result that illustrates the need for what the organizer X explored in 'Educate Our People in the Science of Politics,' for example, a militant, Pan-Africanist tract now collected with many others in *February 1965: The Final Speeches* (1992). An individual rebel where a collective movement is not in place, yet, Kebebe hangs himself rather than give himself up to the state or the police, self-sacrificing for the cause like the non-celluloid martyr. One among many, Berihun is left to carry on his grassroots message or that of *Harvest 3000 Years* as a whole, chasing a truck 'full of goods' to be carried city after city and then abroad – in the wake of Beletech's sacrifice by the current order of things: 'I thought the exploitation was limited to my family, but it's everywhere.'

Conclusion

Coming to the United States was also a decisive step in the shaping of Gerima's sociopolitical consciousness and the rediscovery of his cultural heritage. ... Having been raised in a society where caste and class were more significant than the shade of one's skin, he became profoundly affected by the issue of racism in the United States and increasingly shared the problems and aspirations of the African-American community. At this time he began reading the writings of Malcolm X and other black militants of the 1960s, and came to identify with their struggle. Interestingly, it is through their search for African roots that Gerima reasserted his own Africanness.

Making commentary in *Ouaga: African Cinema Now!* at FESPACO (Pan-African Film and Television Festival of Ouagadougou), the 'triangular' cineaste would assert that 'mad' people have a greater freedom than anyone else.[18] He explains that Kebebe of *Harvest 3000 Years* was partly based on one of these people, a 'free spirit' from his childhood (Nee-Owoo and Owusu 1988), in Gondar, near Lake T'ana, the source of the Blue Nile. In addition, he has explained that all of the film's characters are dramatic rather than documentary figures (Quam 1981: 7). The oratorical, semiotic and ideological connections between this character, this childhood, this cinema and Malcolm X, this should make for an African film criticism in line with a radical Pan-Africanism which is appropriate for an African cinema of liberation.

Haile Gerima is consistently clear about his sources of influence and inspiration, before and after his arrival in North America: 'Even when I had the opportunity to grab the camera, I did not have a mentor, until African Americans embraced and sanctioned me' (Ukadike 2002: 255-6). The struggle he identifies with is a Black world struggle for Pan-African liberation. Various fans, interviewers and critics are told time and again who were the folks who helped shape his consciousness: Frantz Fanon, W.E.B. Du Bois, Malcolm X and Amilcar Cabral as well as Che Guevera in addition to fellow filmmakers Ousmane Sembene and Med Hondo. These are the individual names most often mentioned. The collective name is the movement for Black liberation struggle that helped him reverse the effects of his colonial mis-education once he reaches Chicago en route to Los Angeles (or UCLA and, ultimately, Howard University in Washington, DC) from Gondar via Addis Ababa: 'In fact, without the African-American community's support, there is no way I could have made any kind of film, including *Harvest 3000 Years*' (Pfaff 2004: 207). Dialectically, this personal political connection calls to mind the historical significance of Ethiopia or literary, spiritual and political 'Ethiopianism' in Black communities all across the Americas, not to mention the African continent, from as early as the late eighteenth century to the present.[19]

Beyond this Biblical school of thought's *Psalms* 68:31 ('Princes shall come out of Egypt; Ethiopia shall soon stretch forth her hands unto God'), Malcolm X invoked another, equally iconic Ethiopia himself on the way to his own African revolution when he recalled his self-re-education during his years in US prisons. In the midst of a debate on compulsory military training, his white opponent made a passing reference to Italy's invasion of Ethiopia and belittled Ethiopian resistance to this Italian colonialist aggression: 'I said the Ethiopians' black flesh had been spattered against trees by bombs the Pope in Rome had blessed, and the Ethiopians would have thrown even their bare bodies at the airplanes because they had seen that they were fighting the devil incarnate' (Haley 1965: 212-13). For Malcolm and other 'Ethiopianists' throughout the diaspora, Ethiopia was a synecdoche for Africa at large, not a sign of investment in any given country or state, anywhere. For Malcolm, 'America' (as in 'African-Americans') refers to the Americas (North, South, Central and the Caribbean) and 'Africans' refers to all Africans at home and abroad. This Malcolm X is showcased marvelously in *February 1965* (X 1992: 46-64; 143-170; 257-69).

Hence, just as Hip-Hop artists rap to erase the white and Black elite public erasure of Malcolm X, Sizzla has sung to reinvigorate an Ethiopianism of Pan-Africanism in Dancehall Reggae on *Royal Son of Ethiopia* (1999). The neo-colonial or neo-slavery condition of Black folk here and there is a constant theme, as is state corruption, exploitation and repression. 'Break Free' begins with a mantra which refers to tiers of government men who are pictured as spawn growing wildly out of control: 'Age to be protected / The sick to be cared for / The hungry must be fed.' Sizzla chooses Zion over Babylon, as is tradition, vowing to burn the latter down. His chorus calls for the wretched, beloved masses to come, as 'Ethiopia's last judgment.' They are personified alternatively by Black youth, prisoners, and Black women, who must 'break free from the slave' today in the present tense as African ancestors struggled to break free from slavery in times past. Lyrically, breaking free also means breaking free from white masters in Black face. Interestingly enough, then, Sizzla's *Royal Son of Ethiopia* sounds like an audio version of Elaine Brown's *The Condemnation of Little B: New Age Racism in America*, his version being launched from a different part of this hemisphere. And despite the fact that he shouts out 'Selassie I' (and 'Emmanuel') in due course, his complex, blistering sing-song criticism of neo-slavery and neo-colonialism could not and should not logically leave quasi-feudal monarchies intact.

Now a 'Cannes Classic,' *Harvest 3000 Years* was filmed in the middle of the military takeover of power from the reign of Emperor Haile Selassie. It is a mistake to assume that Haile Gerima had to wait to move to North America in order to make contact with US imperialism, which in the wake of the Italian invasion was responsible for regimatic aid, expanded class division and the Peace Corps whom the filmmaker so often derides as a principal source of cultural alienation.[20] This is the same phenomenon that Malcolm X had derided (in 'Not Just an American Problem, But a World Problem') as 'benevolent colonialism. Philanthropic imperialism. Humanitarianism backed up by dollarism' (X 1992: 160); and this political economic analysis led him to analyze what he would call the 'science of imagery' in media without which no modern political economic domination or hegemony could possibly be secured (152). Therefore, when the filmmaker says he militates against the 'plantation school of cinema' (Woolford 1994: 92), and cinema as an 'effective imperialist venture' (Ukadike 2002: 255), El-Hajj Malik El-Shabazz and Haile Gerima work in unison once again. A mass-based Pan-Africanism makes their struggle one struggle: *Harvest 3000 Years* or *Mirt Sost Shi Ami* amply demonstrates this much, (if ironically for another, nation-bound paradigm or point of view), as a Black world classic now for decades.

NOTES

1 See *PROUD FLESH* 2 at http://www.proudfleshjournal.com for a special issue of this journal ('The Damned Issue') entirely devoted to a discussion of this book.

2 Sylvia Wynter is brilliant on this distinction between 'Black Studies' then (in its original conception as a radical challenge to the whole white West) versus now (in its more current conception as 'African-American Studies' on a mere ethnic, 'multicultural' model of Western bourgeois liberalism). See her 'On How We Mistook the Map for the Territory and Re-Imprisoned Ourselves in Our Unbearable Wrongness of Being, of *Désêtre*: Black Studies Toward the Human Project' (2006).

3 Dasun Allah and Joshua Fahiym Ratclffe discuss 'Rap COINTELPRO' in *The Source* magazine's 'Law and Disorder' (2004); and, alone, Dasun Allah publishes a different, *Village Voice* version of this article which is available at http://www.villagevoice.com /news/0414,allah,52443,1.html.

4 Of course, the very useful formulation of 'Black radical tradition' comes from Cedric J. Robinson's *Black Marxism: The Making of the Black Radical Tradition* (1983).

5 The Black Panther Brown sings a song of liberation ('Seize the Time!') for one scene on the soundtrack of *Hour Glass* (1971), a short film which was Gerima's first film ever and which is now distributed on video with *Child of Resistance* (1972).

6 This means that the same argument could be made for at least one of Gerima's current, major works-in-progress, *The Maroon Project.*

7 More information on Haile Gerima's films and their distribution can be found at http://www.sankofa.com.

8 Writing of *Harvest 3000 Years* in his book, *Black African Cinema* (1994), Ukadike contends: 'Although he has made several other features in the United States, their themes concern black American experiences, and those films are consequently seen as belonging to the African American independent film movement' (Ukadike 1994, 192).

9 She asks, 'Haile, you have been in the United States for more than thirty-five years, more time than you have spent in Ethiopia. Should you be defined as an African or an African-American filmmaker?' (Pfaff 2004, 206). This is before Gerima reaffirms his Pan-Africanism when posed a question about his children, their upbringing in Washington, DC, and their fluency in Amharic (213-14).

10 This is not a simple question of diaspora, either. The crisis of classification does not follow continent-born African intellectuals and filmmakers who are based in France, interestingly enough, be their countries French-colonized or not: Paris is thus presented as the capital of Africa, in effect, to the extent that it is thought to be logical for African filmmakers to live and work in Europe – as if a completion of personal and aesthetic-political identity is found there; as if only an erosion of African identity takes place in the Americas, among Pan-African Black communities no less.

11 http://www.festival-cannes.fr.

12 Writing on Sembene and Gerima, Cham adds: 'Thus, we see a struggle between the rich and the poor, the exploiter and the exploited, the honest and the dishonest, the progressive and the reactionary, the powerful and the powerless, the landlords and the peasants, the political and economic managers and those who are politically and economically managed' (Cham 1984, 11).

13 Elsewhere, he proclaims in an April 1965 interview with *Flamingo*, a magazine oriented toward the Black population of Britain: 'When you put a fire under a pot, you learn what's in it. Anger produces action.' (X 1992: 43).

14 This press conference and statement are treated further in Orlando Bagwell's documentary, *Malcolm X: Make It Plain* (1994).

15 Likewise, Malcolm X defines 'colonialism or imperialism' as simply 'the slave system of the West' in a speech at Ford Auditorium in Detroit, February 1965 (X 1992: 79).

16 See George Jackson's magnificent *Soledad Brother* (1970), of course, for more on 'neo-slavery.'

17 Perhaps refreshingly, Davis punctuates her 'Meditations on the Legacy of Malcolm X' (1992) with a moment of political fantasy: 'I have a fantasy; I sometimes daydream about masses of Black men in front of the Supreme Court chanting 'End sexual harassment by any means necessary,' 'Protect women's reproductive rights, by any means necessary.' And we women are there too, saying 'Right on!" (46). Still, all the examples of anti-sexist politics offered here remain reformist and state-centered, as if this liberalism is the only or correct means by which a Malcolm X-informed Black radical struggle could be waged in anti-sexist ways. This would be a dangerous assumption animated by many an academic critic, nowadays especially. By contrast, bell hooks focuses on

personal relationships almost exclusively in 'Malcolm X: The Longed-for Black Feminist Manhood' (1994). It can be read as a critical corrective to Davis's assumption that Betty Shabazz (or 'the woman') must have been the most sexually progressive person in their marriage. In conclusion, hooks is adamant: 'Contemporary thinkers do Malcolm a great disservice when they attempt to reinscribe him iconically within the very patriarchal context he so courageously challenged' (192). However, her analysis of Malcolm X and his transformative politics of gender never moves beyond the politics of the personal, or romantic relationships, much like neither Davis nor hooks moves this analysis beyond the geopolitical confines and constructs of the 'United States.'

18 See Gerima's 'Triangular Cinema, Breaking Toys and Dinknesh vs. Lucy' (1989), for his articulation of 'triangular cinema.' In an interview for Ukadike's *Questioning African Cinema*, he recapitulates: 'It is not enough to be just a filmmaker and especially a traditional filmmaker. It is not enough to be a critic and especially a traditional film critic. It is not enough to be a traditional passive audience. This is the triangle.... So the triangular cinema is the idea to make all of us activists' (Ukadike 2002, 277-8).

19 Erna Brodber provides an excellent treatment of Ethiopianism as a Black, Pan-African tradition in 'Reengineering Blackspace' (1997).

20 Michael D. Quam writes in '*Harvest 3000 Years*: Sowers of Maize and Bullets' (1981): 'Following the unsuccessful colonization attempt the Italian fascists, Haile Selassie moved to further centralize and bureaucratize political power and to stimulate some economic modernization through the encouragement of foreign techniques and businessman. He also greatly expanded the size and destructive power of the military with the assistance of major aid from the United States. These efforts transformed Ethiopian society by creating a much more elaborate class structure' (5).

WORKS CITED

Allah, Dasun and Joshua Fahiym Ratcliffe. 2004. 'Law and Disorder.' *The Source* (June): 41-6.

Black Market Militia. 2005. *Black Market Militia*. Nature Sounds.

Brodber, Erna. 1997. 'Re-engineering Blackspace.' *Caribbean Quarterly* 43:1&2 (March–June): 70-81.

Brown, Elaine. 2002. *The Condemnation of Little B: New Age Racism in America*. Boston: Beacon Press.

Cabral, Amilcar. 1969. *Revolution in Guinea: Selected Texts*. New York: Monthly Review Press.

Cham, Mbye. 1984. 'Art and Ideology in the Work of Sembene Ousmane and Haile Gerima.' *Présence africaine* 129:1: 79-91.

Clarke, John Henrik. 1992. *Notes for an African World Revolution: Africans at the Crossroads*. Trenton: Africa World Press.

Common. 2005. *Be*. Geffen Records.

Davis, Angela Y. 1992. 'Meditations on the Legacy of Malcolm X.' *Malcolm X: In Our Own Image*. Ed. Joe Wood. New York: St. Martin's Press: 36-47.

Diawara, Manthia. 1989. 'Oral Literature and African Film: Narratology in *Wend Kuuni*.' *Questions of Third Cinema*. Ed. Jim Pines and Paul Willeman. London: BFI Publishing: 199-211.

Ethioguide. 2005. 'The Mis-Education of Haile Gerima: The Ethioguide Interview.' http://www.ethioguide.com/aaethioguide/ethioguide/spotlight/morehaile.htm.

Fanon, Frantz. 1963. *The Wretched of the Earth*. Trans. Constance Farrington. New York: Grove Press. Originally published as *Les damnés de la terre* (Paris: Francois Maspero, 1961).

——. 1967. *Black Skin, White Masks*. Trans. Charles Lam Markmann. New York: Grove Press. Originally published as *Peau noire, masque blancs* (Paris: Éditions du Seuil, 1952).

Gabriel, Teshome. 1982. *Third Cinema in the Third World: The Aesthetics of Liberation*. Ann Arbor, MI: UMI Research Press

Galeano, Eduardo. 1973. *Open Veins of Latin America: Five Hundred Years of the Pillage of a Continent*. New York: Monthly Review Press.

Gerima, Haile. 1976. *Bush Mama*. Mypheduh Films, Inc.

——. 1976. *Harvest 3000 Years*. Mypheduh Films, Inc.

——. 1989. 'Triangular Cinema, Breaking Toys and Dinknesh vs. Lucy.' *Questions of Third Cinema*. Ed. Jim Pines and Paul Willeman. London: BFI Publishing: 65-89.

——. 1995. 'Visions of Resistance.' *Sight and Sound* 9: 32-33.

——. 2005. 'The Mis-Education of Haile Gerima – The Ethioguide Interview. http://www.ethioguide.com/aaethioguide/ethioguide/spotlight/morehaile.htm

Haley, Alex. 1965. *The Autobiography of Malcolm X as Told to Alex Haley*. New York: Random House.

hooks, bell. 1994. 'Malcolm X: The Longed-for Black Feminist Manhood.' *Outlaw Culture: Resisting Representations*. Boston: South End Press: 183-96.

Jackson, George. [1970] 1994. *Soledad Brother: The Prison Letters of George Jackson*. Chicago: Lawrence Hill Books.

Lil' Kim. *The Naked Truth*. 2005. Atlantic Recording Corporation.

Masilela, Ntongela. 2002. 'The Los Angeles School' *Ijele: Art e-Journal of the African World* 5: http://www.africaresource.com/ijele/issue5/masilela.pdf.

Nee-Owoo, Kwate and Kwesi Owusu. 1988. *Ouaga: African Cinema Now!* Effiri Tete Films.

Pfaff, Françoise. 1977. 'Towards a New Era of Cinema.' *New Directions* 4:3 (July): 28–30.

——. 1988. 'Haile Gerima.' *Twenty-Five Black African Filmmakers: A Critical Study with Filmography and Bio-Bibliography*. Ed. Françoise Pfaff. New York: Greenwood Press: 137-55.

——. 2004. 'From Africa to the Americas: Interviews with Haile Gerima (1976-2001).' *Focus on African Films*. Ed. Françoise Pfaff. Bloomington: Indiana University Press: 203-20.

Quam, Michael D. 1981. '*Harvest 3000 Years*: Sowers of Maize and Bullets.' *Jump Cut* 24-25 (March): 5-7.

Robinson, Cedric J. 1983. *Black Marxism: The Making of the Black Radical Tradition*. London: Zed Books.

Rodney, Walter. 1972. *How Europe Underdeveloped Africa*. Washington, DC: Howard University Press.

Safford, Tony and William Triplett. 1983. ''Haile Gerima: Radical Departures to an New Black Cinema.' *Journal of the University Film and Video Association* 35;2 (Spring): 59-65.

Sizzla. 1999. *Royal Son of Ethiopia*. Greensleeves Records, Ltd.

Ukadike, Nwachukwu Frank. 1994. *Black African Cinema*. Berkeley: University of California Press.

Ukadike, Nwachukwu Frank (ed.). 2002. *Questioning African Cinema: Conver-*

sations with Filmmakers. Minneapolis: University of Minnesota Press.

Woolford, Pamela. 1994. 'Filming Slavery: A Conversation with Haile Gerima.' *Transition* 64: 90-104.

Wynter, Sylvia. 2006. 'On How We Mistook the Map for the Territory and Re-Imprisoned Ourselves in Our Unbearable Wrongness of Being, of *Désêtre*: Black Studies Toward the Human Project.' *Not Only the Master's Tools: African-American Studies in Theory and Practice*. Ed. Lewis R. Gordon and Jane Anna Gordon. Boulder and London, Paradigm Publishers: 107-169.

X, Malcolm. 1989. *Malcolm X Speaks: Selected Speeches and Statements*. Ed. George Breitman. New York: Pathfinder Press.

——. 1992. *February 1965: The Final Speeches*. New York: Pathfinder Press.

The Video Film Industry & its 'Substitution' for Literature & Reading in Africa: A Case of Nigeria's Nollywood

Ignatius Chukwumah & Raphael Obinna Amalaha

Drama is not a new concept to Africa. It originally arose from the religious ceremonies prevalent in the pre-colonial era. We can see similarities, for example, with the Dionysian festivals of ancient Greece which used masks, miming and costumes to illustrate the activities of the gods in Mount Olympus. Africa's dramatic origins can still be seen, particularly in masquerade, most especially during the New Yam festivals. Chinua Achebe captures this in *Things Fall Apart*:

> The *egwugwu* with the springy walk was one of the dead fathers of the clan. He looked terrible with the smoked raffia body, a huge wooden face painted white except for the round hollow eyes and the charred teeth that were as big as a man's fingers. On his head were two powerful horns. (1958: 64)

In the above, the primary elements of drama – impersonation, costume, and spectacle – are interlocked into an inseparable whole. This is further exemplified by the imitation of 'the dead fathers of the clan' by living men via the use of masks and raffia palm.

During the colonial period in Nigeria, urban centers sprang up, and the populace migrated to them from the villages. These people experienced a vacuum which had hitherto been filled by festivals. It was only a matter of time before the borrowed habits and tastes of the people would make the Popular (Travelling) Theatre adapt the creative instinct for drama into full theatrical performances. Beginning in

> ...Victorian Lagos in the 1930s and 1940s where church plays were combined with Yoruba masquerade performances, music, dance, and acrobatics, the travelling troupes were to become popular in the Yoruba dominated areas of Nigeria and even along West Africa's coastal cities. (Kunzler 2007:1).

From the 1950s to the early 1980s, reaching a peak in the 1970s, there were no less than a hundred troupes travelling and perfoming in the Yoruba language alone. (Ogundele nd: 46)

The emerging replacement of live stage performances reached a climax in 1959 when Chief Obafemi Awolowo, the pioneer Premier of the then Western Region of Nigeria commissioned, ahead of his times, the first ever television station in Black Africa. With this technological break-through, live performances were filmed and shown on television at chosen times just as they were previously shown in public centers with the aid of video projectors (Kunzler 2)

The Nigerian video industry, also known as Nollywood, a term derived from Hollywood, and which will be used hereafter when referring to Nigerian videos (except when particular reference is to be made to a regional video, in which case their regional appendages will be referred to – categorized as Yoruba-, Hausa- and Igbo-videos). This classification of Nigerian film is doubtless faulty. If we take Delta State, for instance, we find that due to multi-lingual and multi-ethnic affiliations, since the early 2000s, there have been films with local language dialogue meant for the consumption of local audiences. We have the Urhobo, Isoko and Ukwuani videos. Examples of Ukwuani videos are *Onye-Ebiai* (2006) and *Action of the Gods* (2007), to mention a couple. How far this trend is replicated in other multilingual parts of Nigeria is a subject of research. Granted, they may be few in the number of copies produced, but although eclipsed by the major ethnic nationalities they can still give a more representative picture of the nation. One characteristic they all bear is that they have had so much to borrow from their 'forebears' – the Yoruba and Igbo videos. For example, the Ukwuani video: *Action of the Gods* has parts 1 and 2, a feature borrowed from the Igbo video pattern. There are also those which fit into neither of these categories but which are in English. As for the ascription: 'Igbo video', Kunzler says:

> If the term Igbo is used here, it is thus designating an origin in South-eastern Nigeria. An analysis of 36 Igbo-comedies showed clearly that the central positions of executive producer, director, screenplay and story are consistently occupied by people from South-eastern Nigeria. (7)

The Igbo video gradually metamorphosed to win nation-wide acceptance because it is written in English and constitutes the bulk of what is today known as Nollywood, an aspect that will be fully examined during this paper.

The upsurge in videos started with the establishment of Igbo film production. Although Haynes and Okome say it is of uncertain origin, (cited in Kunzler 2), the 'commercial potential of videos' was identified in 1991 by Kenneth Nnabue, a film promoter and dealer in electronics by producing *Aje Ni Iya Mi* (Kunzler 6). A year later, *Living in Bondage* was produced by him which sold about 750,000 copies. *Glamour Girls*, a video in English, marked the starting-point of the retention of English and the eschewing of Igbo, as dialogic mode.

With the use of English comes the attendant success of wider markets especially in English-speaking West Africa. This, however, does not preclude the fact that videos in Hausa or Yoruba could also be commercially successful:

> Thousands of movies have been released. One of the first Nigerian movies to reach international fame was the 2003 release *Osuofia in London*, starring Nkem Owo, the famous comedic actor. Modern Nigerian cinema's most prolific *auteur* is Chico Ejiro, who directed over 80 films in a five-year period and brags that he can complete production on a movie in as little as three days. ('Cinema of Nigeria' 12)

The success outlined here is progressive and continual.

Nollywood & Reading

The question that underlies Nollywood and reading is: how is the video going to influence the reading culture not only of Nigeria, but Africa as a whole?

From the 1960s to the mid-1980s, reading literary works in Nigeria was a leisure activity, actively enjoyed by every literate and semi-literate Nigerian. If no trustworthy documentary evidence exists, the existence of Onitsha Market Literature, Kano Market Literature, the huge difference in the statistics of literary works published then and now, and the number of flourishing publishing houses for both the semi-literate and the literate are enough indices. Since the late 1980s, the publishing houses that are still in business have now diverged into publishing secondary school curriculum-based text books. Besides, they also focus on 'publishing only political writings' and 'personality works' (Wase 2007: 253). The poor state of publishing is tied to the poor reading culture that discourages the publishers in the publishing industry. Theodore Wase argues that this situation results in the best literature of Nigeria's new age being published outside its shores.

If the reading culture had been sustained, the formal phase of language learning in schools would also have been sustained. Akwanya puts it thus:

> Language teaching in the school system is one phase of language learning. Probably the more important phase is the non-formal aspect of language learning by direct encounter with the language where it is concretely used in conveying of information and where it takes place as the representative of thought. This demands that all the four main language skills, listening, speaking, reading, and writing are continuously in exercise; which means that in this language thought is fully engaged – in description, documentation, analysis, ordering and interpreting experience. (2005: 254).

The 'more important phase' which is 'the non-formal aspect of language learning by direct encounter with the language' where 'it takes place as the representation of thought' is literature. It is here that thought lavishly abounds. With the advent of the video film, visual alertness and picturesque scenery are given prominence just as seeing retains images to the detriment of the exercise of thought which trains the mind. Today, a visit to public library will confirm this trend.

Reading has become seasonal at most, say in the approach to and during the Senior Secondary Certificate Examinations (SSCE) May/June and November/December. So we might be right in saying that curriculum-based reading impacts on curriculum-based publishing, or vice versa. This nexus is not going to foreseeably abate because after this period, the number of library users drastically reduces. As it is to those of secondary school age, so it is with the adult, whether gainfully employed or not.

On 27 July 2007, Dr Aduba, a medical doctor in Onitsha complained to the authors about the contrast in reading behaviour between his son and himself at the same age and class. He mentioned Cyprian Ekwensi, Onuora Nzekwu, and a host of others whose works fell within the ambit of children's literature in the 1970s and 1980s – all of which he had read. But his son would have read none of these. What is true of Dr. Aduba's son is true of his mates. It has also affected students' enrolment of literature in the SSCE, their excuse being – 'there are too many texts to be read'.

The present state of reading literary works reminds us that there 'was a time when things were different, when it seemed that God dwelt in the world' but now no longer does. (Miller 1965: 2). The 'in the world' is not the whole world but Nigeria's world, and by extension Africa's.

Nigeria is still very influential across Africa. So just as Nollywood film has depleted the reading culture in Nigeria, it could do (and is already doing) so in other parts of Africa. If 'money is the primary limiting factor in production of videos', it is also its enhancing factor (Whittaker 1989: 322) because of the gains that the producers and actors make. Some actors in Nigeria could earn up to $4,000 for one movie (Kunzler 9). Hausa films for example:

> Are distributed in the surrounding countries where Hausa is spoken: in parts of Cameroun, Chad, Niger, Benin, Burkina Faso, Togo, Ghana and even Sudan. From Kofar Wambai Road market in Kano, the videos are sold to retailers and wholesalers in other major cities, from where they are distributed to smaller cities and even the rural areas. This trade uses established trade network based on the credit and trust and thus the social capital of Islamic trade. (Kunzler 6)

Apart from the Hausa videos, Igbo comedy videos starring the small in stature actors: Chinedu Ikedieze and Osita Iheme 'can be found in sub-Saharan Africa particularly in regions where English is not spoken' (9), for example, 'In Lome (Togo), Kinshasa (Democratic Republic of Congo), Kigali (Rwanda), Manzini (Swaziland), Durban (South Africa) and even in remote areas as Marsabit on the edge of the Chalbi desert in Kenya' (13).

Again, in manipulating technology to full commercial advantage, the marketers make use of the internet 'to sell Nigerian videos directly to consumers in the Diaspora' (13). Apart from the informal and individual foreign patronage, Lequeret tells us that:

> Nigerian videos are also shown on television in other African countries, e.g. on Zambia National Broadcasting among others. A South African satellite programme (*Africa Magic*) broadcasts them across Africa and even in Asia. (Kunzler 13)

There is also a 'European satellite programme showing Nigerian videos' (13). The prospect is really bright abroad but that is not the only influence of the Nigerian videos. As Kunzler highlights:

> There are other ways the Nigerian video industry is influencing other sub-Saharan African countries. In several African countries, the popularity of Nigerian videos led people to think about producing their own videos, without other video industries yet emerging on the same scale. (13)

This is the case in Ghana where Nollywood could challenge 'the local production' and subsequently attain a prime place in that market (14). There is, evidently, international and intra-national influence. The former is Ghana's while those of local ethnic nationalities within Nigeria belong to the latter. An example is Ukwuani (a community in Delta State) video.

As for the audience:

> The lower classes without these facilities at home are probably the main *clientele* for the *video parlors*, where videos are shown on ordinary televisions at low prices. The audience is dominated by ... young men, ranging from the mid-teens to the mid-twenties. (11)

More reasons abound as to why the video parlours are frequented. Even those who have the equipment visit them. The reason is that with the rate of power outage in Nigeria, it is quite unpredictable whether the voltage would be sustained until the film ends. This predicament is made worse when one does not have a power generating plant. Even when one does, the extra cost of fuelling it deters one. The other reason is that it offers itself as a point of relaxation and socialization. Considering all these, and noting that the videos possess themes that readily appeal to the audience of secondary school age and the middle class adults, a 'substitute' for reading literary works as a past-time could be said to have evolved. With the tremendous rate of production and spread of Nigerian videos that have taken place from 1994 to 2005 (from few videos to above 2000 videos per year (Kunzler 11)), the future of reading as leisure is really bleak for Nigeria if the trend continues – especially as the Nigerian video industry is described as 'a developing industry' ('Cinema of Nigeria' 1). If this growth continues, the ways the Nigerian video industry will influence other sub-Saharan African countries will be inexhaustible.

Two Faces of a Face?

It is possible that the factor facilitating the substitution of reading culture by Nollywood could be the similarities in the thematic preoccupation and plot-structure in both the video film and literature.

Literature has characteristics that distinguish it from the other forms of art. It deploys language for communication, but depends on tradition for the suffusion of meaning. The Aristotlian term 'poetry' or 'poem' often raises some concern because it hardly covers the whole of 'literary studies' or 'literature'. Aristotle's usage appears to be our authority. Although its currency applies to anything in a metrical and stanzaic form, rather than see it as a category of generic classification, it might help us to use it in a more extended sense since we cannot dispute that there are great works of prose, which in all manners and specifications, deserve to be called poetry. *The Odyssey* is an example.

In Aristotle's account of human action (*praxis*), we find that it could be 'primarily imitated by histories, or verbal structures that describe specific and particular action' (Frye, 1957: 82) while *mythos* is a secondary imitation of an action (83) as differentiated from reality and histories. *Theoria* is imitated by 'discursive writing' with some specific definiteness. Now, a *dianoia* is a 'secondary imitation of thought' (*theoria*) which is pre-occupied with 'typical thought, images, metaphors, diagram, and verbal ambiguities' from where flow specific ideas. This is the primitive core of our beings as humans and the appurtenance of every man; except one that does not exercise genuine thinking, for 'the speech of genuine thinking is by nature poetic' (Heidegger 1971: x). Heidegger further posits that the needfulness of taking 'the shape of verse is uncalled for,' as 'the opposite of the poem is not prose', for 'pure prose', if it qualifies as literature, 'is as poetic as any poem' (x). With these, therefore, we can surmise that the *mythos* is the '*dianoia* in movement', 'the *dianoia* is the *mythos* in stasis' (Frye, *Anatomy* 83). Along with Frye's analysis is Ricoeur's that '*mimesis* does not mean the duplication of reality; *mimesis* is not a copy; *mimesis* is', ultimately '*poiesis*, that is, construction, creation' and the *mythos* must be written and coherent (Ricoeur 1989:180).

Aristotle describes the *mythos* as fable, which can also be referred to as the story-line. The story-line (*mythos*) is the seeming meeting point between literature and the video. Both are constructions (Ricoeur); they are not the real. Both could embody characters that perform the actions as well as play out their thematic preoccupations. While literature or the literary text is *deceased* as a sign-signal (Derrida 1978: 12) beyond which there is no reality, the video is merely a moving signal devoid of reality.

It is this similarity that enables literary works to be adapted into video film and, in some instances, for example in Hausa popular literature and Hausa videos the reverse is the case (Kunzler 4). When Chinua Achebe's *Things Fall Apart* running into several series, was shown by the Nigerian Television Authority in the late 1980s it was watched with rapt attention. Possibly, it is this link that Theodore's intuition grasped when he said that as a panacea for their poor storylines, Nollywood should enter into a working relationship with the Association of Nigerian Authors (ANA) ('Creative Writing'). However, he fails to indicate how this will be done. The above assertion extends the issue of the similarity too far because the video film has not got a body of critical approaches or theories by which they could be criticized.

Their similarity is further enhanced by themes or plots that appeal to the audience's existential capacities/statuses. For the literary, Frye says that every poem is a product of its time and to some extent a record of the anxieties of its time ('Mythos and Logos' 1969:14). One might be reduced to think that this is subtle historicism. But there is no doubt that Frye meant the record that the mind makes of the vibrations of his day, rather than his reality. In this could be seen the reflection of the struggles of Africans in everyday life (Kunzler 10).

Amongst Yoruba videos there are some that portray the accumulation of wealth by means of witchcraft instead of by hard work. The wealth is used to entice women. Others emphasise love, Christianity, crime, conservative morals, existential response to change in the society – all of which are not uncommon themes to the ordinary Nigerian or African. As for Hausa video, the influence of the local theatre tradition and other socio-cultural modes are apparent (3). The latter deals with the tension between the traditional and the Western with respect to love, marriage and arranged marriage, individual freedom and collective responsibilities, as well as religion (in this case Islam). Unlike the Hausa videos, the Igbo videos show core concepts that govern the traditional Igbo worldview and value-systems. Others display such issues as witchcraft, money, women, social success, urban life and marriage. These themes are found in *Living in Bondage* (1992), the archetypal Igbo video, and to a large extent, the archetypal Nigerian Nollywood video. The reason is that all aspects of life are blossoming in all Nollywood irrespective of regional (ethnic) affiliations. It is indeed a template for all – where a man, having joined a cult to get money, is under duress to use his wife for ritual purposes which he does but not without emotional and psychological trauma, and the Pentecostal church remedies the situation through prayers and deliverance sessions.

Based on the above, it is clear that Nollywood, Nigerian literature, and indeed African literature are closely related. This fact will be given more impetus if we consider a few Nigerian/African literary works and attempt to relate some themes of Nollywood with them. The first work of Nigerian literature to be considered is the heroic narrative, *Things Fall Apart.* To different degrees, most themes in Nollywood: love, religion (Islam, Christianity and traditional ones), crime (against the community and the state), conservative morals, existential response to change, the tension between the traditional and the Western, marriage, the clash between individual freedom and collective responsibility, the orientation of achievement and success, are displayed in *Things Fall Apart.* Further resonances are seen in Amos Tutuola's *The Palmwine Drinkard* where fantastical incidents could be likened to the witchcraft and 'juju movies' of the Yoruba video. The use of witchcraft to acquire money as exemplified in *Living in Bondage* is also of relevance here.

The socio-political themes such as money, power and women in such videos as *Living in Bondage*, *Glamour Girls*, and *Onye-Ebiai* (2006) are also found in Achebe's *A Man of the People* where the lust for power in Chief Nanga makes him crush his opponents including by seducing Samalu's girlfriend. Similarly in Gabriel Okara's *The Voice,* Okolo, its protagonist, because of his fertile consciousness, attempts to look for 'it' – an ideal. Unable to match the usurping power of Chief Izongo, he is banished to live his 'charred' life elsewhere. Another video whose theme relates back to literature is *Mortal Inheritance* starring Omotola Ekeinde where she performs the role of a woman afflicted by sickle-cell anaemia. She fights for her life even when she thinks she will not live, but later has a baby and lives on in the end. This displays the theme of hope for survival amidst hopeless circumstances. It is related to the doctrine of the absurd in Albert Camus's *The Plague*. But it goes beyond the absurd by the ultimate survival of the protagonist and even in her having a baby. The film is a major landmark and one of the best of Nollywood videos.

The Action of the Gods exudes consipiracy – a Joseph motif. The video relates to literary works such as Isidore Okpewho's *The Last Duty* where Toje ensures that his 'enemy' does not come out of the hold in which he has put him at Idu. The same issue of conspiracy or oppression is visible in Wole Soyinka's *Season of Anomy* and Echewa's *The Crippled Dancer*. Marriage and its intrigues are a common thematic preoccupation of Nollywood videos. They are also portrayed in Zaynab Alkali's *The Stillborn*. These issues determine the fall or triumph of each character in the novel. The tension between traditional ways of living and an encroaching modernity that some Hausa videos display as their theme is the preoccupation of Echewa's *The Land's Lord*. In the work, Father Higler's sojourn with the indigenes is described by Philip, his servant as a history of naturalization, which leads to the massacre of the gods as well as the desecration of the Eucharist. This does not stop Philip from killing himself in the wake of the clashes. Similar clashes are seen in *Things Fall Apart* and *Arrow of God* although the clash in *Arrow of God* upon which the tragedy hinges is intra-communal. These and many others too numerous to outline and compare are instances where Nollywood and literature could be said to have thematic meeting-points. However, it could also be said that these thematic meeting-points have enhanced the gradual 'substitution' of literary reading culture for leisure with Nollywood videos especially as they appeal to Nigerian (African) experience? But there is still a failing which makes Nollywood incomparable to literature on critical standards.

The Lack of a Critical Framework for Nollywood

What the videos lack is an enduring critical framework. Even Nollywood's casual viewers hint at this indirectly through their complaints about the poor quality. According to Kunzler:

> Videos reflect ... the struggles of Africans in everyday life and an analysis might help to understand popular discourses. This approach seems far more fertile than complaining about the poor artistic quality of Nigerian videos or the fact that they are like 'television programmes packed in movies'. ...Nigerians are not unaware or uncritical of these technical and aesthetic shortcomings, and ... discussions ... usually included mention of their dissatisfaction with poor sound quality, misrepresentations of cultural practices. (10)

Essentially, the above reveals the emergence of a sharp critical attitude, albeit, at an inchoate stage. But where are the harmonized, tested, and tried sets of critical theories or approaches by which the videos can be assessed? This is an open question concerning a blank space – a space that only scholars can fill. By 'an analysis might help to understand popular discourses', Kunzler hints at critical attitudes; perhaps those that border on character and theme.

Generally, the approaches would facilitate the interpretation and understanding of the scenes, images, metaphors, figures, symbols and words that are conveyed in the videos. Unlike literature where analysis *is* the duty of the literary critic, the videos cannot be so subjected. Until parameters for the evaluation of Nollywood videos are evolved, there will continue to be complaints about the poor artistic quality of Nigerian videos. In fact, the complaints may rather increase. And as they increase, it behoves the scholars to devise enabling critical theories for Nollywood and indeed, videos in general. The theories should qualify to be applied to a broad spectrum of videos and the peculiarities from where all the '-ollywoods' originate. The tools should be able to take care of technical and aesthetic shortcomings, poor sound quality, misrepresentations of cultural practices and in the long run, help the audience to make their choices where possible. As for misrepresentations of cultural practices, it ought to be noted that Nollywood, like literature, does not have a documentary mandate to discharge. They are as fictitious as fiction could be. Akwanya asserts that:

> It would be foolish to treat *Moby Dick*, for instance, as a source book on whales or even on whaling. In any event, the literary work does not surprise either by telling the truth, defined as adequation between language and the real, or by falling short of adequation; it will not surprise by telling no truth at all, only by telling nothing but the truth. (110)

Conclusion

In Nigeria, video making is a lucrative venture. It has also opened up employment opportunities for many Nigerians and non-Nigerians. Kunzler cites the results of the collection of statistics on Nollywood sales, output, cost per video, and cost of production:

> Average sales of 32,000 copies sold for 250 Naira, the annual production of 1,500 videos would generate a turn-over of 12 billion Naira (52 million

pounds). This turn-over is not including the money made in *video parlors* and with rentals. (Kunzler 12)

The video industry is economically important. Apart from the oil, telecommunications, and banking sectors, very few nations or corporations have had the courage to invest 12 billion Naira in the Nigerian economy in any year. Therefore, the resilience of Nollywood and its hold on Nigeria's reading culture are and will continue to be difficult to wish away. This is especially true as the recent administration of President Umaru Musa Yar'adua had threatened to declare a state of emergency in the power sector if that organ of government did not improve its services. The enhancement of the power sector will mean more television sets accompanied by video CD players and recorders. As a result more Nollywood videos will enjoy more sales, have more actors/actresses, more income, more job opportunities. Correspondingly, reading habits will decline amongst non-academics, whether as a pastime or otherwise. Already, families are having difficulties making their children sit down and face their studies. In addition, in villages that are newly connected to a source of power, the first acquisitions of many homes are television sets and CD players/recorders, which are of course also status symbols. The future of reading culture looks bleak.

WORKS CITED

Achebe, Chinua. *Things Fall Apart*. Ibadan: Heinemann, 1958.

Akwanya, A.N. *Language and the Habits of Thought*. Enugu: New Generation Books, 2005.

Aristotle. 'On Poetics'. Ed. Mortimer J. Adler. *Great Books of the Western World: S... Aristotle II*. Chicago: Encyclopaedia Britannica, Inc. Vol. 8.

Campbell, Richard. *Media and Culture*. Boston: Bedford/St. Martins, 2000.

'Cinema of Nigeria.' http//en.wikipedia.org. 2007.

Derrida, Jacques. *Writing and Difference*. Chicago: The University of Chicago Press, 1978.

Echewa, T. Obinkaram. *The Crippled Dancer*. London: Heinemann, 1986.

Frye, Northrop. *Anatomy of Criticism: Four Essays*. Princeton: Princeton University Press, 1957.

——. 'Mythos and Logos.' *Yearbook of Comparative and General Literature*, 18 (1969): 3-18.

Heidegger, Martin. *Poetry, Language, Thought*. New York: Harper & Row, 1971.

Kunzler, Daniel. 'The Nigerian Video Industry as an Example of Import Substitution.' http://www.suz.unizh.ch/kuenzler/grey/index.html. (2007).

Miller, J. Hillis. *The Disappearance of God: Five 19th Century Writers*. New York: Schocken Books, 1965.

Ricoeur, Paul. *Hermeneutics and the Human Sciences*. New York: Cambridge University Press, 1989.

Wase, Theodore. 'Creative Writing and Apathy: Book Publishing in Nigeria.' Radio Nigeria News Analysis. 29 August, 2007. http://www.radionigeriaonline.com (2007).

Whittaker, Ron. *Video Field Production*. Mountain View, California: Mayfield Publishing, 1989.

Ogundele, W. 'From Folk Opera to Soap Opera: Improvisation and Transformations in Yoruba Popular Theatre.' Ed. J. Haynes. *Nigeria Video Films*.

The Portrayal of Mothers-in-Law in Nigerian Movies: The Good, the Bad, & Oh, So Wicked!

Agbese Aje-Ori

In the February 2, 2010 episode of the *Dr Oz Show*, Mehmet Oz listed in-laws as constituting a major cause of stress in marriage. Although this is an American show, the Internet is filled with web sites, blogs, discussion boards, books, and articles from around the globe that indicate that stressful in-laws are not just an American phenomenon. According to Radcliffe-Brown (1950), men and women across cultures cite mothers-in-law as the 'principal points of tension created by a marriage' (cited in Fischer, 1983:187). The husband's mother, especially, is frequently presented as being the most 'problematic' and most 'troublesome' in-law (Prentice, 2008: 75). Take this story, for instance, from http://www.motherinlawstories.com:

> At our wedding, my mother-in-law asked me (the bride), and her other daughter-in-law and son-in-law to step out of the pictures so the photographer (who we were paying for) could take some pictures of '*her* family.' So, there I was, the bride, standing on the side, watching her set up pictures of '*her* family.' Her son-in-law told me to get used to it, as she does this at all occasions (I still can't get used to it!).

On another site, single ladies talked of their fears regarding mothers-in-law, and they had very low expectations of them. In her study on how new in-laws were assimilated into the family, Carolyn Prentice (2008) found that people's expectations of their in-laws came indirectly from acquaintances, their own experiences and the media.

Television shows, movies, advertisements, and books from as far back as the 1950s are filled with representations of mothers-in-law (MIL) as problematic, meddlesome, seductive (usually the wife's mother), materialistic, domineering, jealous and controlling (Fischer, 1983; Jackson & Berg-Cross, 1988; Vera-Sanso, 1999). From *The Flintstones* cartoon series to TV's *Everybody Loves Raymond* and 2005's *Monster-in-Law*, popular culture has maintained a stereotypical image of a MIL as conniving, intrusive, abusive, and prone to using emotional blackmail. In 1997's *Too Close to Home*, a MIL wants her son to herself so much that she assassinates her daughter-in-law (DIL). Bad MILs exist, but the problem with these images is that they are stereotyping MILs and therefore creating 'inaccurate and negative perceptions and expectations for both future mothers- and daughters-in-law' (Mikucki, 2008: 3). A stereotype is a mental judgment about a person or a group of people on the basis of race, ethnicity, nationality, age, or many other variables. The danger with media stereotyping is that because mass media are not objective mirrors of social reality, there is a high probability of people simply accepting what they see as true.

According to Gorham (1999), the media maintain myths and stereotypes through repetition. Media are not just organs of information, entertainment or education. They are also cultural sites where people can learn acceptable and expected morals, attitudes and behaviors. According to George Gerbner's (1969) cultivation theory, heavy television users, especially, can internalize the messages they receive and end up with a generalized worldview (a stereotype). Bandura's (1994) social learning theory also suggests that people learn and imitate the behavior that they see. The media, according to Bandura, symbolically produces models for most social learning. When people are repeatedly exposed to stereotypical characters, behaviors or roles, they form attitudes and stereotypes, and in some cases, model them.

Extensive research exists on the media's relationship with society, and its effects. However, research on the evil MIL myth is scarce. According to Mikucki (2008), 'Family research across disciplines – communication, psychology, sociology, and family studies – often treats in-law relationships as peripheral or secondary to other family issues or dilemmas' (Mikucki, 2008: 3). However, the mediated image of MILs is an important area to study, considering that MILS can impact the entire family system (Rittenour and Soliz, 2009). Moreover, from a cultural standpoint, if MILs in the West are seen as secondary to other family issues, they are a primary concern in non-Western societies like Nigeria where a new couple is an extension of the family, not an independent unit. This paper seeks to contribute to the scarce literature on media portrayals of MILs by examining their image in Nollywood movies.

Nollywood, the Nigerian movie industry, is popular across Africa and abroad. In many cases, Nollywood movies have replaced television programs in many African homes as satellite television companies like MultiChoice/Digital Satellite Television (DSTV) broadcast them daily (Ebewo, 2007). According to Osei-Hwere and Osei-Hwere (2008), Nollywood movies comprise one of Nigeria's 'fastest growing cultural exports' and it is now the second largest employer after oil (1). More than 65 percent of the movies are produced in English and feature stories that cut across cultural lines. With such a broad appeal, Nollywood movies could have the same cultivation effects as Gerbner suggests. So, what are these movies teaching women, who are Nollywood's largest audience, about mothers-in-law? (Haynes, 2007)

Using some of these movies as units of analysis, this paper will answer two questions: (a) How are mothers-in-law portrayed in Nollywood movies? and (b) Will the portrayal of mothers-in-law follow the typical image of Nigerian women in Nollywood movies? These questions will also be addressed by examining the literature on Nollywood and its impact on women.

This paper recognizes that MILs are a sub-group, or sub-culture, of the larger culture of women. Not every woman is a MIL, but every woman is a potential MIL when she has children. In that regard, there are gender role expectations for being a MIL and stereotypes about this subculture could affect their interactions with others, particularly their DILs, and how they see themselves. According to Fischer (1983), women are society's kin keepers who have the responsibility of preserving the kinship bond. According to her, the MIL and DIL relationship is a 'primary' link in maintaining the 'tenuous balance in two sets of intergenerational kin' (187). Their relationships could determine the relationship of children and grandparents, nephews, nieces and uncles or aunts, and children and parents. The continued media perpetuation of MILs as intrusive, domineering, bad, jealous and meddlesome could significantly impact the self-esteem of MILs and their family relationships in general. As people repeatedly observe such stereotypes of MILs, being a MIL will carry a social stigma.

Nollywood – The Rebirth of Nigerian Cinema

The Nigerian movie industry, popularly called Nollywood, was resurrected in 1992 when Kenneth Nnebue produced *Living in Bondage* to sell a stock of blank video-cassettes (Ebewo, 2007). His company, NEK Videos, sold about 750,000 copies of the movie and marked the beginning of a $200 million to $300 million industry that produces about 1,000 movies annually (Hays, 2005). Prior to this, the Nigerian movie industry was almost extinct. Soap operas and made-for-TV movies dominated the Nigerian television screen in the 1980s. A few film producers turned to video production in the late 1980s to stay in the movie business. However, they had limited funds and very small audiences. Nnebue's success provided an alternative. Moreover,

> With the global world united under the sway of visual culture, the emergence of the video film in Nigeria is timely and crucial as it serves as the voice of its people and responds to the drudgery of a socioeconomic existence characterized by high unemployment and dwindling oppor-

> tunities. It has taken all on board, including religious-minded people. (Ebewo, 2007: 47)

Nollywood movies differ from Hollywood movies largely in terms of production and distribution. The movies are shot using video technology (including high-definition video technology) and shooting can take 10 to 14 days to complete on a $15,000 to $24,000 budget (Osifo-Dawodu, 2007). The industry's major source of funding comes from marketers, individuals, non-governmental organizations or corporations. The Nigerian government has not invested in the industry, though a few states such as Cross River, Akwa Ibom and Benue have contributed to a few. The movies are commonly produced in multiple parts. It is not unusual to find a movie with four parts, sometimes under a different title. Movies are also re-released under different titles. More than 65 percent of them are produced in English and the rest in indigenous languages, with English subtitles, including Hausa, Yoruba, Igbo, Idoma, Benin, Ibibio and Pidgin English. There are some with French subtitles to reach the francophone audience.

In terms of distribution, television, not film or movie theatres, is the major channel for Nollywood movies. The movies come in video CD (VCD) and DVD formats, which are intended for home use (hence its other name, home videos) for about $2.50. There are many ways to watch the movies without buying them directly. State- and private-owned television stations in Ghana, Kenya, Cameroon and Uganda feature the movies on their programming schedules (Osei-Hwere & Osei-Hwere, 2008). In the United States, Ireland and the United Kingdom, Nollywood channels are available through DishNetwork and Sky, as well as through The African Channel, a video-on-demand channel in the United Kingdom. Some flights to African countries also feature Nollywood movies, and they are free through YouTube and sites like onlinenigeria.com and africanseer.com. The movies are so popular that they have driven foreign films off the shelves in Nigeria (Ozele, 2008). Ebewo (2007) explains that Nollywood movies are very popular because 'they have indigenous content and address issues relevant to the audience' (47). 'In spite of the ethnic differences, there are core values that transcend ethnic and regional boundaries. These include: religiosity; extended family; tradition and rituals; community; respect for elders and veneration of ancestors' (Ozele, 2008, 14).

The movies also feature the cultural hybridity of modern (Western) and traditional (African) cultures in Nigeria, as well as the resulting tensions between old and new, extending their appeal to an international audience. Despite its success, filmmakers estimate that the industry loses at least $20 million annually to piracy, duplication and online streams (Osifo-Dawodu, 2007).

In terms of storylines, Nollywood tells melodramatic stories. According to Abah (2008), 'Melodrama is a powerfully conservative social artifact' that draws its audience 'into both the prescriptions and the proscriptions of mainstream cultural values' (338). 'Nollywood films tend to be full of moralizing messages, cautionary tales in which citizens are handed dire warnings about the perilous consequences of infidelity, crime and greed,' a common trend in melodrama (Hays, 2005: 2). Melodrama is a genre with local and international appeal (Haynes, 2000; Casas-Perez, 2005; Martin-Barbero, 2006). The common themes deal with social and cultural issues, including religion, corruption, women's rights, materialism, culture, immigration, AIDS, marriage, unemployment, and gender roles. In its depiction of women, however, Nollywood is widely criticized.

Images of Women in Nollywood

According to Haynes (2007), Nollywood films are 'oriented towards female viewers' because the audience is predominantly female. However, women account for less than one percent of producers, directors and writers. Abah (2008) found that though Nollywood movies 'celebrate African women of all shades, shapes, and sizes,' and portrayed women in 'varying professional roles' from wives and CEOs to prostitutes, many videos showed a stereotyped image of women (339).

An ideal woman was depicted as married, submissive, and with children. Women were dangerous when they were 'economically, socially, or politically independent' (Abah, 2008, 339). Movies like *Women's Cot, Women in Power* and *Unchained*, which dealt with the empowerment of women and gender rights, thematically cast women in the 'culture bound definition of domestic roles for women' (Abah, 2008, 353). Women who acted outside expected and culturally defined gender roles were depicted as bad and doomed. In *Power Tussle*, a rich and single woman was portrayed as bad. She became good only after a male servant beat her, daily, into submission. In other movies like *Girls' Cot, Aristos, Be My Val, Sleep Walker I – IV, Fishers of Men, Koko Babes* and *Runs*, the Nigerian woman's 'only asset is her sexuality' (Ozele, 2008, 20). She is frequently punished for doing the same things that men are rewarded for, and she is someone that her fellow women cannot trust.

> This image of women as portrayed in Nigerian home video films cuts across the country from North to South, though with differing intensity. The difference being that the rituals and murders, which occur in Southern films, do not yet appear in Northern movies. Still, women in the Northern films are not reflected any better; they are seen as greedy, fickle minded,

> weak, unable to make their own marital decisions and are available for purchase by the highest bidder. (Anyanwu, 2003: 84-85)

For instance, Chinyere Okunna (1996) notes that Igbo movies portrayed women negatively. She found the images 'unrealistic, counter-productive and damaging to the cause of women' (34). Furthermore, she argues that the movies could 'lead to the subjugation of women because they can increase men's disdain for women, *sow mistrust between women*, undermine their confidence in themselves and strengthen the forces which push women to the background in this patriarchal society' (Okunna, 1996, 34, emphasis added). 'Nigerian movies perpetuate sex role stereotypes and reflect the patriarchal social values dominant in Nigerian society' (Ebewo, 2007, 49). 'The general impression is that women are negatively portrayed' to appeal to men. (Ebewo, 2007, 48)

Ozele (2008) also criticizes Nollywood's image of women, and stresses that 'the industry has still to critically address fundamental issues of gender equality and equity, violations of the rights of a woman, traditional stereotypes of females, and the struggles of the female child for equal educational opportunities' (20). He adds that:

> Such uncomplimentary depiction of the *'Africanness'* in women undermines the lofty virtues of the African woman, especially in other spheres of life. The influence of these negative portrayals on adolescent minds who view movie actors as their heroes could only be left to the imagination. (20)

This study is interested in seeing how MILs, a subgroup of women, are portrayed in Nollywood movies.

Mikucki identifies six types of MILs. The first type is the Jealous Mother-in-Law. This MIL sees her daughter-in-law as an intrusion to the family unit. According to Mikucki (2008):

> The *Jealous Mother-in-Law* feels as though she is in direct competition with the daughter-in-law for her son's resources, which elicits high degrees of possessive dependency. The *Jealous-Mother-in-Law* desires a high degree of connection with her son and attempts to retain this connection at any cost; her primary desire for connection is with her son, not with her daughter-in-law or the couple as a marital dyad.

This type of MIL does not allow her son to express his independence. If he tries to assert himself, he is controlled or manipulated through emotional blackmail. She cannot resist the urge to wield parental control. In terms of communication, the Jealous Mother-in-Law openly expresses herself to her son and ignores the DIL. She does not include the daughter-in-law because she sees her as an outsider. She openly expresses her dislike for the DIL. However, she understands that she must tolerate her to keep the connection with her son.

The second type is the Ambivalent Mother-in-Law, who has 'mixed feelings about being a mother-in-law. The mother is glad that her son has become an adult, yet ... she has a hard time letting go' of her son and allowing a new member' into the family (20). She sees her son as a man and a child and wants to stay connected, but not too connected, with him. She is characterized by 'moderate degrees of possessive dependency' (21). Though she would like the son's loyalty to remain with his family of origin, she understands that he should also be loyal to his new family. In terms of communication, this MIL features open and closed communication with her son and keeps issues relating to the DIL private. She does not initiate communication or engage her in conversation, but does not avoid it either. She does not intentionally exclude her DIL from family activities and rituals, or go out of her way to include her. Her DIL is family in the legal sense, but treated like a distant relative, niece or cousin. This MIL could also be described as jealous.

Next is the Embracing Mother-in-Law, who is 'characterized by her genuine love and affection toward a daughter-in-law and high degrees of differentiation acceptance. The *Embracing Mother-in-Law* abandons her need to 'parent' and does not feel the desire or the need to exert parental authority' (22). She can have an adult relationship with her son and his wife, and does not interfere in their marriage. She sees the couple as adults, a marital dyad, and provides emotional support. This MIL openly communicates with her DIL and son, and uses accommodative communication to include the DIL in family rituals and activities. To her, the DIL is part of the family.

The Accepting Mother-in-Law type is similar to the embracing one, except that she is not as enthusiastic about her son's differentiation. Her DIL is seen more as a friend than a member of the family and so her communication with her could be limited or excluding, thereby limiting her inclusion in family activities and rituals. Also, unlike the embracing MIL, the accepting MIL communicates with her DIL as a friend and opens up more about herself when they meet.

Next is the Indifferent Mother-in-Law, who has 'a moderate to high desire for connection with the son, but an extremely low desire or even aversion to connection with a daughter-in-law. In fact, the Indifferent Mother-in-Law views her daughter-in-law as her son's family, not her own' (24). She does not see her DIL as a threat to her relationship with her son, has a moderate level of possessive dependency, and is really apathetic toward her DIL. When she communicates with the couple, she exhibits mixed communication, but is especially closed in her communication with her DIL. She restricts what she tells her concerning family matters. One could say she is not malicious towards her DIL. But since she is indifferent to her, the DIL is no more than a stranger.

Finally, there is the Aloof Mother-in-Law who is characterized as lacking 'desire for connection with both the son and daughter-in-law. She is not concerned about retaining a connection with her son and by default does not desire a connection with a daughter-in-law or the marital dyad' (25). For this mother, it is expected that her son will leave the nest and so she exhibits low levels of possessiveness. Her communication is closed with both DIL and son. She did not have a strong relationship with her son before he got married and the relationship will remain the same when he gets married. Therefore, by default, the DIL is treated the same way.

To understand how MILs are portrayed in Nollywood movies, this study chose to examine Nollywood movies with mother-in-law themes. I selected movies with in-law in the title or movies that fit the description from their cover. These movies were *Demon-in-Law I* and *II*, *The Monster* (*Demon-in-Law* III), *Desperate Mother-in-Law* (also released as *Divided Home I* and *II*), *Si Gbogo Obinrin* (to all women), *Mothers-in-Law I* and *II*, *Mama Commander*, and *Woman in Red I* and *II*.

Demon-in-Law (2006) and *Monster-in-Law* (2007) are the story of Lillian and Emeka who are engaged. However, Emeka's mother, Okwudili, does not want a city girl as a daughter-in-law and has already chosen Amaka for him from the village. Amaka is mentally and physically retarded. When Emeka refuses Amaka and marries Lillian, Okwudili commits herself to destroying the relationship. After the wedding, she visits her son and discovers Lillian is pregnant. She is visibly upset, because she still wants Amaka in Emeka's house. But she pretends to be happy and is nice to Lillian. When Emeka travels, she takes Lillian back to the village with her. Then she visits a voodoo priest, whom she asks to terminate Lillian's pregnancy and 'close' her womb (make her barren). She also got a charm to make Emeka to love Amaka and hate Lillian. Okwudili is a jealous MIL. She saw Lillian as competing with her for her son's affections and resources, and openly expressed her dislike for her. Though Okwudili is portrayed as an evil MIL, the movie makes it clear that she is evil to everyone. When Emeka's uncles supported his plans to marry Lillian, she inflicted one with stroke and another with sores. Okwudili even inflicted a bride with paralysis for not greeting her.

The twist in the movie is that Okwudili is no ordinary woman. She is a witch, who killed her husband to save her son from a life threatening ailment. Apart from the human sacrifice, she also agreed that her son would marry Amaka, whose grandmother led the coven. The repercussion for breaking the promise was death. This is why she destroyed the love between Lillian and Emeka.

Lillian's friend then takes her to a pastor, who not only exposes Okwudili's secret identity, but takes on the fight for deliverance at

Okwudili's house with his prayer warriors. Okwudili tries to stop them but is unsuccessful. The pastor tells her she must confess in three days, or suffer a 'public and painful death. The birds of the night will feast on your flesh.' In the end, Okwudili dies, the spell is broken and Emeka returns to Lillian.

Desperate Mother-in-Law (2008) tells the story of Nnamdi and Lola, an inter-ethnic couple. Lola is Yoruba and Nnamdi is Igbo. They have a son and are expecting a second child. This movie also deals with the issue of ethnicity in marital relationships. They were a happy family until Nnamdi returned from the village with news of a son, Emmanuel, whom he had before he married Lola. He wanted to bring Emmanuel and his mother, Ifeoma, to the city. He pleads with her to forgive his omission and welcome the child to the family. But Lola becomes very upset, and complains to her mother, who advises her to stand her ground, because Nnamdi's parents want to use Emmanuel as an 'excuse to get an Igbo wife' for him. She may not be wrong.

On their part, Nnamdi's parents have not accepted Lola as Nnamdi's wife because he did not observe the Igbo rites of marriage. Nnamdi married Lola in court and church, but not customarily. In the eyes of the law, Lola is his wife. But in the eyes of tradition, Ifeoma is his wife because his parents performed the traditional marriage rites on his behalf. Technically, Nnamdi has two wives. When Ifeoma and Emmanuel come to the city at Nnamdi's mother's prompting, things fall apart for Lola and Nnamdi. Both wives deviate from the cultural definition of a good wife, particularly Lola, who becomes rude and physically abusive to her husband. She also exhibits the Yoruba stereotypes for women as she is loud and troublesome.

Lola's mother does not help matters. She sees Emmanuel as a threat because he is the first son. That means he, not her grandson, would inherit Nnamdi's property. She feels that this is unfair because she 'laid the foundation for his riches to favor' her daughter. Lola's mother is an example of a wife's mother who can also cause problems in a marriage. Though she has the characteristics of a jealous MIL type, she is not jealous of her daughter's relationship with her husband. She believes that her daughter should have her own family, but does not want to let go. She knows everything that happens in her child's marriage and always supports her daughter, even if she is wrong. When the daughter is incapable of handling things, she takes over. She is a combination of a jealous and an ambivalent MIL. She is very intrusive and stops at nothing to achieve her goal or what she thinks is in her child's best interest.

For instance, Lola's mother uses diabolical means to protect her daughter's marriage and her grandson's rights. She uses voodoo to remove Ifeoma from the house (and later kills her) and hires people to kidnap Emmanuel. When Emmanuel returns home, she plans with

Lola to poison the boy when Nnamdi is out of town. Just as Emmanuel begins eating, his father returns to take a document he forgot. He plays with his sons and wants to eat from Emmanuel's plate. Lola stops him, and tells him that the food is poisoned. Emmanuel is taken to the hospital in time and he survives. Lola regrets her actions and ends her relationship with her mother, whom she said destroyed her. Her mother in turn blames her for the plan's failure, saying she should have allowed Nnamdi to eat the food and die because 'that would have been the best thing that ever happened to you.'

The movie sends two serious warnings to women. First, a woman who refuses to submit to her husband will destroy her home. A good woman should submit to her husband, even if her mother's connections made him wealthy. Lola is portrayed as a bad wife, especially within the context of having Emmanuel join the family. Since he involved her, a good wife should have deferred to his wishes and cooperated with him to keep her family together. She had a husband who provided for, loved and respected her, and she allowed selfishness and pride to destroy her marriage. Second, women who listen to their bad mothers will always regret it.

Si Gongbo Obirin is a Yoruba movie that deals with the relationship between MILs and DILs. It tells the story of two friends, Moyo and Fisayo, who prayed that their future husbands' mothers would not be alive when they got married. They saw MILs as intrusive, problematic and troublesome. However, their prayers were not answered as they both married men whose mothers were alive. Their excuse was that the men were good to them. Moyo married Sunny, a businessman, whose mother instantly disapproved of Moyo when they met. She expressed her dislike not only non-verbally, but also verbally. She tells Moyo that her definition of a good wife is one that allows her frequent access to her son. Moyo's MIL is typical of a jealous MIL who wants to control her son. She sees Moyo as competing for her son's time and money and believes that by marrying Moyo, Sunny is abandoning her so she requires him to visit her every weekend. When he misses a weekend visit, she comes to them. She calls daily and never sees anything positive in Moyo. Unable to withstand the interference, Moyo decides to fight her MIL.

One day, during an argument with her, Moyo slaps her MIL. Her husband walks in and sees the slap. He apologizes to his mother, who expects him to beat Moyo. When he does not, she leaves. Moyo apologises to Sunny, but is actually very happy for standing up to her MIL. Sunny then goes to his MIL's house and beats her with a stick in retaliation. When Moyo finds out, she deprives him of sex for more than a year. A friend of Sunny's advises him to have an affair because he is wasting away. He does and gets another woman pregnant. When the child is born, he nonchalantly invites Moyo to the naming ceremony.

Moyo is ashamed and ends the marriage, but notes the importance of tolerating a MIL.

On her part, Fisayo married Olaseni ('Seni), also a businessman. They dated for five years before they got married at 'Seni's mother's prompting. Unlike Moyo's MIL, Fisayo's MIL was an embracing MIL. She saw the couple as adults and treated them equally. She helped around the house and treated Fisayo like her daughter. Her communication style was open with son and DIL. However, as a Nigerian MIL, she saw the couple as an extension, not an abstraction, of the family. She often visited without warning. This time, it was Fisayo who showed the characteristics of the jealous MIL. She was jealous of the relationship between her husband and his mother, even though the MIL saw her as part of the family. In her jealousy, when the MIL visited, she gave her spoiled food disguised in lots of sauce. The MIL went to the hospital several times as a result, but 'Seni blamed it on his mother buying food from canteens when she was at home. In the end, Fisayo killed her MIL with poisoned food.

After her MIL's death, Fisayo's son died. Three years later, she was still not pregnant. The issue of childlessness is important because many Nigerian cultures have children as the basis for the marriage. 'Women are highly valued for their childbearing capabilities. Therefore, a childless woman' is of 'little or no value to her husband, her family, or the community at large' (Wilson and Ngige 2006: 252). Concerned, her mother took her to a soothsayer who divined that Fisayo could only have children if she confessed her deed to her husband. If he forgave her, she would succeed in life. When she confessed, he did not forgive her and she died.

The movie was filled with messages for women about marriage. One message was that women should be patient with their MILs, even when the MILs maltreated them like Moyo's. Good wives were advised to be submissive and patient and treat their in-laws with the same affection as they treated their husbands. From Moyo's story, women are told not to destroy their happiness, especially when they have rich and hardworking husbands. Women must not forget that tradition allows a Nigerian man to marry multiple wives. When they misbehave, a man can simply replace them. Women do not have that luxury. Moyo is portrayed as being responsible for her husband's adultery. The movie also teaches that there are different types of DILs, some with similar traits as MILs. Women who are MILs will also learn from this. As one elder put it, MILs are 'obsessed with their sons. When your daughter is ripe for marriage, you pray she marries a well-to-do man. You will always like your son-in-law to cater for you. But when it's your son, you wouldn't want him to cater for his wife's family.'

Mama Commander is a Yoruba comedy about a controlling MIL. As in *Desperate Mother-in-Law*, this movie is about the wife's mother's role in marriage. Dayo and Yewande have a happy marriage with one problem – Yewande's mother. Nicknamed 'Mama Commander,' Yewande's mother is portrayed as a rude, intrusive and aggressive MIL. Her characteristics match those of a Jealous-Mother-in-Law, with aspects of the embracing MIL. She is not jealous of her daughter's relationship with Dayo, but she wants to control it. She changes things around the house that she does not like, including Dayo's favorite toothpaste. She sleeps in the couple's room, which is considered private in many Nigerian cultures. If servants do wrong, she fires them without consulting Dayo. She also has a key to the house and comes round at will. Nevertheless, her communication pattern with her daughter and son-in-law is open. She expresses herself freely with the couple and anyone else as a matter of fact. She is very rude and physically abusive to men. The movie is filled with scenes where she slaps men, even those older than herself. No matter what she does, her daughter, Yewande supports her.

Sometimes, Yewande's support for her mother's actions goes too far and her husband beats her for it. Domestic violence is presented as deserved in this context because Yewande, like Lola, is not submissive. When Dayo beats her after she catches him at a hotel with another woman, her intrusion is the problem, not his adultery. When Mama Commander finds out how badly Dayo beat Yewande, she has him arrested. It is Yewande who leaves the hospital with a bandaged head, to bail him out. When she gets him out, Dayo tells her she is no longer his wife. He leaves and does not contact her. Yewande is then shown begging his friends to tell her where he is and that she is sorry. Unfortunately, they receive information that Dayo is dead. In regret, Yewande drinks poison. But before it takes any effect, she calls her mother to thank her for destroying her marriage and killing her husband and herself. Her mother rushes to her house in time and Yewande's life is saved at the hospital. Mama Commander is so distraught by what happened that she suffers a heart attack. While she is in a coma, Dayo and Yewande enter her room and her spirit hears them praying for her recovery. She recovers and begs Dayo to forgive her, promising to stop 'shooting trouble.'

Though the movie portrays Mama Commander negatively, it also makes light of domestic abuse. It implies that women should stay with men who beat them and cheat. We never learn what Mama Commander does for a living, but we see that she is affluent. Yet, she is defined by her excessive behavior. She is defined very stereotypically as a Yoruba woman who is loud, aggressive, intrusive and over-protective. Punishing Dayo for beating his wife is portrayed as intrusive and disrespectful and Yewande suffers the consequences since she is portrayed as a bad wife.

Woman in Red tells the story of three siblings – Ikechukwu, Nneka and Oluchi – their marriages, and the influence of MILs in marriages. Ikechukwu has been married to Doris for four years. They have no children. Ikechukwu's mother, Theresa, is unhappy about this and constantly blames Doris for their childless state. She tells Doris that her marriage is useless because they have no children and she will continue to cause trouble in their marriage until she sees a child. Again, Theresa fits the description of a jealous MIL, who sees her son as a child and not an adult. She often exaggerates incidents between her and Doris so Ikechukwu will scold his wife. She comes to the house without notice and openly shows her dislike for Doris verbally and physically.

When she arrives at the house, Doris offers her food. In response, she attacks her for not having children. She falls asleep on the couch and when she wakes up, calls Doris and asks for food, which Doris provides. But while eating, Theresa complains that Doris is wasteful (because she put eggs and meat in the food and gave her juice instead of water) and a bad cook. After eating, she goes back to the couch and sleeps. Doris wakes her up later, to go to the guest room, but she kicks her and tells her to go away. When Ikechukwu arrives and sees Theresa in the living room, he is upset. Theresa then tells him that Doris had ignored her ever since she arrived. She complains that Doris neither gave her food nor offered to take her things to the guest room. Doris breaks down in tears as her husband scolds her for not performing her duties. But when he hears her story, he gets upset with his mother for her treatment of Doris, but says nothing until the next morning when Theresa again attacks Doris for waking her up to eat breakfast. 'Food! Food! That is all your mother taught you to do. Did your mother not teach you how to make babies?' Ikechukwu is enraged at that and confronts his mother. She threatens to leave and he encourages her. Seeing that she cannot manipulate Ikechukwu, Theresa leaves the house in her night-gown, an action supposed to embarrass Ikechukwu in the eyes of his neighbors or anyone who sees her because they will think her children are irresponsible or that she is insane.

Oluchi is married to Harry. They also have no children after five years of marriage. Oluchi's MIL lives with the couple and is presented as an embracing MIL. She treats Oluchi as her own child and is surprisingly not bothered by the childless issue. Her communication with the couple is open and she offers motherly advice to Oluchi and her siblings. Oluchi has a very good relationship with her MIL, which is not the case with her own mother, Theresa. The two are always fighting and things come to a head when Oluchi accuses her mother of being a witch who is responsible for her and Ikechukwu's childless state. She says she got the information from a prophet. Theresa banishes herself to the village, promising never to return.

Nneka is engaged to Chinedu. When Chinedu introduces her to his parents, his father insists that Nneka must get pregnant before the marriage to get his blessing. A stranger comes to the house and tells him that Nneka cannot have children because she has had several abortions. Chinedu's father believes the information and becomes the troublesome in-law in the movie. Chinedu marries Nneka secretly, but when his father finds out, he disowns Chinedu and removes him from his company and his apartment. The couple care for themselves and two years later, their childlessness affects the marriage as Chinedu starts to think his father was right. 'Are you an abortionist?' he asked Nneka. 'You come from an unfortunate family. Something is wrong with your family. Otherwise, how do you explain why your brother and sister have no children?' When Nneka protests against his accusation, he slaps her.

On her part, Oluchi discovers that her MIL is really bad after all. One night, she overhears a conversation between Harry and his mother. His mother tells him to find a new wife. In fact, she has already gotten him a new wife, someone who can give him children. Harry is surprised because he thought his mother liked Oluchi. His mother explains that she is tired of pretending because Oluchi is 'fruitless. She is bewitched.' When Harry refuses, she insists that he must obey her because she is his mother. We see Oluchi's MIL as a jealous MIL, manipulative and controlling. She does not live with the couple because she wants to help them. She is there to intrude on their lives. Her communication also becomes closed toward Oluchi as she speaks to Harry in private. Oluchi learns her MIL's true nature after a period of prayer and fasting. She comes home and sees her MIL as she truly is – a witch.

Harry's mother, not Theresa, is actually responsible for the siblings' problems. She paid someone to lie to Chinedu's parents and cast a spell that made the couples barren. She did this in retribution for Theresa insulting her years before at a women's meeting. In fact, she never wanted Harry to marry Oluchi. After the spell is broken, the couples conceive and have children. Harry's mother dies and Theresa and her children reconcile. Though childlessness is a strong theme in the movie, the movie also warns women about trusting themselves. If you do not have children and your MIL is unconcerned, she might be the reason why.

Finally, the *Mothers-in-Law* movie looks at the issue of MILs from the marriages of two couples – Joy and Chike, and Austin and Amara. Chike and Amara are siblings. Chike and Joy have a very good relationship. In the beginning of the movie, the couple is presented as happy, loving and respectful. One interesting thing about their relationship is that they do not care about traditional gender roles.

During a trip to the village, Joy talked while Chike did the laundry. Nollywood commonly shows women or servants, not husbands, performing such duties. However, Joy's MIL, Ugochi, hates her because 'since my son married her, he has ceased to respect me. He no longer buys those small, small gifts he used to give to me. That girl has succeeded in confusing my son.' Ugochi is a jealous MIL, who does not like anything about her DIL, and does not hide it. She is jealous of their relationship and often looks for ways to destroy it. Her communication is very open with her son, but closed with Joy. She does not include Joy in family activities and is jealous of her relationship with her father-in-law. As she tells Chike, 'she cannot snatch your attention from me and that of your father as well.' She calls their affection for each other 'nonsense' and said she felt 'insulted' when they display affection (such as Joy feeding her husband meat) in her presence. Joy is constantly shown trying to control her temper and be nice and respectful to her MIL because she does not 'want to be labeled a stubborn daughter-in-law.'

Austin and Amara had just got married. When Amara first met her MIL, they were good friends. Her MIL, Ogechi, treated her like a daughter and visited them often. Her communication with the couple was very open and she never discussed anything with them separately. Though Austin was cautious in his relationship with his mother, Amara saw her as a wonderful person, until after the wedding. She soon learned that Ogechi was a jealous MIL, who believed in controlling not only her sons but also her DILs. Ogechi was very critical of Amara, condemning her cooking and forcing her to do chores instead of spending time with her husband. She always called Amara useless and mannerless, a home breaker who came to divide her family. She also slapped Amara. When that happened, Amara reported it to her mother, Ugochi, who was very upset because 'nobody has the right to molest my daughter in her matrimonial home.' Ugochi was so angry that she followed Amara home and confronted Ogechi. Both women got into a fight that was reminiscent of MILs gone wild. After Austin apologized, Ugochi went to Chike's house, while Austin sent his mother away.

These two women were contrasted with Ojeli who had a very good relationship with her DIL, Kate. Whenever Ojeli visited Kate, she took her gifts of food. She called Kate her 'baby' and treated her son and DIL equally. If she pampered one, she pampered the other. Her communication was open and honest with the couple and she was very affectionate with them. Ojeli symbolized an embracing MIL, who saw her DIL as her daughter too. In fact, she was the only MIL in the movie who called her DIL 'my daughter.' Ojeli believed when MILs treated their daughters with respect, they enjoyed their relationship with their sons. Incidentally, Ojeli and Ugochi were friends, with the former always advising the latter to love her DIL.

After the fight at Amara's house, Chike made the connection between Ugochi's treatment of Joy and Ogechi's treatment of Amara. He asked his mother – 'How did it make you feel?' She replied that she felt very bad and angry when she saw how Amara was treated. 'That is how my wife and her mother feel every time you maltreat my wife.' Ugochi was ashamed and later apologized to Joy. Ogechi also realizes her faults and the two women become fast friends. They promise never to maltreat their DILs.

The movie, like all the others, was filled with messages for MILs and women in general regarding marriage. The evil MIL myth is made real in the movie through Ugochi and Ogechi's treatment of their DILs. However, an example is also given of a good MIL like Ojeli. Austin also advised women that 'Any daughter-in-law today, is a potential mother-in-law tomorrow. And in the course of any conflict between the two, the men bear the brunt.' Women must also 'work hard for the success of any marriage and the betterment of the family.'

Findings & Discussion

The goal of this paper was to answer two questions: (a) How are mothers-in-law portrayed in Nollywood movies? (b) Will the portrayal of mothers-in-law follow the typical image of Nigerian women in Nollywood movies?

To answer question (a) the study found that MILs were negatively portrayed in Nollywood movies in many ways. The common stereotypes were that MILs were vindictive, manipulative, troublesome, problematic, controlling, jealous, intrusive, talkative, wicked, forceful, and critical. Ogechi, Ugochi, Mama Commander, Sunny's mother, and Harry's mother all conformed with these stereotypes. They did not want their sons' loyalty to go to their wives, nor did they see their DILs as part of the family. They saw their DILS as their rivals. In some cases, the MILs were very abusive of the DILs.

One area in which they all used emotional abuse was cooking. All the mothers condemned the cooking of their DILs. The kitchen is seen as the woman's domain in Nigerian societies and a woman who can cook is often synonymous with good upbringing and a happy husband (the way to a man's heart is through his stomach is a popular Nigerian saying). To insult a woman's cooking is to insult her mother, upbringing and capabilities as a wife. For instance, Ogechi complained of stones in Amara's cooking. When Amara explained that it was foreign rice (which is usually stone-free in Nigeria), Ogechi chastised her for being careless and lacking proper training. Sunny's mother criticized Moyo's cooking too, saying she used too much seasoning. Ugochi complained of too much salt in Joy's cooking. The MILs always made the complaint in front of their sons, hoping that they would compare their mothers' cooking with their wives'. But in each case, the sons praised their wives' cooking, which offended the mothers. Chike even said his wife was a better cook than anyone else he knew. This made his mother very angry.

Another area the MILs showed control was in their visits. Though Nigerian families are extended and therefore little or no privacy is guaranteed, these MILs did not give the couples any privacy. If they did not live with them like Harry's mother, they paid frequent, unscheduled visits. When the couples tried to live their lives, the MIL interrupted everything they did. The husbands' mothers especially believed that since the house belonged to their sons, they could come and go at will. Their favorite statement to their DILs is: 'This is my son's house.'

Mothers-in-law in Nollywood movies were also very selfish. They cared more about their own happiness than their children's. Some went to great lengths to portray this selfishness like Okwudili, Harry's and Lola's mothers who used charms and connived to get their children to do their will. Mothers-in-law in these movies were fetish. Interestingly, though the movies featured most of the bad MILs as village-based, when it came to using voodoo, it did not matter where she was. Lola's and Harry's mothers lived in the city and still used voodoo.

It was also interesting that when the women had good MILs, their fathers-in-law were bad as was the case with Ojeli's husband and Nneka's father-in-law. Both men did not like their DILs and though they did not intrude in their lives like the bad MILs, they expressed their dislike for their DILs. Ojeli's husband was jealous of his wife's relationship with Kate. He described Kate as ill-mannered and difficult. Chinedu's father also disliked Nneka because his son had disobeyed him by marrying her. He decided to make life difficult for them.

It is also important to note that though the husband's mother is often portrayed as the problematic one, Nollywood movies also featured wives' mothers as problematic. However, this was usually the case when the husband was not wealthy when he married the daughter, or the MIL was wealthy. Social standing seemed to be the reason why the wife's mother was a bad in-law. She either intruded because she had the money to do so, or because she was the reason for the man's success as Lola's mother constantly reminded Nnamdi. Such portrayals are bound to create or support the stereotype that a successful woman is a threat. If a man gets financial help from his MIL, he will always be reminded of it. The wife and MIL will see him as weak. This was a strong message in *Desperate Mother-in-law*, where Nnamdi appeared incapable of making decisions or asserting his authority in his home. His MIL practically ran the household. His wife did not respect him and took decisions without consulting him. His friend was always advising him to man up. Also, though a bad MIL did not mean a bad husband, the reverse was the case for women. A bad MIL meant a bad wife who must be made submissive.

To answer question (b) 'Will the portrayal of mothers-in-law follow the typical image of Nigerian women in Nollywood movies?' This study found that in many ways, the portrayal of MILs in Nollywood movies followed the typical negative image of Nigerian women in Nollywood movies.

Only one movie, *Desperate Mother-in-Law* was co-written by a woman. Men wrote the rest and directed all of them. All the English-language movies typecast one actor, Patience Ozorkwor, as the bad MIL. Since the producers and writers of these stories are predominantly male, they have maintained the status quo of the negative portrayal of women in this genre. Mothers-in-law are a subgroup of women and when women are portrayed this negatively, it undermines the contributions that women make to society. Furthermore, it teaches women to expect maltreatment from their MILs when they get married. They will also learn that if they fight their husband's mother, their marriage will fail like Moyo's. Such images might lead women to fear marriage. Women could also imitate these portrayals as what society expects of them. Bad in-laws exist, but when the bad is depicted more than the good, it cultivates a mean world syndrome in people.

Also, though some MILs were punished for their actions, the movies predominantly saved the harsh treatments for the husbands' mothers who used diabolic means, or the wives' mothers. Theresa did not suffer for maltreating her DIL, nor did Ogechi, Ugochi or Sunny's mother. Their relationships with their sons stayed intact, while Lola and Yewande had to end or limit their relationships with them. Ogechi and Ugochi regretted their actions, but that only made their relationships with their sons stronger.

The negative behavior of MILs was also presented as a natural trait in women. Women were presented as mischievous and very pretentious people, whose true nature only came out in marriage. Ogechi was nice to Amara until she married Austin. Harry's mother pretended to like Oluchi but was really the force behind her infertility. Fisayo pretended to like her MIL but was slowly killing her.

Women were also portrayed as selfish and ungrateful. The husbands' mothers were jealous of their sons' relationship with their wives, despite getting anything they wanted from their sons and, in some cases, their DILs. Fisayo was not content despite the love and material things her husband provided for her, as were Lola and Moyo. Women were rarely shown working together for the good of the family. In fact, only Kate and her MIL had a good relationship and this was presented as an unreal ideal.

Apart from Mama Commander and Lola's mother, MILs were also portrayed in a traditional sense. They lived in the village, while their children lived in the cities, and depended on their sons or husbands (or both) for money. This was not the case for the MILs in the city who were independent and rich. This symbolized the struggle between traditional and modern Nigeria. The MILs from the village saw marriage as an open and extended institution. Couples had little or no privacy and parents were involved in their children's marriages. However, people in the city saw the family more in the nuclear sense, with couples expecting some level of privacy in their marriages. They understood that culturally their family unit was an extension of their families of origin, but wanted to maintain some individuality. The struggle between these two worlds was apparent and told more on wives than husbands.

Women were expected to have modern ideas in the city but were defined by cultural and traditional expectations. They were supposed to welcome their MILs, no matter when they came, and exercise enormous patience. Mothers-in-law were supposed to understand that their children needed privacy but to also to maintain their traditional roles as mothers by intruding in their children's lives, particularly when the couple had not produced offspring of their own. If their sons married bad women and beat them, these MILs did not scold them because they were performing their roles as husbands. When MILs lived in the city like Mama Commander and Lola's mother, they were shown as culturally abnormal and unnatural because they dared to be different by supporting their daughters. It appears that Nollywood producers want women to be dependent on men, meek and extremely patient in the face of adversity. When city women get out of line, tradition, in the person of the village MIL, will put them in line.

Women will also learn from these movies that if the husband is rich before marriage, there is a 99 percent chance that his mother will be a problem. The competition will not only be for his affection but his money as well. The men in these movies, except Austin, were cast in powerful male roles as first sons or the only child or son. That means they are responsible to their families of origin too. The MILs, except Ojeli and Seni's mother, saw their DILs as coming to enjoy what they had not suffered for. However, for those who want to marry poor men, the movies suggest they should not have rich mothers like Lola's mother and Mama Commander because their marriages will fail. It was also interesting how these movies portrayed a good wife's mother as one who never came to the house and minded her own business. Moyo's mother never visited the couple and she was praised for being a good mother and in-law. We never saw Joy's mother either, but learned that she did not approve of Ugochi's treatment of her. But the husband's mother was not bad because she came (after all, it was her son's house). She was bad for other reasons.

Also, though Chike said men were affected by the tension between their mothers and wives, they rarely showed any efforts in handling the situation. When they did, it was either to the extreme ('Mama, leave my house') or complete silence ('She is my mother. What can I do?'). The men mostly had a hands-off attitude to the situation. When women faced the problem head on, they were portrayed as bad wives who had to be beaten into submission. Men should have been more involved in finding a solution to the problem.

In conclusion, this paper has attempted to examine the portrayal of MILs in movies by looking specifically at Nollywood movies. The image of this group of women was found to be very negative and capable of influencing the perception of women, who are the dominant viewers of these movies. Rather than contribute to the work of Nigerian women in the age of gender empowerment, these films could cause men to look down on women and for women to distrust themselves. It is quite unfortunate that the loudest voices in the industry are of those who use the traditional angle to keep women down. There is a need to present an alternative perspective of the MIL/DIL relationship, one that celebrates the positive or presents a more balanced perspective because the relationship is an important one. Many Nigerian cultures are patriarchal and therefore a woman marries into a family. In some cases, marriage causes a break with her family of origin. If DILs and MILs, who are supposed to see themselves as family and not strangers, have a bad relationship, the entire family unit will be affected since women are kin keepers, the people who maintain relationships between both sides (Fischer 1983). Movie producers cannot afford to continue portraying the MIL through negative stereotypes because they will not only undermine women's self-esteem when they marry but could also make women fear the marriage institution.

Noting the significant impact that film can have on viewers, it is important that Nollywood movie makers understand that film should reflect the contradictions in society to make people aware of social problems, particularly those affecting women. But when movies exaggerate the issue or routinely portray a group negatively, the consequences could be devastating, not only for the group, but the society as a whole. There are many Nollywood movies that portray MILs using negative stereotypes. This paper just looked at a small sample. Therefore, Nollywood movie producers are encouraged to actively engage in creating movies that push for positive change. Nigerian women are under immense pressure to simultaneously achieve their goals of self-realization and actualization without being seen as anti-family or anti-men. Nollywood movies should send messages that understand the tension between modernity and tradition and project solutions that will aid the cause of women's contributions to national development.

WORKS CITED

Abah, Adebayo L. 'One Step Forward, Two Steps Backward: African Women in Nigerian Video-Film.' *Communication, Culture & Critique* 1(2008): 335–7.

Bandura, Albert. 'Social Cognitive Theory of Mass Communication.' In *Media Effects: Advances in theory and research* ed. Jennings Bryant and Dolf Zillman, 61-90. Hillsdale, NJ: Lawrence Erlbaum Associates, 1994.

Bequette, Sarah. 'Nollywood Rising: Global Perspectives on the Nigerian Film Industry.' http://lists.lsit.ucsb.edu/archives/ihcevents/2005–May/000102.html 2005. (accessed January 10, 2010).

Chukwuma, Anyanwu. 'Towards a New Image of Women in Nigerian Video Films.' In *African Video Film Today* ed. Foluke Ogunleye, 81-90. Manzini, Swaziland: Academic Publishers, 2003.

Ebewo, Patrick. 'The Emerging Video Film Industry in Nigeria: Challenges and Prospects.' *Journal of Film and Video* 59, no. 3 (2007): 46-57.

Fischer Lucy R., 'Mothers and Mothers-in-Law.' *Journal of Marriage and the Family, 45*, (1983): 187-92.

Fisher, Christy. 'Demographic Trends: Marketers Straddle Asia-America Curtain.' *Advertising Age* 65, no. 47 (1994): S- 2, S-18, S-19.

Gerbner, George. 'Toward Cultural Indicators: The Analysis of Mass Mediated Message Systems.' *AV Communication Review* 17 (1969): 137-48.

——. 'Cultivation analysis: An overview.' *Mass Communication and Society*, 1(1998): 175-94.

Gorham, Brad W. 'Stereotypes in the Media: So What?' *The Howard Journal of Communications*, 10 (1999): 229-47.

Haynes, Jonathan. 'Introduction.' In *Nigerian Video Films* ed. Jonathan Haynes, 1-36. Ohio University research in international studies. Africa series No. 73, 2000.

——. 'Video Boom: Nigeria and Ghana.' *Postcolonial Texts* 3, no. 2 (2007): 1-10.

Hays, Mathew. 'A Thousand Films and One Queen.' *The Globe and Mail*, 2005 (Accessed December 20, 2010).

Jackson, Jacqueline C. and Linda Berg-Cross, 'Extending the Extended Family: The Mother-in-Law and Daughter-in-Law Relationship of Black Women.' *Family Relations* 37 (1988): 293-7.

Jèsus, Martin-Barbero. 'The Processes: From Nationalisms to Transnationalisms.' In *Media and cultural studies key works*, ed. Meenakshi Gigi Durham and Douglas Kellner, 626-57. Revised ed. Malden, MA: Blackwell Publishing, 2006.

Lippmann Walter,. *Public Opinion*. New York: Macmillan, 1922.

Okunna, Chinyere S. 'Portrayal of Women in Nigerian Home Video Films: Empowerment or Subjugation?' *Africa Media Review* 10, no. 3 (1996): 21-36.

Osei-Hwere, Enyonam and Osei-Hwere, Patrick. '*Nollywood*: A Multilevel Analysis of the International Flow of Nigerian Video Films.' *Paper presented at 2008 Annual Convention of International Communication Association.*

Osifo-Dawodu, Egbe. WIFV-DC Member Promotes the Nigerian Film Industry in the U.S. http://www.wifti.org/news.cfm?nf_nfid=51 2007. (Accessed January 10, 2010).

Ozele, Anthony. *Representations of Cultural Resilience and Perceptions of Religiosity in Nigerian Movies and the Crisis of Personal Identity among Nigerian Adolescents.* Paper presented at 2008 Annual Meeting of the Religious Education Association, Chicago, IL.

Pérez, Maria Casas. 'Cultural Identity: Between Reality and Fiction: A Transformation of Genre and Roles in Mexican Telenovelas.' *Television New Media* 6 (2005): 407-14.

Prentice, Carolyn M. 'The Assimilation of In-Laws: The Impact of Newcomers on the Communication Routines of Families.' *Journal of Applied Communication Research* 36, no. 1(2008): 74-97.

Rittenour, Christine E. and Jordan E. Soliz, *Communicative Predictors of Shared Family Identity, Future Contact, and Caregiving in Mother-in-Law/Daughter-in-Law Relationships.* Paper presented at the 2007 Annual Meeting of the National Communication Association, Chicago, IL.

Stephan, Wilson M. and Ngige Lucy, 'Families in Sub-Saharan Africa.' In *Families in Global and Multicultural Perspective* edited by Bron B. Goldsby and Suzanna D. Smith, 247–71, 2nd ed. Thousand Oaks, CA: Sage, 2006.

Sylvia, Mikucki. 'A Theoretical Typology of Mother-in-Law Types.' *Paper presented at the Annual Meeting of the NCA 94th Annual Convention, San Diego, CA*, Nov 20, 2008.

Tan, Alexis, Yuri Fujioka and Nancy Lucht, 'Native American Stereotypes, TV Portrayals and Personal Contact.' *Journalism & Mass Communication Quarterly* 74 (1997): 265–84.

Vera-Sanso, Penny. 'Dominant Daughters-in-Law and Submissive Mothers-in-Law? Cooperation and conflict in South India.' *Journal of the Royal Anthropological Institute* 5, no. 5 (1999): 577–93.

Charting Nollywood's Appeal Locally & Globally

Moradewun Adejunmobi

One of the great accomplishments of Nigerian video film is that it has succeeded where African high literature and African cinema have failed thus far, that is, it has succeeded in generating an experience that is both African and popular with audiences. In advertising the works of famous African filmmakers like Djibril Mambety Diop or Sembene Ousmane, one would have to say, 'Coming soon to an American campus near you' or 'Coming soon to a European film festival near you' for it is in those locations that one might have an opportunity of watching their films. As anyone who has lived in or traveled through much of Africa can confirm, outside of events like the FESPACO film festival, you are not likely to come across the works of famous African film directors anywhere in Africa,[1] to borrow the title of another film that you probably will not see in most African locations. By contrast, it is hard to miss Nigerian video films in Nigeria itself, sold as they are by itinerant traders in market places, viewed on government-owned television, on private television, and sold in shacks that describe themselves with such high sounding names as 'video mart' or 'video superstore.'

What is more, audiences for Nigerian video films have emerged around Africa and beyond the borders of Nigeria. According to reports, the films are being viewed in South Africa, Zambia, Kenya, Liberia, Sierra Leone, the Gambia, the Congo, Tanzania, and Ghana among other countries.[2] On the cable television channel, DSTV, broadcast across the continent, 80 per cent of the films reportedly shown on *Africa Magic*, a program introduced in 2003 and dedicated to African film, are in fact Nigerian video films.[3] Such success has created resentment among professionals working in the same or allied fields in some African countries. In Ghana, the popularity of Nigerian video films led to the introduction of a law to protect Ghanaian film production in 2004. Pressure from members of local theater groups who felt that Nigerian video films were drawing away their audience also prompted the government in the Democratic Republic of the

Congo to request that private television stations cease showing Nigerian video films.[4] There is no indication yet that these measures have diminished the appeal of Nigerian video films in both countries.

Nigerian films are equally popular with African immigrants outside Africa, wherever they may come from. Stars in the industry have reported enthusiastic welcomes from fans in locations from Greece to the Netherlands. In several instances, the fans were not even Nigerian. Today, it is almost certain that any store serving the needs of mostly African immigrants in the United States and which also sells or rents films, will have a regularly updated stock of Nigerian video films. Personal acquaintances have told me, for example, of Cameroonians selling Nigerian video films in San Jose, and Congolese traders of Nigerian video films in the New England states.

Though cinema theaters are operational in some African countries, the majority of viewers in Nigeria watch Nigerian video films at home in the company of friends and family. As a result, ticket sales cannot be used as a reliable indicator of the size of Nollywood audiences.[5] Exact figures are also hard to come by when it comes to the sales of tapes, since most of the distribution and marketing occur in the African informal economy, and piracy is an integral part of the sales networks that have developed around Nigerian video and foreign films in many parts of Africa.[6] It would be almost impossible to determine how many Nigerian video films are sold outside Nigeria, but according to some estimates, a successful film might sell between 50,000 and 120,000 copies within Nigeria (Ogunbayo 2004: 48). A Nollywood blockbuster like *Osuofia in London* is reported to have sold 400,000 copies in 2004 (Barrot 2005: 42). One would have to multiply these figures several times over to come close to the number of people who might actually watch each film within and outside Nigeria.

The question I would like to address here is why Nigerian video film has been so successful in drawing a large, popular, and predominantly African audience. What is it that explains the appeal of Nollywood within Nigeria and especially beyond its borders? Furthermore, what projections can be made about Nollywood's ability to generate audiences outside Africa and outside communities of African immigrants? Scholarly and non-scholarly discussions of the appeal of Nigerian video film often reference the question of culture. Writing for example about Nigerian video films and Congolese audiences, Ngoloma Katsuva (2007: 92) explicitly invokes cultural similarities between Nigerians and Congolese, stating 'In every video film that is watched by the Congolese, the audience will, in most cases, find some similarities with their own way of living and their own cultural background.' Similar conclusions have been drawn with respect to other film practices around the world. For example, Cindy Wong (1991: 91) attributes the fact that rentals of local films apparently account for over 90 percent of video rentals in Hong Kong to a preference for indigenous local products. Joseph Straubhaar and Gloria Viscasillas (1991:192) have suggested that in developing countries, 'audiences tend to prefer cultural products that are as close to their own culture as possible.' Straubhaar proposes the term 'cultural proximity' to account for this tendency to prefer products that appear culturally similar, though he also acknowledges that some audiences in developing countries, comprising mostly the elite, may continue to seek out 'internationalized productions from outside both nation and region' (1991: 56), even when more culturally proximate materials are available.

Straubhaar's observations appear entirely reasonable. Undoubtedly Nigerian audiences consider Nollywood films to be more culturally proximate than Hollywood productions. The same principle probably applies for audiences further afield in countries like Sierra Leone and Kenya where Nigerian video films are also popular. One could refer here to what Straubhaar (55) describes as a secondary layer of cultural proximity, where audiences in countries that do not have their own media industries will show a preference for regional products that are more culturally proximate than materials from more distant locations.

But if this principle is generally true, how do we explain the fact that Nigerian video films have generated significant audiences in the one West African country that does have its own video film industry, namely Ghana? Nigerian films are still widely available in Ghanaian markets and still frequently shown on Ghanaian television stations. Furthermore, Nigerian films appear to be at least as popular if not more popular with Ghanaian audiences than films by Ghanaian directors made in Ghanaian languages. If cultural proximity sufficed to explain the convening of audiences around texts and performances, how would we account for the fact that some Nigerians, mainly in northern Nigeria continue to watch Indian films, and probably as many audiences in several English and French speaking countries in West Africa have acquired a taste for Latin American telenovelas broadcast on private and government owned television stations? How do we explain the fact that outside of film festivals, African cinema rarely generates a popular audience in Africa in spite of the attention given to cultural detail, particularly in earlier films by Francophone directors? Indeed, what exactly do we mean if we claim that audiences in the Congo watch Nigerian video films because they find them culturally similar? If cultural proximity were the overriding element in the emergence of most audiences in developing countries, could we therefore conclude that Nollywood's audiences will remain overwhelmingly Nigerian and or African? Zeb Ejiro, the well-known

Nollywood director and producer, recently said and without sounding in any way regretful: 'Look, we're never going to crack the American market' (Trenton 2004: 115). Is Ejiro right on this score and are there other markets that Nollywood might not 'crack' apart from the American market as he describes it because of cultural remoteness?

I would argue that what is at stake in the appeal of Nollywood films across Africa is not cultural proximity in the sense of shared cultural heritage, shared cultural patrimony or devotion to a common store of values. Congolese and even Ghanaian viewers may or may not recognize *akpu* and bitter leaf soup displayed on screen, but they understand when meals are meant to be read as signs of excessive consumption, and when they are meant to be read as signs of indigence and poverty. Zambians may not have a practice of 'spraying' as do Nigerians and other West African societies on a more limited scale, but grappling with the challenges posed by structurally adjusted economies, they understand the display of wealth involved in showering wads of local currency or more amazingly, US dollar bills all over some man or woman in the context of a party.

Even if a shared cultural heritage did exist, Nigerian video film directors and especially producers and marketers are, by and large, not in the business of promoting cultural heritage as an end in itself.[7] That is, the depiction of elements supposedly drawn from an existing cultural patrimony might be considered useful to the extent that it sells film narratives by sheer shock value. This explains the frequent association of indigenous spirituality with 'witchcraft' and bloody rituals in many films. African cultural heritage as presented in most Nigerian video films has few redeeming qualities, and its insertion into the narrative often marks the beginning of a time of moral regression, torment and suffering for major characters. Given the way in which African cultural heritage is portrayed in Nigerian video films, it is questionable whether Nollywood's audiences watch the films mainly because they desire to see what is claimed as their own heritage on screen.

Nigerian video film narratives are created and watched primarily for purposes of entertainment. They succeed in generating significant local and regional audiences to the extent that they address widespread fears and fantasies in what viewers consider to be a satisfactory manner. More so than accurate representations of cultural heritage, Nollywood's mainly African audiences appear to have a particular appreciation for the portrayal of what they perceive to be familiar struggles represented on screen as subjects of high dramatic tension and conflict. The recognizably local identity of the actors, the settings, and the director/authors seems to have value for viewers insomuch as it enables them to feel that the challenges depicted apply more directly to the experiences of people living in African settings. However, what Straubhaar calls cultural proximity, I would prefer to describe as phenomenological proximity, so as to clearly differentiate the motivations which propel audiences towards these local narratives from an identification with cultural heritage. In my opinion a distinction needs to be made between an audience's recognition of varying degrees of cultural proximity in a narrative and an audience's interest in and preference for depictions of local and especially traditional culture.

Audiences for Nigerian video film, as for other commercially driven texts, respond above all to perceptions of substantive relevance, that is to outcomes presented as having implications for the interests or concerns of viewers, and presented as plausible for people in the personal, social and political circumstances of viewers. Paradoxically, both the desire for escape from everyday life and the desire for relevance to everyday concerns, are high on the list of reasons why people consume commercial fiction. Video film directors understand that they can misrepresent the culture as long as the story is considered sufficiently entertaining and relevant. Different kinds of texts generate different kinds of audiences, but substantive relevance often holds greater significance than cultural and even phenomenological proximity for audiences of commercially driven texts, or what I call popular audiences. And this is the reason why overlapping and popular African audiences may find certain kinds of narratives produced by non-Africans as entertaining or even more entertaining than narratives produced by Africans. Indeed, both phenomenological proximity and distance in texts offer different types of popular audiences equal opportunity for experiencing substantive relevance.

To the extent that a creative form can be produced and reproduced locally, it is marked as local and embraced by many precisely because it has become familiar. For some audiences, then, phenomenological proximity is a factor in their experience of substantive relevance. Yet other audiences have an appreciation or preference for texts marked as foreign in content and style, in order to experience displacement vicariously, in order to engage with practices seen as desirable but not yet applicable to the local environment, in order to have temporary access to, while distancing oneself from practices seen as not desirable for the local environment.[8] The unfamiliar elements depicted in a narrative of foreign origin do not automatically render it irrelevant to the concerns of all local consumers. Whether particular audiences privilege the phenomenologically proximate depends on what priorities they set for their educational, political or leisure activities. Given a choice, some audiences for a certain type of text will prefer similar types of texts that are more phenomenologically proximate while other audiences in the same location will choose texts that are less phenomenologically proximate, and yet others are able to appreciate both types equally.

In the case of Nigerian video films, their appeal for many African audiences derives in the first place from perceptions of substantive relevance. It is the types of conflicts, confrontations and struggles appearing in the films that are considered familiar rather than the specific rituals used to gain wealth, the language spoken, the clothes worn, and the food eaten etc. I find remarks made by the Nigerian actress Ajoke Jacobs, pertinent here. She argues that the films appeal to the Nigerian public 'because it's about them' (Trenton 115). Indeed, Nollywood films in English are able to generate audiences in diverse locations in Africa because they present recognizable struggles, they appeal to widespread fears and familiar aspirations. These films travel so well across state and cultural boundaries in Africa because the conflicts they represent and the resolutions they offer are perceived to be experientially proximate for postcolonial subjects. The situations depicted are within the realm of possibility and could occur in the societies where the viewers live even if they have no personal experience of such crises. The stories are true to expectation if not precisely to history and cultural heritage. Furthermore, and even where audiences do not find the narratives proximate to expected occurrences within their own society, they may consider the actions and conflicts displayed appropriate to the particular fictional world projected in the film narrative. Within that imaginative realm, the story obeys its own logic and is believable. Audiences are willing to engage with the narrative on its own terms, and to that extent find it a feasible and entertaining fiction.

Above all, and in terms of substantive relevance, Nollywood's audiences are entranced by the spectacle of odious human behavior matched only by the certainty of commensurate judgment. Shorn to bare essentials, the story in many films coming out of Nigeria consists of two basic sections. The first section organized around shock value is the exposition of scandal, and of socially unacceptable conduct, often in discontinuous fashion. The reprehensible actions that bring leading characters to a crisis are rarely culturally specific in the English language films. Nollywood's villains have only human failings, but taken to excess. There are men attracted to beautiful women, which is not unusual, only the beautiful woman desired is the wife of one's best friend or the best friend of one's wife. There are characters who want money, an aspiration shared by many, only they are willing to murder spouses, siblings, children, neighbors, and friends to become rich.

To this extent, Nollywood's characters are unlike those found in the high literature of disillusionment produced by African authors since the 1970s and as the failure of the postcolonial state became more and more apparent. Whether they are agents of the state as in Sony Labou Tansi's fables, or free agents pursing their basest instincts as in the urban hell of Calixthe Beyala's novels, the characters of African high literature of disillusionment appear to be mindless caricatures of human beings when they embrace excess without expectation of improvement in their circumstances. Characters in Nigerian video film are not beholden to strange fetishes without reason, nor are they carnivores and cannibals like the 'Providential Guide' in Sony Labou Tansi's *La Vie et demie*, they desire only the good life, and who could quarrel with that? Their acceptance of excess always serves a tangible purpose directly tied to the quality of life they pursue for themselves.

Perhaps even more importantly, immediate judgment is rarely visited upon the instigators of mayhem in the fictional universe of African high literature and high cinema. We may see in those texts the suffering of victims but rarely the punishment of evildoers. By contrast, the second and final section of a typical Nigerian video film reveals the dire consequences that are certain to befall exploiters, oppressors, and all manner of evildoers, while also showing how victims of injustice will be avenged. Though directors and producers of Nigerian video films have been engaged in a long running battle with Nigeria's National Film and Censor's Board over the morality of the films,[9] I would in fact take the position that the films are very much informed by a clearly articulated moral vision that consistently delivers punishment to those who do evil. No matter what has occurred earlier, and no matter how implausible the conclusion of the narrative, in the end, the wicked and the immoral are always punished as is common in melodramatic narratives, preferably experiencing a slow, painful and agonizing process of decline following a supernatural intervention.

Audiences for Nollywood films expect to see the wicked punished, the arrogant brought down, and the innocent rewarded by the time narration ends. As such, the decisive conclusions of many Nollywood narratives contribute to the popularity of the films with various African audiences. Elizabeth MacArthur's (1990: 16) definition of narrative closure as 'an attempt to preserve the moral and social order which would be threatened by endlessly erring narratives' is relevant here and again marks a distinction between Nollywood productions and some more recent texts of African high literature and cinema. In those texts, narration ends, often without bringing closure to the central conflict of the narrative. One could cite Sony Labou Tansi's novels as examples in African literature and films by Djibril Mambety Diop as examples in African cinema. As Richard Neupart (1995: 31) observes, the 'more classical genre films constantly reaffirm viewer expectations.' This is precisely what Nigerian video films do for their audiences, even if the ending often depends on a most improbable sequence of events.

The fact that production of Nigerian video films occurs almost exclusively within the ramifications of commercial enterprise is not incidental to this tendency to reaffirm viewer expectations. Like commercial narratives everywhere, Nigerian video films use imaginative narrative to offer decisive resolutions to the fantasies and fears of the moment, in contrast to African cinema texts, that either do not offer such decisive resolutions or focus on actual trends and events within African societies that have not, however, entered into the popular imaginary as subjects of widespread fears and fantasies. Consequently, and though directors of African cinema narratives may strive for a more comprehensive representation of cultural heritage, their films cannot compete with and attract as large a local audience as a narrative style specifically designed to entertain interested viewers in the local community by reaffirming rather than questioning their expectations.

In situations of permanent insecurity as might be experienced for any number of reasons around the world, the predictability offered by an interpretation of events founded on the certainty of moral absolutes holds considerable attraction. Much of Nollywood's appeal lies, then, in its melodramatic mode of storytelling and acting. Whatever the theme, we see in Nigerian video films a preoccupation with what Peter Brooks (1976: 5) has called the 'moral occult' or as he defines it 'the domain of operative spiritual values which is both indicated within and masked by the surface of reality.' The seemingly unstoppable manifestation of excess within a framework suffused by morality in Nigerian video films is typical of melodrama. Melodrama requires excess, for without excess, there would be no need for judgment and for the moral template used to adjudicate these incarnations of excess. Mysterious, magical and spiritual forces are often a necessary component of melodrama, effecting the justice that the institutions of society can no longer deliver.

Melodrama offers a mode for reconciling personal experiences of suffering with continued admiration for the institutional framework within which suffering occurs. In the case of Nigerian video film in English, the setting in which various crises unfold is unmistakably modern and the characters embrace modernity without reserve. And yet they encounter tragedy and torment in this modern world. Since there is no desire on the part of the audience to hold modernity responsible for the difficulties encountered, failure and success become a function of personal morality. As such, the failures that precipitate tragedy in the lives of key characters are almost always personal rather than institutional, and are brought on by the propensity of significant individuals for excess.

Brooks (15) locates the origins of melodrama in the emergence of a post-sacred era following the French revolution. For Brooks (16), '[m]elodrama represents both the urge towards resacralization and the impossibility of conceiving sacralization other than in personal terms.' Melodrama has apparently captured the imaginations of some African publics, and notably Nollywood audiences though we do not, at this time, have a post-sacred era in Africa. On the contrary, the dominant idioms in many African societies today for confronting political and institutional failure draw from the realm of spirituality. Likewise, morality in most Nigerian video films in English is explicitly tied to religion and often to Pentecostal theology. Apart from supernatural agents, pastors, priests and other acolytes of organized religion, are in Nigerian films the characters who most frequently initiate the process through which the wicked get their just deserts and through which the virtuous are rescued from their oppressors.

Unlike Brooks, therefore, I would associate melodrama, not so much with the needs of a post-sacred era as with attempts to rationalize a form of social organization that remains popular despite its inability to deliver expected benefits. What is at stake in melodrama is the inclination to account for political and institutional failure by displacing such failures onto the realm of morality and individual character deficiencies. In this instance, the melodramatic narratives of Nollywood provide a medium for rationalizing the continuing attractiveness of modernity as an ideal notwithstanding the increased poverty and social dislocation that have come to characterize Africa's experience of modernity. If the expected gains of modernity appear beyond reach, the perversions of those in positions of authority in the political system, in places of worship, and on the domestic front among others can be held responsible. Moral reform is expected to achieve the desired goal, but in the meantime, and as to be expected in settings where social and political institutions cannot be relied upon to provide assistance to those in need, magical and mysterious forces intervene to bring relief to the suffering.

For Nigerian video film audiences, the attractions of melodrama do not only operate at the level of narrative organization. Melodramatic acting also travels well across linguistic and cultural divides and can be interpreted by audiences who do not speak the language being used on screen. Despite the language barrier, audiences in the Congo whose working languages are Lingala, Kikongo, Kiswahili, Chiluba, and French among others, are apparently watching Nigerian films in English. In the case of Nollywood films and any commercial film narratives that circulate transnationally, the well-known aphorism is true: actions speak louder than words.[10] And from the point of view of Nigerian video film directors and producers, the expressive body remains an accessible and useful resource where technological and financial means are not available to enable the creation of elaborate stunts or special effects.

The dissemination of mass-produced narratives in West Africa and probably much of the continent is associated more and more with what I am choosing to call a practice of circumvented literacy. Nigerian video film narratives frequently communicate with audiences not so much by disregarding as by circumventing where possible advanced literacy and verbal signs. Brooks (70, 56) identifies gestural communication and non-verbal means of expression as important features of melodrama. It is no accident that the aesthetics of melodrama are so pervasive in the mass-produced narratives originating from and circulating in postcolonial societies where mastery of advanced literacy and the standard form of dominant languages is less widespread for large segments of the society, since such mastery depends on sustained access to formal education.

To secure the interest of as many potential viewers as possible, individuals involved in the creation of mass-produced narratives in multilingual societies with variable levels of literacy, often cannot rely on verbal communication alone, but supplement the verbal with gestures, with music and dance. Nigerian video film, Latin American telenovelas and Bollywood texts are melodramatic to varying degrees and all make liberal use of non-verbal means of communication. In Nigerian video film, sighs, weeping, shouting, and other speech forms that do not actually involve the use of words can take up significant swathes of time. Exaggerated facial expressions and other gestures also serve purposes of communication more effectively than words. Audiences around Africa that either do not speak English at all or have difficulty following Nigerian English are able to decipher these gestural signs as they are deployed in Nigerian video films. It is from this perspective that we can begin to make sense of the growing popularity of Nigerian video films in countries like Côte d'Ivoire and the Democratic Republic of Congo that are officially French speaking and even in the supposedly English speaking African countries where the level of proficiency in English is quite low.[11]

No discussion of Nigerian video films is complete without reference to one of the great mysteries of this cultural form, namely the fact that enthusiastic audiences have emerged for these films in spite of the poor production quality on many films. Sound quality in particular has been a major source of concern, especially when the films are viewed outside Nigeria. Noise in the background and background music drown out speech on many films. The South African cable television station, DSTV, which has been showing mostly Nigerian video films on its *Africa Magic* program was sufficiently worried about the sound quality of the films to dispatch two specialists to Nigeria to train Nigerian sound technicians working in the video film industry in 2004 (Barrot 61). The foregrounding of non-verbal means of expression in Nollywood productions has so far turned out to be an advantage here, enabling communication to continue where mastery of technology remains approximate and a hindrance to the deciphering of speech.

Thus far, Nollywood's African audiences have responded towards the deficiencies in technical quality with a curious mixture of tolerance and pride. On the one hand, the mere fact that the films exist indicates a degree of African familiarity with modern technology and is therefore a matter for some pride among Nollywood's Nigerian and African audiences. It is no longer that foreign nationals make films about Americans and other foreigners with an African setting as in *Black Hawk Down*, *Tears of the Sun*, or *Blood Diamond*, Africans now have sufficient skill with the technology to make their own films about Africans with, if they so choose, a Western setting. On the other hand, the poor quality of production and reproduction communicates as well as the narrative what it means to live in poor societies around the world. What Brian Larkin (2004: 291) has described as an 'aesthetic of piracy' which affects the visual images and sound quality of the film among other elements, is part of what makes this film something other than an American film and creates the ambiance of phenomenological proximity for African viewers. Africans may not all share the same wedding rituals, but most know what it is like to lead one's life in a place where the output of various technologies is highly unpredictable.

While African immigrant communities outside Africa are perhaps less inclined to put up with poor sound quality and poor visual images, they are similarly tolerant of other lapses attributed to the films, such as the slow and discontinuous narrative, or the melodramatic acting. Immigrants anywhere in the world seek images of home and products from home. African immigrants are in this regard no exception. But, and in addition, for Africans living outside Africa who must contend with the rarity of televisual images about their place of origin, and the tendency of those images to concentrate on certain types of crises, Nollywood films offer the opportunity to see Africans in a context other than that of AIDS, war, and famine. In the end, Nollywood films humanize Africans, and create stories that mirror the current concerns and aspirations of Africans themselves, which is more than can be said for much of what either Hollywood or the news media around the world projects of Africa.

Some of the criticisms leveled against Nollywood video films have been made about film practices elsewhere in the world and are apparently accepted by the audiences that have emerged for those film practices as elements of a distinctive style. The mixing of the supernatural and the 'realistic', the melodramatic acting style, and slow paced narrative development are also features of Indian cinema.[12] According to Srinivas (2002: 158), for example, Indian viewers 'complain that Hollywood movies or 'English pictures' are too short.' Perhaps such audiences would find the duration and pace of the Nollywood narrative better suited to their sensibilities. In the case of Hong Kong movies, Cindy Wong (1999: 101) comments that American viewers who watch these films appear to consider 'an incoherent plot as a characteristic of Hong Kong films.' The occasionally discontinuous and digressive narrative that we find in many Nollywood films will not work for all audiences, but there are apparently film viewers around the world who are less interested in the continuity of the narrative than in other dimensions of the film.

Given the problems to which I have just alluded, can Nollywood's audiences extend beyond the circle of Africans at home and abroad? Would such an expansion even be a worthwhile goal? Nollywood films may yet attract a non-African audience, but it is likely to be among the kinds of viewers around the world who are not seeking narratives that offer the phenomenologically proximate. Furthermore, and in explaining why and how some mass-produced narratives generate popular audiences across state and cultural boundaries, we must also not overlook the determination of marketers, producers and directors of commercial film to circulate their works as widely as possible and to make them legible and attractive to as dispersed a public as possible. We know that within West Africa, the penetration of Nollywood products into various countries is not solely the handiwork of individuals involved in piracy and counterfeiting of tapes. Nigerian directors and producers have played an active role in this expansion of the market for what are essentially Nigerian film projects by recruiting well known local actors in countries like Ghana and Sierra Leone to perform in their movies. The appropriation of local talent in this way puts a new twist on Straubhaar's concept of cultural proximity.

To this end, interested film producers invest in narratives offering substantive relevance and or legible aesthetics, while also selectively leveraging the possible advantages and disadvantages of cultural proximity. Some filmmakers are content to target a somewhat more circumscribed audience using a less accessible and more grounded depiction of particular cultures. This appears to be the strategy of producers of Hausa and Yoruba language films whose films circulate mainly among Hausa and Yoruba speaking audiences within and outside Nigeria.[13] It is a strategy that is especially appealing when the language community in question is reasonably large, thus guaranteeing satisfactory financial returns, as is the case with the Hausa and Yoruba speaking communities. Other filmmakers, especially those producing English language films, however, choose to deploy a highly accessible and lightly marked representation of localized practices in order to reach an even larger audience that is more linguistically and culturally heterogeneous. If in addition, such producers can ensure that viewers find the aesthetics of the film entertaining, and the core conflicts of the narrative relevant to their immediate preoccupations, the narrative form is likely to attract a significant following locally and across various state boundaries.

Nollywood's current audiences view the remarkable tales of scandal and excess as the films' strongest assets, and for this reason, have been willing to disregard the technological deficiencies associated with the reproduction of narrative as video film. Poor production quality may turn out to be an obstacle to further expansion of Nollywood markets and audiences in locations around the world where, even given the fact of piracy, the technology is in better working order, and reproduced video tapes, DVDs and VCDs do not show the signs of deterioration that are both visible and audible in the materials sold in Africa. In the absence of channels of distribution that are adequately managed and policed to protect intellectual property rights, Nollywood producers and directors have at this time minimal incentive to invest in improving quality of production and reproduction. Even if they undertook such a project so that their films could sell massively in Thailand, what is the likelihood that they would reap the benefits from such investments unless the marketers and counterfeiters were actually willing to pay more to the actual producers for releasing a higher quality product?

The fact that Nollywood might not as Zeb Ejiro puts it, 'crack the American market,' is in the short term, a blessing in disguise. It means that Nollywood producers and directors will concentrate on cultivating an audience that is African, that spans the continent, and that reaches immigrant communities from the continent around the world. It also makes it more likely that they will continue seeking to perfect their own distinctive style of storytelling since it is not in their best interests to produce films that are completely identical with those of Hollywood or Hong Kong, though borrowing narratives from other film traditions is an article of faith in Nigerian video film production as in many other popular narrative styles around the world.[14] Nollywood's focus on African audiences is especially important since financial considerations and the challenges of infrastructure have made it more difficult to remain as attuned to specifically African audiences in other areas of cultural production associated with Africans.[14] Hopefully, enforceable solutions will emerge to address the very serious problem of intellectual property rights confronting Nigerian video film directors, which may or may not lead to a global expansion and diversification of the Nigerian video film audience. But even if that never happens, it is Nollywood's great accomplishment that it has generated this African popular audience, and is for the moment, one of the few media that offers contemporary Africans the possibility of sharing a relatively well disseminated store of 'vernacular' narratives, that are peculiar to Africa, that cater to local tastes, and have an almost continental reach.

NOTES

1 I am referring to the German film, *Nirgendwo in Afrika*, which appeared in English translation as *Nowhere in Africa*.

2 See Fuita and Lumisa, Ondego, Katsuva, Muchimba for more on this.

3 See Barrot (2005: 49). In fact, on the occasions when I watched Africa Magic in Nigeria during the summer of 2005, all of the films shown were Nigerian video films.

4 See Fuita and Lumisa (2005).

5 The term Nollywood, crafted after Hollywood and Bollywood remains controversial among scholars of Nigerian video film, however, it has passed into popular use in Nigeria and that is why I have chosen to use it here.

6 See Larkin (2004) for more on the role of piracy in Nigerian film production and distribution.

7 One of the exceptions to this trend is the film director Tunde Kelani, who has shown a definite commitment to using video film as a medium for exploring aspects of Yoruba history, literature, and folklore. When most professionals in the Nigerian film industry speak of showing what they describe as 'our culture,' they are generally referring to depiction of contemporary fashion styles which are generally distinct from Western fashions, but cannot be described as traditional either.

8 Apart from the elite identified by Straubhaar, young men in the developing world seem to constitute another group that is often very attracted to narratives and products marked as foreign.

9 In the interview that Daniel Trenton conducted with a selection of Nigerian video film actors and directors, the sense of frustration with the Nigerian Censor's Board was palpable. I heard similar evaluations of the role of the Nigerian Censor's Board in interviews I conducted with two well known Nigerian video film directors in 2005. Barrot (2005: 43-4) too refers to the problematic impact of the Censor's Board on film production in Nigeria.

10 Cowen (2002: 93) makes a similar point with Hollywood films: 'As Hollywood markets its films to more non-English speakers, those films become more general. Action films are favored over movies with subtle dialogue. Comedy revolves around slapstick rather than verbal puns.'

11 See Adejunmobi (2004) for an extended discussion of how African audiences respond to European languages in mass produced narrative forms like Nigerian video film.

12 See for example, Srinivas (2002: 158)

13 Yoruba language films are apparently popular with Yoruba language speakers in southern Benin, while Hausa language films are gaining ground in Niger.

14 Tejaswini Ganti (2002) comments on and describes the apparently widespread practice of remaking Hollywood films by Bombay filmmakers in India. Though

published studies of similar practices on the part of Nigerian filmmakers are not yet available, it would seem, to consider one Nigerian example, that the narrative strategies in the early parts of the Nigerian video film, *Osuofia in London* share certain elements in common, with the famous South African film, *The Gods Must Be Crazy*.

15 I am thinking here in particular of the future development of African literature, and the African novel, at a time when the most celebrated authors are increasingly published by publishing houses outside Africa that have no special interest in cultivating an African audience or promoting an entity that might be described as 'African' literature.

WORKS CITED

Adejunmobi, Moradewun. *Vernacular Palaver: Imaginations of the Local and Non-Native Languages in West Africa.* Clevedon, UK: Multilingual Matters, 2004.

Barrot, Pierre. *Le Phénomène vidéo au Nigeria.* Paris: L'Harmattan, 2005. Eng. Transl. *Nollywood: The Video Phenomenon in Nigeria.* Oxford: James Currey; Bloomington, IN: Indiana University Press, Ibadan: HEBN, 2008.

Beyala, Calixthe. *Tu t'appelleras Tanga.* Paris: Editions J'ai Lu, 1988.

Brooks, Peter. *The Melodramatic Imagination: Balzac, Henry James, Melodrama and the Mode of Excess.* New Haven: Yale University Press, 1976.

Cowen, Tyler. *Creative Destruction, How Globalization Is Changing the World's Cultures.* Princeton: Princeton University Press, 2002.

Fuita, Franck and Godefroid Lumisa. 'Kinshasa: quand les vidéos nigérianes chassaient les démons.' In Pierre Barrot (Ed.) *Nollywood, le phénomène vidéo au Nigéria.* Paris: L'Harmattan, 2005, 111-16.

Ganti, Tejaswini. 'And Yet My Heart Is Still Indian: The Bombay Film Industry and the (H)Indianization of Hollywood.' In Faye Ginsburg, Lila Abu-Lughod, Brian Larkin (Eds) *Media Worlds.* Berkeley: University of California Press, 2002, 281-300.

Katsuva, Ngoloma. 'Nigerian Home Videos and the Congolese Audience: A Similarity of Cultures.' In Foluke Ogunleye (Ed.) *African Video Film Today.* Manzini, Swaziland: Academic Publishers, 2003, 91-104.

Larkin, Brian. 'Degraded Images, Distorted Sounds: Nigerian Video and the Infrastructure of Piracy.' *Public Culture* 16.2 (2004): 289-314.

MacArthur, Elizabeth. *Extravagant Narratives: Closure and Dynamics in the Epistolary Form.* Princeton: Princeton University Press, 1990.McCall, John. 'Nollywood Confidential.' *Transition,* 95 (2004): 98-109.

Muchimba, Helen. 'Yes-O to Nollywood.' *BBC Focus on Africa,* 15.4 (2004): 46

Neupart, Richard. *The End: Narration and Closure in the Cinema.* Detroit: Wayne State University Press, 1995.

Ogunbayo, Modupe. 'Boom Time.' *BBC Focus on Africa,* 15.4 (2004): 48-50.

Ondego, Ogova. 'Le Kenya sous dépendance.' In Pierre Barrot (Ed.) *Nollywood, le phénomène vidéo au Nigéria.* Paris: L'Harmattan, 2005, 117-21.

Srinivas, Lakshmi. 'The Active Audience: Spectatorship, Social Relations and the Experience of Cinema in India.' *Media, Culture & Society.* 24.2 (2002): 155-73.

Straubhaar, Joseph. 'Beyond Media Imperialism: Assymetrical Interdependence and Cultural Proximity.' *Critical Studies in Mass Communication.* 8 (1991): 39-59.

Straubhaar, Joseph and Gloria Viscasillas. 'The Reception of Telenovelas and Other Latin American Genres in the Regional Market: The Case of the Dominican Republic.' *Studies in Latin American Popular Culture* 10.5 (1991): 191-214.

Tansi, Sony Labou. *La Vie et demie.* Paris: Editions du Seuil, 1979.

Trenton, Daniel. 'Nollywood Confidential, Part 2.' *Transition*, 95 (2004): 110-128.

Wong, Cindy Hing-Yuk. 'Cities, Cultures and Cassettes: Hong Kong Cinema and Transnational Audiences.' *Post Script: Essays in Film and Humanities.* 19.1 (1999): 87-106.

The Rise of the Video Film Industry & its Projected Social Impact on Ghanaians

Africanus Aveh

Historical Overview

Motion picture production in Ghana dates back to the colonial era when the British colonial government organized what is said to be the first film school in sub-Saharan Africa for a group of Africans of whom three were from the then Gold Coast. The three, Robert Ofoe Fenuku, Samuel Aryeetey, and Bob Okanta pioneered the Gold Coast Film Unit established in 1946 under British producer/director Sean Graham. The unit was charged with the production of socially educative films to assist in the governance of the Gold Coast and other British colonies. The first feature film produced in this country, *The Boy Kumasenu* (1952) is the story of a young boy who drifts from a village to the city of Accra and encounters problems as he tries to settle. There were several documentaries on civic education and social responsibilities of citizens to their nation.

After independence in 1957, the first republican government under President Kwame Nkrumah changed the unit to the State Film Industry Corporation and upgraded it into a modern film production outfit with state-of-the-art facilities and equipment. Nkrumah was convinced of the power of cinema in the shaping of popular opinion which forms an integral element in governance. It is on record that almost everywhere that the president went either within the country or abroad, a camera crew accompanied him.

Successive governments after Nkrumah have neglected the film sector and the corporation's equipment and facilities grew obsolete with time. State-funded celluloid film production and exhibition ground to a halt in the late 1970s. Independent productions however kept aloft the flag of Ghana in the cinematic world with Kwaw Ansah's *Love Brewed in the African Pot* (1980) receiving, among others, the Jury's Special Peacock Award at the eighth International Film Festival in New Delhi, India and the Oumarou Ganda Prize at the seventh Pan-African Film and Television Festival (FESPACO) in

Ouagadougou, Burkina Faso, both in 1981. Ansah's *Heritage Africa* (1988) won the Grand Prize, the *Stallion Yennenga* at FESPACO in 1989. King Ampaw co-produced, among others, *Kukurantumi Road to Accra* (1984) and *Juju* (1985) with NDR Television of Germany.

It must be noted that lack of adequate funding, coupled with the hassle of doing post-production abroad worked against celluloid film production in Ghana during this period. Cinema houses were turned into warehouses and churches as box-office returns dropped as a result of bad projectors and poor sound amplification that made film shows less enjoyable. A near film vacuum was created in the country in the late 1970s up to the mid-80s.

It was this vacuum that preceded the era of the video boom, that is, the massive scale of production of motion pictures in video format from the start of the industry. Several factors made this possible. Ghana Television began colour transmission around this period and that made Ghanaians returning from abroad bring in colour television sets, which together with video cassette recorders (VCRs) became symbols of affluence in Ghanaian homes. Video cassette rental shops sprang up in the middle-class residential areas in the cities of Accra and Kumasi stocking Hollywood movies released on tape. Several screening centres (basically equipped with a VCR and an average size television set) were established in the working class neighborhoods and enthusiastic youth paid token entrance fees to watch the video shows. A number of mobile units also began operating, carrying screening sets especially to school campuses where shows could not be organized regularly. Such operations did brisk business, and the Ghanaian government was compelled to institute licensing fees and taxes for operators to generate income for the state.

The National Film and Television Institute (established in 1978 with German Government assistance to train people for the television and film corporation) offered practical training in video production and graduates from the institute were available to handle video cameras and video post-production benches when the video boom got underway. At the same time cheap consumer camcorders became available for hire and affluent people began to rent them to cover funerals, weddings and other social ceremonies. With playwrights and television script-writers ready with stories and energetic actors and actresses from the popular television soaps and other stage performers around, it was just a matter of time before video production burst onto the Ghanaian creative scene. Enterprising youths managed to raise small amounts of capital and plunged into movie production by gathering friends and relations to shoot stories on tape. The scene was now set for a major outpouring of screen productions which lasted over two decades. The full-length commercial video film that opened the floodgate is *Zenabu* (1986) by William Akuffo who was then an entrepreneur with no filmmaking knowledge. Since then Ghana has produced close to a thousand video titles.

Video Film Production

How the Ghanaian video film grew in popularity is an interesting phenomenon. Ghanaians saw very familiar stories easily understandable on the screens, identified familiar faces among the cast, recognized known neighborhoods and towns that formed the backdrops and locations of these productions. The language of the video films, easily understood as 'Ghanaian English,' was spoken in a mixture of local dialects. There were productions made in Akan, a language which is predominantly understood in Ghana. With screening centers dotted over several neighborhoods, one only needed to walk a short distance to watch a movie at an affordable fee. Also, as the producers kept on churning out new titles regularly, patrons always had something new with which to entertain themselves. At the peak of the video boom in the late 1980s to the early 1990s, there were as many as five new titles released every week.

The technical quality of many of the productions was deplorable for the industry was dominated by untrained filmmakers. As I have already mentioned, people with stories to tell found the means of raising small capital sums, assembled friends and relations to form the cast and crew, and armed with a camcorder, usually a VHS or a Video 8, went shooting movies. The shots were chained together, some music dubbed over them, and instant video films were released. Actors in the productions became stars and were mobbed wherever they appeared. Some producers made profits on their investment in the video venture and established production companies, a few of which have survived the economic turmoil and are still in operation to date.

It is unfortunate that professionally trained and experienced older Ghanaian filmmakers at first shunned the video format and saw it only as suitable for training or television production. This really created room for the amateurish productions that dominated the video scene as these film enthusiasts developed the notion that there is no need for training in order to make movies. However, a few professionals braved the odds and produced in the video format, helping to raise the standard of video production in the process. International award-winner Kwaw Ansah co-wrote and directed *Harvest at 17* (1992) for the National Commission on Culture as part of a youth sensitization campaign on teenage behaviour concerning sex, abortion and problems of parenting in Ghana. Professionally trained cast and crew were used and the video can be said to be one of 'the few good ones' of the time. Wallace Bampoe-Addo produced *Mataa – Our Missing Children* (1992), the story of a drug baron who rules a village with his money and influence despite his involvement with child abduction and ritual sacrifice. Tom Ribeiro directed *Out of Sight, Out of Love* (1993) which focuses on a mother's role in the choice of a man for her daughter to marry. However, the absence of a national policy on motion picture production and the lack of organized sources of funding continued to work against any attempt at standardization of video film production in Ghana (Aveh 1996).

Video Film Distribution

Distribution has been a headache for producers of video films in Ghana. In the earlier stages of video film development, producers had to organize their own screenings by booking theatres in Accra and Kumasi, the two major cities. To avoid pirating the producers or their trusted agents carried the video tapes to the screening centres at the scheduled times and kept a vigilant eye on the operators during the screening to prevent illegal dubbing. In addition the box office had to be monitored since most of the time the business deal was a splitting of the proceeds on agreed percentages.

Later, two distribution companies won the confidence of several producers and took over the business of distributing video films in Ghana. They were Alexiboat Productions and Kama Marketing Company. They either bought the full rights of a movie and duplicated the tapes for sale to individuals or they monitored the screening centres to ensure the payment of returns.

In recent times, producers have tended to organize premiere shows of the productions for specially invited guests as well as paying patrons at high profile venues like the National Theatre in Accra and the International Conference Centre. The following day or two after the shows, they hit the streets on carnival-style floats, selling the video films for people to screen at home. This was understandable since the screening centres were no longer in mass operation and it was now more common for households to have their own VCRs, VCDs and DVD players.

The Nigerian 'Invasion'

Since the turn of the millennium, local video film production in Ghana has dropped considerably. Several Ghanaian video film producers have complained of losses and have instead become distributors of the Nigerian video films that were imported into the country during this period. The Nigerian producers cut good deals with the local distributors that assured them of some income though, as it turned out, some of the Nigerian productions brought to Ghana were found to have been banned by Nigerian authorities for some unacceptable scenes.

This Nigerian 'invasion' can be traced to the beginning of co-production ventures between Ghanaian and Nigerian video film producers. Mention can be made of the collaboration between Miracle Films of Ghana and Igo Motion Pictures of Nigeria in the production of *Asimo* and *The Visitor* (1999) with a combined Ghana-Nigerian cast and crew. These were followed by some popular Nigerian directors working for Ghanaian producers with locations for the movies in both countries. Nigerian producers then began producing video films with wholly Ghanaian casts, making it difficult to classify these video films as either Ghanaian or Nigerian. Then the onslaught of 'full-blooded' Nigerian video films began to displace the few Ghanaian productions in the shops and on Ghanaian television screens. Some Ghanaians see this 'Nigerianization' of the Ghanaian screen as adversely affecting Ghanaian cultural and social behaviour while others see it as a threat to the survival of the local Ghanaian movie industry that must be addressed in some way. This is a controversy I shall return to later in this essay.

The Kumasi Productions

In recent times there has been another development in the Ghanaian video production industry: a steady flow of particular kinds of video films labeled 'Kumasi Productions', partly because of their place of origin and also because of their targeted viewers. The locations depicted in these video films are mainly Kumasi and its environs and the language used is Twi occasionally mixed with English. The majority of these productions have no English sub-titles and the few sub-titles found are often riddled with grammatical errors and some serious spelling mistakes.

These productions are mainly improvised dramatic pieces whose strengths rely mostly on the abilities of the lead characters to develop the stories through their interactions in the various situations that are created. While the cinematography in these productions is generally poor, the acting is often good especially with the use of the local language, Twi, and the absence of rigid scripts whose lines had to be memorized. Agya Koo, a popular comedian and performer from the concert party tradition, features in many of these productions. He is witty and cracks rib-splitting jokes in every situation in which he finds himself. The various sequels developed out of single titles in these productions have helped to sustain audience interest.

Themes

The main focus of local video films has been on social issues confronting the nation either at the family or national level. The movies have explored themes of love and marriage especially generational conflicts related to the choice of partners on the part of sons and daughters. We have the popular image of the shrewd mother-in-law who will burst into her son's marital home, throw out his wife for not producing a child and replace her with the woman of her choice.

Other interesting subjects in these films are what I term 'mini-skirt leeches' – young sexy-looking ladies in skimpy mini-skirts whose appearance provokes older married men to abandon their marital homes and obligations to be at the whims and caprices of these ladies. Very often, established marriages are disrupted and hitherto peaceful families torn apart in these marital dramas. Award-winning *A Stab in the Dark* (1999) and its sequel *Ripples* (2000) focused on this theme. A young lady named Efe comes to spend the holidays with her friend Kate and ends up in a relationship with Mr Ansah, Kate's father. The relationship tears the family apart when Mr Ansah 'sacks' his wife and daughter for interfering in his affairs. However, as fate will have it, Efe begins to date younger guys, much to the annoyance of Mr Ansah who then has a heart attack and ends up in a hospital bed. He later reconciles with the family. In a retaliatory mood, Efe teams up with two other hardcore ladies to terrorize and blackmail the Ansah family by waylaying Kate, beating her up and holding up her wedding ceremony until ransom monies are paid to them.

Religious themes are also very popular in video films and are specially targeted at the growing church-going population in the country. Many love stories are underscored with elements of religion and spirituality where 'juju' or some other supernatural powers are used to blind men making them submit to all kinds of passions until they are eventually delivered from such evil powers by a Christian pastor. The style of these productions is developed around characters who knowingly or otherwise come under the influence of evil forces and are then liberated by Christian pastors in very interesting circumstances.

Critics have commented on the negativity of many of the local video films associated with traditional African religious practice. (Sutherland-Addy 2000; Aveh 2000). I have commented elsewhere on the negative impact of this practice on the psyche of young Ghanaians, especially as these productions seek to reinforce the

African stereotypes we find in some Euro-American movies. Distinguished filmmakers like Kwaw Ansah have also commented on this practice. In his opinion, Africans have been made to believe through the colonial experience that whatever their ancestors bequeathed to them is heathenish (Ukadike 2002).

In these video films, the traditional priest is presented as an evil and grotesque-looking being who accepts requests to kill or destroy other persons for payment. Women wishing to eliminate their rivals consult the 'juju shrine' as in *Dilemma* (1993), *Double Cross* (1992) and *Jewels* (1999). A man who wants to succeed in his criminal activities solicits spiritual protection from the 'juju shrine' as depicted in *I Want Her Blood* (1992), *Avengers* (1994) and *Mataa – Our Missing Children* (1992). The traditional priest is often associated with murder since he is often made to demand human parts for ritual purposes as in *Nkrabea* (1992). Shrines are depicted as weird-looking unhygienic places filled with odds and ends. Traditional priests are characterized as charlatans who swindle the people who consult them – *Expectations 2* (1999).

How authentic are these images? What about traditional priests as healers and custodians of knowledge about the medicinal powers of plant and tree species? What about their roles as counsellors on social problems? Don't they also act as intermediaries between man and the Supreme Being and foretell looming dangers and how to avert them? Our traditional rulers also function as priests as they sit nearer to the ancestors on the sacred stools that are their symbols of office. They also lead the community in ritual ceremonies during traditional festivals in communicating with the ancestors and the gods.

Religious video films which are meant to help win more converts for the emerging churches oppose these positive, and I will argue, realistic, images of the traditional African priest and priestess. 'Deliverance videos' seek to reinforce the preaching of contemporary charismatic Christian pastors who take the church as serious business because their livelihoods depend on the size of their membership (Meyer 2002). It is common belief that the powers of God could be easily invoked by either a pastor or any other spiritually charged person to deliver any afflicted person from the 'powers of darkness' emanating from a 'juju shrine'. In *The Reward* (1997), a woman who becomes mentally ill as a result of a love affair and goes roaming the refuse dump, is cured by a pastor who casts the evil spirits out of her.

Some video films have tackled the misinterpretation of traditional cultural practices which are confused with religious practices. Traditional marriage is popularly tagged in Christian circles as 'engagement' and as such not accorded due recognition until the couple has had a wedding in a church. *Wedlock* (1999) tells the story of a young couple who go through a traditional marriage ceremony, where the woman is given away to the man by her family. They then decide to follow it with a church wedding which is cut short half-way through when the pastor cannot pronounce them husband and wife because a woman who has had a relationship with the groom objects. As the story develops, opposing factions debate whether the young couple should be regarded as duly married and allowed to live together in matrimony or not.

Video films have also focused on emerging issues like drug trafficking, corrupt officials, smuggling, armed robbery and serial murder. In the late 1990s, the country experienced a spate of serial killings of women mostly in the capital city Accra, and several video films picked on this subject as a theme. Popular among them is *Accra Killings* (2000) which tells the story of an undercover security agent infiltrating a gang that kills women for body parts to be used in rituals by people seeking business success and riches. *A Call at Midnight* (2001) portrays state officials on the run as they are pursued by security personnel for embezzling state funds.

The Role of Television

Television has grown steadily in Ghana since its inception in 1965. The monopoly of Ghana Broadcasting Corporation was broken in the mid-1990s when a government policy enabled private stations to be licensed to operate. Ghana now has four free-on-air television stations broadcasting nationwide. In addition there are numerous other pay/cable and satellite ones. Many homes have their television sets switched on for most of the day as long as there are people in the house. One station now broadcasts twenty-four hours a day. Primarily, television broadcast has concerned itself with news reportage and documentaries, interspersed with light entertainment and sporting activities mostly coming live from the studios or from the stadium. There are also live discussion programmes from panelists in the studio talking about current issues.

In recent times, television has become a major source of entertainment and people are relying on it more and more for regular entertainment throughout the week. The video films screened daily on all channels have popular appeal. Because of the size of television screens, images do not appear as huge and abnormal as those seen in movie theatres and it is easier for viewers to become emotionally attached to whatever unfolds before their eyes. This medium will become more and more important in the unfolding history of video films in Ghana.

Social Effects

As stated earlier, the popular notion among film enthusiasts that there is no need for formal training in order to make movies is at the root of the problems associated with some of the images and sound on the Ghanaian screen. Inadequate research on subject-matter or theme coupled with poor handling of motion picture technique, has produced many titles which bluntly speaking are dangerous visual materials that need to be kept in an underground vault and treated as 'radioactive' waste material. One does not need any technical knowledge to detect the shortcomings of the video films made in Ghana.

These weaknesses have limited the market of the productions to Ghana itself and sometimes to only a particular region of the country. It is often difficult for non-Ghanaians to comprehend the stories or situations contained in these video films. Language barriers, especially with regard to the Kumasi Productions, further limit the interest of non-Akan speaking Ghanaians. Interestingly, a recent survey revealed that South American Spanish-language soaps dubbed into English currently screening on some Ghanaian televisions have more popular appeal even to the non-literate viewers than the local video films. However, these soaps contain some very bizarre and alien social and cultural material that we frown upon here in Ghana. Lesbianism, gay relationships and appalling love relationships where mothers and daughters date the same men are frequently portrayed.

Attempts to copy Hollywood action-style movies with gun-wielding gangsters in car chase scenes have been unsuccessful due to the inability to create convincing stunts and visual effects. Shallow stories and weak plots coupled with poor cinematography render these video films sub-standard.

The 'deliverance videos' with their misrepresentation of African traditional religion have contributed to the low self-esteem of Ghanaians about their ability to function without 'outside' support. The Ghanaian's attitude towards his own cultural values has had tragic consequences. In Kwaw Ansah's view, 'we have been corrupted in such a way that we laugh at our own values' (Ukadike 2002: 9). There are several social practices that are thought to be indigenous but which can be traced to European and Arab origins propagated as part of Christian and Islamic teachings.

Nigerian videos are often full of violent scenes of crime with gangsters on the rampage killing without mercy. Occultism where rivals challenge each others' supernatural powers is also very popular in these films. The impact of these scenes on Ghanaian society can be measured by the many appeals made for their banning. For instance, letters to the editor columns in Ghanaian newspapers are filled with claims that such video films are contributing to an upsurge of armed robberies and other crimes in Ghana.

Nigerian language video films with their mixture of pidgin English with Igbo, Yoruba or Hausa, have also influenced the Ghanaian way of speaking to the extent that you find Ghanaians slipping expressions picked up from Nigerian productions into their day-to-day speech. *Tufiakwa, Oya, Oga,* are popular examples. It is very common in Ghana now for people to be addressed with the title 'chief' though they may not necessarily be traditional rulers or chiefs. A children's game has emerged called *Issakabar* where one child jumps and pounces on another from behind unawares. This was borrowed from a Nigerian video film of the same title in which a ruthless, armed gang goes round pouncing on people and subduing them. This movie, which was apparently banned in Nigeria, surprisingly found its way into Ghana and was even shown on national television.

Of special interest to educators is the impact of video film culture on reading in Ghana. Concern has been expressed about a dwindling interest in reading. There is a growing tendency among students at both the second-cycle and tertiary levels to 'watch' rather than read. They prefer to watch videos of prescribed literature texts than to read the originals. Shakespearean plays on video abound especially at the British Council library. This has prompted the production of some African dramatic works on video. An example is Efua Sutherland's *The Marriage of Anansewa* now on video. Video films have now also become integral components of public education on major national exercises or policy dissemination. They are, for instance, currently used as part of a public education campaign on the ongoing National Identification System project.

Conclusion

It can be argued that the video film in Ghana has come to fill a vacuum created by the decline in celluloid film production as a result of lack of resources in the industry. Jobs have been created and creativity has been maintained. I have argued elsewhere that despite the technical flaws in most of the video films produced here, they still constitute an important body of Ghanaian creative and literary work that will be studied for many years to come. Additionally, the video films as artifacts constitute important collections that document Ghana in several ways. They can be regarded as historical records deserving proper archiving for posterity. What is needed is for the state to foster initiatives to improve their content, to mitigate their adverse impact on the psyche of Ghanaians, and to maintain and preserve Ghanaian identity in the face of globalization.

NOTE

1 The debate is still raging and the attempt to delve into it in this paper will cause a massive derailment. My own thoughts on this issue are the subject of a paper in preparation.

WORKS CITED

Aveh A. 2000, 'Ghanaian Video Films of the 1990s: An Annotated Filmography', *Fontomfrom: Contemporary Ghanaian Literature, Theatre and Film, Matatu Vol. 21–22,* Kofi Anyidoho and James Gibbs (eds), Rodopi BV, Amsterdam/Atlanta, pp. 283–300.

Aveh A. 2000, 'Demons in Raffia, Saints in Suits: Critically looking at Religious Iconography in Ghanaian Video Features', unpublished paper presented at a Consultation on *Media and Religion in Africa* sponsored by International Study Commission on Religion, Media and Culture at GIMPA, Accra (May 2000).

Haynes, J. 2000, *Nigerian Video Films,* Athens, Ohio University Center for International Studies, Africa Series No. 73.

Sutherland-Addy, E. 2000, 'The Ghanaian Feature Video Phenomenon: Thematic Concerns and Aesthetic Resources', *Fontomfrom: Contemporary Ghanaian Literature, Theatre and Film, Matatu Vol.* 21–22, Kofi Anyidoho and James Gibbs (eds), Rodopi BV, Amsterdam/ Atlanta, pp. 265–77.

Meyer, B. 2002, 'Pentecostalism, Prosperity and Popular Cinema in Ghana', *Culture and Religion,* Vol. 3, No. 1: 67–87.

Ukadike, F. 2002, *Questioning African Cinema: Conversations with Filmmakers,* Minneapolis, University of Minnesota Press.

Constructing Identity & Authenticity: The Evolving Cameroon Video Film in English

Joyce B. Ashuntantang

It is over 20 years since the Nigerian video film industry (Nollywood) became a sensation. The industry now produces 600 titles a year and according to a survey on global cinema carried out by the UNESCO Institute of Statistics (UIS), and released last year, Nollywood is now the second largest film industry in terms of output after India's Bollywood. It is also the second largest employer in Nigeria after the government. Since the Nigerian video film phenomenon reached Cameroon in the mid-1990s, Anglophone Cameroonians have responded with films of their own although they have not succeeded in agreeing on a common label. Some video film producers in Cameroon have referred to the evolving Cameroon video films in English variously as Collywood, Camwood or Kamwood, while others have dismissed these appellations as imitative and lacking in originality. It is difficult to give the actual number of films that have been produced because there are no effective legal channels keeping records. However, based on my own knowledge as a practitioner in the field and per the titles available at Magic Touch in Buea and other video stores in different parts of Anglophone Cameroon,[1] there have been well over 500 movies produced in and regarded as Cameroon video-films in English. Compared to the millions of video films already produced in Nigeria, this number may seem insignificant but for a geographical region which still struggles to understand its own socio-political identity, this number is quite illuminating. This paper looks at the way Anglophone Cameroon video film practitioners have sought to situate themselves within this growing phenomena.

Based on this corpus of films, can one even begin to talk of the Cameroon video film in English? This question of identity is one that has confronted Anglophone Cameroon Literature and Emmanuel Fru Doh has attempted an answer in his paper 'Anglophone Cameroon Literature: Is there any such thing?' The impatience of Anglophone Cameroonians and literary critics for answers to these questions is triggered by the the location of Anglophone Cameroon. Wedged between a populous giant, Nigeria, and the dominant francophone majority, it remains a struggle for Anglophone Cameroonians to assert their identity. This identity or lack of identity for Anglophone Cameroon has also framed the production and dissemination of Anglophone Cameroon Literature. When Albert Gerard was editing his 1986 text, *European-Language Writing in Sub-Saharan Africa*, Anglophone Cameroon was omitted. In a last ditch effort to save the situation, Stephen Arnold wrote an informative account on Anglophone Cameroon Literature titled 'Emergent English Writing in Cameroon' and it was included as an appendix to Nigerian literature. In fact because of its apparent isolation, Stephen Arnold has referred to Anglophone Cameroon as the 'orphan of the Commonwealth' (Arnold 1990).

To understand the geo-political position of Anglophone Cameroon, one has to delve into history. The Republic of Cameroon is a classic representation of the complexity of postcolonial realities. Cameroon remains the only African country colonized by three European powers namely Germany, Britain and France. After the defeat of Germany in World War I, Cameroon became a trust territory administered by France and Britain with France gaining four-fifths of the territory while one-fifth went to Britain and was governed as an integral part of Nigeria which was a British colony. British Cameroon was divided into the Northern and Southern Cameroons. While Northern Cameroon was divided administratively among the three Northern Nigerian provinces, Southern Cameroon was governed as a single province of Nigeria. In 1954 Southern Cameroon gained self government and in 1961 it gained independence in a United Nations supervised plebiscite. The region had to choose between joining Nigeria or French Cameroon. Southern Cameroon opted for French Cameroon. The two regions formed 'The Federal Republic of Cameroon' The reasons for this choice can be found in the way the British administered Southern Cameroon as a sort of province within Nigeria (Amaazie). Hence, afraid of total domination by Nigerians, Southern Cameroonians discarded linguistic ties to embrace the relatively unknown French Cameroon.

Thus Anglophone Cameroon began experiencing another colonial influence from 1961, that of the French. With French Cameroonians in the majority, France and French became a pervading force in Anglophone Cameroon. In 1972, after a referendum, the 'federal republic' was scrapped in favor of a 'united Republic' which resulted in a further loss of Anglophone Cameroon identity within dominant French Cameroon. In 1984 the word 'united' was eliminated from the name, a move which most Anglophones saw as a sign of the recolonization of Anglophone Cameroon by La République du Cameroun.

The Anglophone Cameroonian has since complained of his/her second class citizenship within the nation state, Cameroon.

Anglophone Cameroon & Cinema

The Bantu educational cinema experience (launched in 1935) and the Colonial film units (established in 1939) by the British had very little impact in Southern Cameroon which had suffered serious neglect by the British who administered this territory from Nigeria (Todd 1982). An example of this was the absence of any post-secondary school in Cameroon for the first 17 years of British rule. Southern Cameroonians had to go to Nigeria for post-secondary education. This void was only filled in 1939 when the Mill Hill fathers opened a Catholic secondary school in Sasse, near Buea, the former capital of West Cameroon. As Mbassi-Manga explains 'there were no cinemas in the country (southern Cameroons) until 1949 and then only in Victoria…' (1973: 55). In addition to this lone cinema, mobile cinemas were prevalent during the colonial era (Diawara 1992, Butake 2005). Of course this lone cinema in Victoria and the mobile cinema, like that of Nigeria and other African countries was framed in the colonial context (Adesanya 1997, Okome 1997). Thus as Okome suggests, film became 'one of the most significant institutions of dominance' (27), which underscores the fact that images presented through celluloid carried this agenda and therefore projected a foreign identity. However, most of the activities from the colonial film units emanated from Ghana and Nigeria which all had more than one office of the colonial film unit. By 1955 when the colonial film unit closed down, and changed to overseas film and television center, it left behind '16mm cameras, Studios, and laboratories' in its three offices located in Nigeria (Diawara 7).

In 1961 when Anglophone Cameroon gained independence by joining French Cameroon, the British influence was replaced by French. France had an active policy of supporting its colonies and also spreading its assimilationist propagandist mission. (Ukadike 2003) With this new French influence the newly established French Cultural Center in Buea became a strong outlet for Eurocentric cinema. The center showed films which targeted a young audience like *Tarzan*, *Ali Baba and the Forty Thieves* and Charlie Chaplain movies. At this time too, the Lebanese business mogul, Fayez Olabi opened cinemas in major Anglophone Cameroon towns like Kumba, Buea, Tiko, Mamfe and Victoria (now called Limbe). These cinema halls showed Chinese kung fu movies, Indian films and American 'cowboy' films. Besides this avenue for cinema, the Cameroon Development Corporation (CDC) established in 1947 with its headquarters in Limbe (formerly Victoria), had a mobile film unit which became synonymous with the name Mr Ngalle, the man who operated the mobile film unit. It was part of CDC's mission to show films on certain weekends to entertain its employees. Thus Mr Ngale drove the mobile film unit to various CDC camps to show films. The films were usually American Westerns.

While French Cameroon boasts several internationally recognized films by filmmakers Daniel Kamwa, Dikonguè-Pipa, Bassek Ba Kobhio, and Jean-Marie Teno, the earliest known film on celluloid by an Anglophone Cameroonian may be *Ground don change* written by Victor Elame Musinga, the renowned Anglophone popular dramatist. This film was shot in Buea and in Pidgin English. Then in 1997 Ako Abunaw presented a short film at FESPACO titled *Yo Bro.* This film shot in New York City tells the story of Tabi, a Cameroonian student studying in New York who realizes that his visa has expired and he is up for deportation. In order to evade immigration officers, he tries to pass for African American only to discover that under his black skin lies different identities and it is not easy to shed one identity and take on another. Then in 2005, *Sisters in Law* by Kim Loginotto and assisted by Anglophone Cameroonian Florence Ayissi was released. *Sisters in Law* won the Prix Art et Essai at the Cannes Film Festival and has been screened to acclaim at more than 120 festivals around the world. This film dwells on the work of State Prosecutor Vera Ngassa and Court President Beatrice Ntuba as they help women to tackle difficult cases of abuse in the face of a societal culture that requires them to be silent. The cases they deal with include that of six-year-old Manka who has run away from an abusive aunt, Amina, a Muslim woman who wants a divorce from her abusive husband and the young girl, Sonita who has mustered courage to accuse her neighbor of rape. Florence Ayissi followed this success with another documentary entitled *Zanzibar Soccer Queens.* In this documentary, Ayissi explores the lives of Muslim women through their engagement with the game of soccer. Their determination to play becomes a quest for freedom and self determination which often is challenged by religious and cultural view points. Nevertheless, despite the scarcity of Anglophone Cameroonians as filmmakers of celluloid films, they produced several tele-films with the Cameroon Radio and Television Corporation.

The credit of the first Cameroon tele-film in English goes to Victor Pungong's 1987 *Trials of Passion* directed by Kenneth Komtanghi. This film centered on the life of a young girl who is the victim of seduction and rape by a rich tycoon. She dies in the process of an abortion and her fiancé is thrown in jail in a cover up. It took Victor Pungong almost 20 years to pick up the thread again in 2005 in *Trials of Passion II* where the young fiancé, Awa, is vindicated. Then Thomas Gwangwaa wrote and produced *Seminal Dregs* in 1988. The central character in this film is another young girl, Pamela (played by

Joyce Ashuntantang, the present author), who is forced to live with her father's friend, Mr Ngange because of delays at the university dorms. She is raped by her supposed guardian. Underlying this film was a problem faced particularly by Anglophone Cameroon students who had to go to the francophone city Yaoundé to attend the country's one university. With limited space in the dormitories and the absence of relatives in Yaoundé, Anglophone Cameroon students experienced untold hardships in Yaoundé to gain a university education, a fact which was compounded by the need to adapt to French as the main language of instruction in the university. The policy of the University of Yaoundé was that 'the lecturer had a choice between English and French as a medium of instruction (whichever suits him best) whereas the student had no choice...' (Chumbow 1980: 292) With more French lecturers there the university was and continues to be French. Thus Pamela's rape in *Seminal Dregs* becomes a metaphor for the rape of the Anglophone Cameroon language, culture and identity. In fact the mid-eighties were very productive years for Anglophone telefilms with other productions like The Flame Players' *Visitor from the Past,* an adaptation of J.C. De Graft's play, *Through a Film Darkly,* directed by Bob Ekukole. It is this period that Ngwane recalls with nostalgia as he asks 'Who does not know of the mega success of telefilms or plays featuring Godfrey Tangwa, Kwasen Gwangwa, Vanessa Sona, Njikang Placidus, Joyce Abunaw (Ashuntantang) etc.' There was a sharp decline in the production of tele-films in English in the 1990s. Bole Butake has attributed it to 'the marginalization of English and Anglophones' and the dictatorial management of the CRTV boss Professor Gervais Mendoze who only promoted his own works on television. According to George Ngwane 'CRTV itself had dulled the information, education and entertainment psyche of its viewers through programmes that were alienated from Cameroonians, and through a managerial style that was obsessed with patronage and megalomania.'

Thus at the time when Nigerian films like *Glamour Girls* and *True Confessions* entered Cameroon in the 1990s there was a void waiting to be filled. Also, Anglophone Cameroonians enjoyed linguistic as well as cultural proximity with the Nigerian video films, especially the ones from Eastern Nigeria. In a very short time, Nigerian video films had flooded Cameroon and actors like Liz Benson, Zack Orji and Richard Mofe Damijo were household names.

Cameroon Video Film in English

Mfuh Ebenezer released the first Cameroon video film *Love Has Eyes* in 1998. The conflict in this film revolves around a love relationship thwarted by impersonation and false identities reminiscent of *Twelfth Night*. In the end the true lovers, Clen and Wendy, marry as they overcome Abigail's scheme to deny them a most fruitful relationship. Freshly returned from Alberta, Canada in 1996 and armed with a degree in theater arts, Mfuh Ebenezer wrote and directed *Love Has Eyes* as a challenge to prove that Cameroonians too could create a video film that could sell commercially too. This film bore all the marks of a 'carpenter working without his tools'. Mfuh used an old analog camera and had to improvise with lighting and sound. He did not have the necessary funding, so the film took him almost two years to make, between 1996 and 1998. Originally he could only make 500 copies for distribution and it took him another two years to make a thousand more. Despite the amateurish quality of the acting and cinematographic techniques, this film sought to replicate what Mfuh termed an 'authentic Anglophone Cameroon world'. The cast was all Cameroonian, although none of the actors had attained popularity at the national level at home. The next film after *Love Has Eyes* was *Potent Secrets*, released on September 14th 2001 at a grand premier at the Yaoundé Hilton Hotel, followed by sold out screenings in Buea and Bamenda. The current author, scriptwriter and artistic director (Joyce Ashuntantang) and director Ako Abunaw, had just returned to Cameroon from the USA where they had been living. As Joyce Ashuntantang, explained in another article '*Potent Secrets* was my response to a number of Nigerian Video films I had watched. These films were replete with diverse themes, but the representation of women was almost the same. "Woman" was constructed within a patriarchal ideology reinforcing society's dominant values. With Cameroonians watching these films avidly, these films were agents of socialization transmitting stereotyped images of sex roles, particularly to young people.' (Abunaw 2004: 43-4). So for Joyce Ashuntantang and David Abunaw writing and producing *Potent Secrets* was a conscious effort to counteract the stereotypes presented in Nigerian films. These stereotypes have been documented by other film critics such as Anyanwu, who notes that:

> This image of women as portrayed in Nigerian home video films cut across the country from North to South, though with differing intensity. The difference being that the rituals and murders, which occur in Southern films, do not yet appear in Northern movies. Still, women in the Northern films are not reflected any better; they are seen as greedy, fickle minded, weak, unable to make their own marital decisions and are available for purchase by the highest bidder. (Anyanwu 2003: 84–5)

Potent Secrets therefore dwelt on some of the pressures that men and women go through when faced with social problems like rape, abortion and infertility from a decidedly feminist perspective. Set and shot in Yaoundé, Cameroon, the film had an all-star cast from Cameroon led by Godfrey Tangwa and Joyce Ashuntantang. The response to *Potent Secrets* was overwhelming especially amongst the educated section of the population, and the reasons were easy to account for. The director of the film was a trained filmmaker who understood the art of filmmaking and the technical crew was made up of technicians who had several years of experience working with Cameroon radio and television. Thus the film showed a high level of technical superiority which was absent in the pirated Nigerian video films on the Cameroon market. The plot of the film was well articulated with the absence of witchcraft as a 'deus ex machina'. Above all, the presence of recognizable Anglophone Cameroon actors led many to hail this film as the 'real' beginning of Anglophone Cameroon video films. The BBC's Neba Francis confirmed this view when he claimed in his online article that *Potent Secrets* has revived 'Cameroon's sleepy Cinema' and posited that this film may begin the daunting task of challenging the dominance of Nigerian films in Cameroon (2002).

Nevertheless, the share volume of video films pouring in from Nigeria made it impossible for local Cameroon productions like *Potent Secrets* to thrive commercially. The majority of the Cameroon audience was already hooked on the thematic thrust of Nigerian films with their obsession with the occult world (witchcraft, ritual murder and sorcery), prostitution, and the unbridled quest for money. Also the Nigerian actors had become celebrities in Cameroon and thus video films without these actors were not considered 'real films'. Technical logistics also compounded the situation. There were no mass duplicating facilities in Cameroon and the alternative was to duplicate in Nigeria. However, when the *Potent Secrets* director tried to duplicate the film in Nigeria the 2000 copies needed were so insignificant to Nigerian duplicators that they did not want to be bothered with it.

To make local productions commercially viable, some Anglophone directors decided to form partnerships with Nigerian actors and directors. Splash Network founded by Cyrille Akonteh, spearheaded this move. These films which were usually distributed in Cameroon and Nigeria generated the most publicity in Cameroon because of the presence of Nigerian actors but at the same time their identity and authenticity as Cameroonian films were called into question. These films include *Peace Offering, Before the Sunrise, Wendy I and II, Crime of the Heart,* and *Blues Kingdom. Peace Offering* was directed by Nigerian Amayo Uzo Philips and stars Nigerian actors, Patience Ozukwo and Olu Jacobs. With a Romeo and Juliet type plot this film explores the hatred between two families who are eventually forced to confront their destinies when their children fall in love. Although it was shot in Bamenda, Cameroon the fictional world of the movie replicates Calabar/Ibo cultures complete with costumes and tribal marks. Yet the film was hailed as Cameroonian. *Before the Sun Rises*, co-directed by Cameroonian Agbor Gilbert and Nigerian Fred Amata, starred Zack Orji and Dakore Egbuson. This film explores the same theme of estranged families treated in *Peace Offering* but this time the plot was framed within the context of tensions between Southwest and Northwest provinces of Anglophone Cameroon. The costumes and songs here were Cameroonian but for some the presence of the Nigerian actors took away from the authenticity of the film. However, in terms of sales and popularity, these films were huge hits. In fact the Cameroonian filmmaker Agbor Gilbert has continued this trend of involving Nigerian actors/directors in his productions for marketability. His production, *Blues Kingdom,* which is centered on female genital mutilation is directed by Zack Orji who also acts in the film. His latest film *Land of Shadows* also features Nigerian actors Jim Iyke and Zack Orji.

This pattern of including Nigerian actors to sell the films has also been the case with so-called Cameroon films produced in the United States including *Dream Kweens'*. The advert on the film's website claimed 'The acting in African movies until recently was almost like an affair reserved for Nigerians and Ghanaians, just to name a few. But Cameroonian Lady Kate Atabong Njeuma has changed things with the production *Dream Kweens*'. Ironically the lead characters in the film are Nollywood actor, Robert Peters and Congolese artist, Soleil Diva. In fact, francophone Soleil Diva, who plays the lead female character Jamillah, has a hard time articulating her words in English and stumbled on the Cameroon-pidgin lines which were meant to 'Cameroonize' the film. *Dream Kweens* tells the story of a young Cameroonian immigrant, Jamillah who arrives the USA for further studies. When she gets to the USA she finds out to her dismay that the cost of education is prohibitive. Faced with the opportunity, she takes the challenge of pursuing her childhood dream of becoming a model in spite of the cultural stereotypes that frame her choice. The plot itself falters in a number of places as the film ends up being a showcase of the glitz and glamor of America thereby presenting a skewed image of the life of African immigrants in the US.

This quest to create the ultimate Cameroon film also frames the production of *To Kill a Killer* by Ntemfac Ofege. In fact, Ofege asks 'We have seen American films, we have seen Indian and Chinese films and we have seen Nigerian films. Now, what exactly does the typical Cameroonian film look like?' Ntemfac Ofege answers the question he is posing by pointing us to his 2005 video film *To Kill a Killer.* Shot on locations in Bambui and Bamenda, *To Kill a Killer* tells the story of Mr Victor Abango (Cousin Chinepoh), whose greed leads him to viciously trade off his three children to the Inner Circle, a vile and demonic cult. As the director and producer, Ntemfac Ofege explains 'We set out to tell a very Cameroonian story using state-of-the-art equipment and in the best way video can possibly tell'. Yet this film has all the marks of the popular theme of the occult in Nigerian films including graphic images of occult members eating human flesh. What then makes it Cameroonian? The absence of Nigerian actors? This may be the starting point of the construction of films with an authentic Cameroonian identity. This point is reiterated by Asah Elvis. In a telephone interview with this writer, Asah, a film director with over seven films to his credit, claims that he consciously tries to make his films reflect the Cameroonian environment. These films include, *Destiny of Love, Because of a Word, Ndanchi and the Goat, Vendetta, Ancestral Wish, For Salvation.* According to him 'Nigeria is a huge country with millions of people, so everything they do is big, even their houses are huge and their stories look exaggerated. I try to tell my stories to fit Cameroon ... witchcraft is also practised in Cameroon but it is not as graphic as the Nigerians show in their movies ... and even if I could afford a Nigerian actor, I will not use one because I don't want them to influence my story.' Other films along the same lines include Manka Bridget's *Double Set Up,* Chop Samuel's *The Crime of Sinning, The Widow's Tears,* and *The Director.* These films deal with issues of love and betrayal, widowhood and corruption. What unifies them is that they are produced and duplicated locally on a very small scale.

Another development in the constructing of authentic Cameroon films has been the deliberate attempt to replicate the bilingual (French and English) environment of Cameroon. Eric Ntang's *The Price of Cheating* shot in Maryland, USA, fits this mold. When Jeff, played by Eric Ntang himself, cheats on his wife Brenda (Alice Ebongue), it seems like good fun until one of his many girlfriends Abigail (Marlyse Mbanga) gets pregnant with a set of twins and Jeff is forced to face the consequences of his actions. In the film Brenda and Jeff communicate in a mixture of French and English and subtitles are not provided where this happens. Sometimes Brenda follows her lines in French with an English translation but for the most part she does not. The film also showcases the Cameroonian drink 'pamplemousse' and 'kati-kati' a popular Cameroonian dish from the North-west of Cameroon. The jacket of the film carries the phrase 'This is it. No film will boost the Cameroon film industry than Eric Ntang's film.' Yet based on the current author's experiences as a practitioner in the field, one cannot even begin to talk of a Cameroon film industry in the sense of the Nigerian or Ghanaian video film industry. Cameroonian productions are sporadic and are not coordinated by any governing body. There is no marketing outlet for these videos and each producer/director arranges for his/her own videos to be sold. Since each director makes his own rules the actors and actresses are paid arbitrarily and this often leads to disagreements, hence most directors hardly use the same pool of actors twice which has made it difficult for actors/actresses to build stardom.

However, while Cameroon film directors strive to identify their films as authentic Cameroonian products, video film critics like Ukadike actually decry such a label. Pitting video films against celluloid, they contest the question of authenticity. For example, he argues:

> For the Anglophone videos, the target audience is the local population. Deploying alien conventions, sometimes using them regressively to make video-films appeal to the largest common denominator of the audience, may ensure recuperation of capital investment, but it is also tantamount to mimicry of the West, thus eroding knowledge, imagination and skilled direction. (Ukadike 2003: 129)

Although Ukadike's article suggests that the commercial value and popular appeal of video films render them inauthentic, he does not seem to clarify in his article which 'alien conventions' make them so. On the other hand, Carmela Garritano believes that the struggle over which cinematic texts are authentic African art and which are not is based on the fact that 'Critics of African cinema have primarily looked at films through the optic of Marxist or New Critical social and political criticism, which has provided a base for value and an orientation for reading films' (2008: 38). The intention is not to replicate the debate over 'authenticity or inauthenticity' here but the debate will always be present wherever and whenever one is dealing with cultural representations/constructions.

The quest to construct an authentic Anglophone Cameroon identity in video films in this case, certainly goes beyond the film industry. It crystallizes the anxiety of a geographical region whose socio-political identity has often been threatened by the neighboring, populous Federal Republic of Nigeria and the dominant Francophone Cameroon. Therefore, despite the elusive nature of this quest, it will remain a reality for Anglophone Cameroon video film producers because it constitutes a matter of self determination.

NOTES

1 The English speaking section of Cameroon has gone through different names. It was referred to as Southern Cameroons during the British mandate and trusteeship period 1919-1961, West Cameroon during the federal period, 1961-1972 and in the present Republic of Cameroon it is often referred to as 'Anglophone Cameroon'. This is the name I have used in this paper.

WORKS CITED

Abunaw, Joyce. 'Writing Culture, Writing Gender: Scripting Potent Secrets' in *Crossing Borders*. Anne Schroeder, Ed. Münster, Germany: Lit Verlag, 2004. 43-51.

Adesanya, Afolabi. 'From Film to Video.' In *Nigerian Video Films*. Jonathan Haynes, Ed. Jos: Nigerian Film Corporation, 1997. 13-20.

Amaazie, V. 'The Igbo scare' in British Cameroons, 1945-1961.' *Journal of African History* 31 (1990): 281-93.

Anyanwu, Chukwuma. 'Towards a New Image of Women in Nigerian Video Films.' In *African Video Film Today*. Foluke Ogunleye, Ed. Manzini, Swaziland: Academic Publishers, 2003.

Arnold, Stephen. 'Preface to a History of Cameroon Literature in English' *Research in African Literatures*. 14 (Winter): 498-515.

——. 'Orphans of the Commonwealth. An account of the 1978 Guiness Great Writers Contest.' In *Signs and Signals: Popular Culture in Africa*. Raoul Granquist, Ed. Umea: Umea University, 1990.

Butake, Bole. Cinema, CTV and the cable television syndrome in Cameroon. *Cinema Social Discourse in Cameroon*. Alexie Tcheuyap, Ed. Bayreuth: University of Bayreuth, 2005. 40-61.

Chumbow, Beban S. 'Language and Language policy in Cameroon' in Kofele Kale, Ndiva (eds) *An African Experiment in Nation Building: The Bilingual Cameroon Republic Since Unification*, 281-311. Boulder, CO: Westview, 1980. 281-311.

Diawara, Manthia. *African Cinema: Politics and Culture*. Bloomington: Indiana University Press, 1992.

Doh, Emmanuel. 'Anglophone Cameroon Literature: Is there such a thing?' in *Anglophone Cameroon Writing*. Lyonga, Nalova, Bole Butake, and Eckhard Breitinger, Eds.. Bayreuth: University of Bayreuth, 1993. 76-83.

'African "Dream Kweens" Debuts Abroad'. http://nigeriamovies.net/news/news 136.php.

Garritano, Carmela. 'Contesting authenticities: the emergence of local video production in Ghana.' *Critical Arts*, Vol. 22, Issue 1 (July 2008): 21-48.

Haynes, Jonathan. 'Nigerian Cinema: Structural Adjustments.' *Cinema and Social Change in West Africa*. Onookome Okome and Jonathan Haynes. Eds. Jos: Nigerian Film Corporation, 1997. 1-25.

—— and Onookome Okome. Evolving popular media: Nigerian Video-films. *Research in African Literature*. Vol. 29, No. 3 (Autumn, 1998), 106-28

Mbassi-Manga, Francis. 'English in Cameroon: A study in historical contacts, patterns of usage and current trends.' Unpublished PhD dissertation. Leeds: University of Leeds, 1973.

Neba, Ngwa Francis, 'Cameroon's sleepy Cinema'. *BBC News* Tuesday, 5 March, 2002, http://news.bbc.co.uk/2/hi/africa/1855915.stmNgwane, George. 'STV: The Dream And The Drift' http://www.postnewsline.com/2005/09/ stv_the_dream_a.html

'Nollywood success puts Nigeria's film industry in regional spotlight'. *The Times Online*. 03 April 2010. http://www.timesonline.co.uk/tol/news/world/africa/article7086248.ece

Nsom, Kini. 'Movie Preview:Ntemfac Ofege's To Kill A Killer Coming Soon.'

http://www.postwatchmagazine.com/2006/11/movie_previewnt.html

Ofege, Ntemfac. 'Movie Preview: Ntemfac Ofege's To Kill A Killer Coming Soon.' http://www.postwatchmagazine.com/2006/11/movie_previewnt.html

Okome, Onookome. 'The Context of Film Production in Nigeria: The Colonial Heritage.' *Cinema and Social Change in West Africa.* Onookome Okome and Jonathan Haynes. Eds. Jos: Nigerian Film Corporation, 1997.

Takougang, Joseph and Milton Kreiger. *African State and Society in the 1990s: Cameroon's Political Crossroads.* Boulder: Westview Press, 1998.

Todd, Loreto. *Cameroon (Varieties of English Around the World. text Ser. 1).* Heidelberg: Julian *Groos*, 1982.

Ukadike, N.F. 'Video booms and the manifestations of 'First' cinema in Anglophone Africa'. In A. Guneratne and W. Dissanayake (eds), *Rethinking Third Cinema*, 126-143. New York: Routledge, 2003.

Reviews

Edited by James Gibbs

Jago Morrison, *The Fiction of Chinua Achebe: A reader's guide to essential criticism*

Basingstoke and New York: Palgrave Macmillan, 2007, 185 pp., $24
ISBN 978-1-4039-8672-6

Achebe's fiction is, Morrison notes, 'a staple of the university curriculum throughout the English-speaking world.' The body of criticism of Achebe is by now 'vast and bewildering', and includes over a hundred book-length studies let alone anything else. Morrison's book is designed as a tool by which to navigate the most significant of this criticism.

The Introduction focuses on the immediate success of *Things Fall Apart*, its canonization and problems that have to do with this: the way it overshadowed other work produced since the early mid-twentieth century (to strengthen his point, Morrison could have mentioned here the early African fiction in French) and the way the 'empire strikes back' novel then took centre stage to the exclusion of practically all else.

Two subsequent chapters on *Things Fall Apart* set the matrix for the rest of Morrison's book – hence my concentrating on these in this review. Early academic criticism is dealt with first. There is some eyebrow-raising material here: for instance, G. D. Killam's fixation on the question of whether the novel passed muster in relation to the Anglo-Irish literary canon. As throughout, quotation from the criticism is extensive. Morrison's gloss on this work is deft and lucid and he makes a very good job of positioning critical trends as they emerge.

Turning to later, often 'revisionist', criticism, separate sections deal with language issues and feminist readings. The former summarizes Achebe's views and Ngugi's on language choice (though Ngugi's recognition of Achebe's genius but classification of his work as 'Afro-European' is not quoted) and moves on to Gareth Griffiths' (in a sense) medial position in his analysis of the novel as an inquiry into narration. The latter section centres on Rhonda Cobham's seminal exploration of the novel's handling of gender issues and on the now well-established recognition of Achebe's masculinist approach and his disinclination to explore male / female power relations.

The next chapter deals with two questions: the novel's status as historical inquiry and its insertion within the discourses of Nigeria's independence struggle. Key texts here are Neil ten Kortenaar's project (cognate to the work of Anthony Appiah) to problematize the novel's epistemology and Ode Ogede's critique of Achebe's use of satire and tragedy, structures that bear 'core Western ideas and attitudes', thus disabling any meaningful break with Western liberalism. Morrison's structuring of these sections – one critic's perspective segueing into or setting up a disjunction with another's – is extremely effective and forms a powerful narrative in itself.

Turning to *No Longer at Ease*, Morrison traces a growing recognition by critics – after an initially cool response – of the novel's ingenuity and thoughtfulness, especially in respect of its intertextuality. *Arrow of God* is seen by Morrison as an examination of the collision between 'African sophistication and European naivety' and as a more concentrated attempt than *Things Fall Apart* to explore historical change. Working on similar lines, Tejumola Olaniyan sees it as questioning 'the foundational issue of institutions and their legitimacy.' Again, in this chapter much attention is paid to intertexts. Charles Nnolim's charge of plagiarism (arguing for a 'parasitic relationship' between the novel and a 1953 historical pamphlet) and a forensic scrutiny of this charge by Caroline Innes are covered in some detail.

A Man of the People and *Girls at War* are dealt with in a single chapter. Ezenwa-Ohaeto's biography is drawn upon to trace the tense relationship in the 1960s between Achebe and the Nigerian establishment, which he often portrayed critically through his work for the Nigerian Broadcasting Corporation. On Achebe's apparent clairvoyance regarding the 1966 coup, Bernth Lindfors observes astutely that the novel is 'an African parable, not a Nigerian prophecy'. In his own reading, Morrison describes it as 'a provocation to debate about the future of the Nigerian state'. On *Girls at War* – still neglected – important observations mark Achebe's turn to a concern with gender issues and the ways in which the stories draw on the oral aesthetic.

Finally, *Anthills of the Savannah*, which is seen as Achebe's 'most subtle and sophisticated' novel, and, in Simon Gikandi's view, 'a sweeping meditation on the meaning and failure of nationhood.' A crucial section here is on the novel's handling of gender issues, in the forefront as never before in Achebe, and on the interpretation of this by feminist critics. Excellent work has been done here, notably by Ifi Amadiume and Elleke Boehmer.

At the time of publication, Morrison's book was the only one of fifty-odd volumes in the Reader's Guide series to be devoted entirely to African literature. It is a very useful work indeed. Standards of accuracy and production are exemplary, though I do note that Femi Osofisan appears to have undergone a sex change.

Chris Dunton
Department of English, National University of Lesotho, Roma

Mia Couto, *A River Called Time*

Translated by David Brookshaw, London: Serpent's Tail, 2008, 231 pp., £10.99
ISBN 978-1-84668-671-9

Mia Couto is Mozambique's best known writer, with many short stories, poems and novels to his name, most famously the ground-breaking *A Sleepwalking Land* (Terra Sonâmbula) of 1992. Born in 1955, his Portuguese parents brought him up as part of Mozambique, so that doubts about where his loyalties lay were, as he said in an interview given in September 2007, settled during adolescence. A journalist and environmental biologist, Couto was an activist for Frelimo (Mozambique Liberation Front) in his country's liberation struggle and civil war, but he has also been concerned about its subsequent development, a theme that permeates much of his writing.

Reading Couto is a pleasure because his writing captivates and enchants in its mix of reality and fantasy. As Doris Lessing points out on the back of the UK edition, he is 'quite unlike anything else ... from Africa'. His ability to create expressive new words in Portuguese reminds the Brazilian reader of Guimarães Rosa, who wrote in the 1950s and 1960s. Like Couto, Rosa created a very distinctive literary language by using both regional forms and sophisticated neologisms. The nature of such a creative process must make translating Couto an even greater challenge than usual, so it is a pleasure to read this edition in English of *A River Called Time* (*Um Rio Chamado Tempo, Uma Casa Chamada Terra*). David Brookshaw has done a fine job, producing a text that reads and flows well without sacrificing the resonances of the Portuguese names of some of the characters.

Summoned to attend his grandfather's funeral, Mariano travels from the city to the island after many years away. But, even though the wake has begun and the grave has been dug, his grandfather is not quite dead. The island's Goan doctor says he is clinically dead, but in a cataleptic sate. His demented grandmother wants Mariano to take charge, apparently going against the tradition of seniority, with varying reactions from relatives. Then unsigned letters start appearing for Mariano, written as if from his grandfather. Furthermore, the body of his grandfather is found lying outside the coffin the morning after his death. The letters warn against machinations of the family, guide Mariano forward and eventually illuminate as events unfold.

The reader's natural curiosity about just what is happening here, as if reading a detective novel, is dominated by the captivating tone of the book, its dream-like narrative, inconclusive dialogues, and Mariano's unanswered questions. *A River Called Time*, like other novels by Mia Couto, incorporates several deep and interlinked themes: fantastical events among everyday reality, halfway stages between life and death, voices from the dead that gradually reveal hidden truths, the surge of a crude modernity at the expense of traditional African identity.

There are also hosts of characters and relatives with marvellously evocative names such as Miserinha, Mariavilhosa, and the two aunts, Abstinência and Admirança. Many have varying views on the grandfather's death. Some represent different aspects of Mozambique, such as Ultímio, a politically connected and rather sleazy uncle who symbolises the urban face of Mozambique that has become disconnected from the rural traditions of the island. Ultímio contrasts starkly with his brother, Mariano's father, an ex-guerrilla, now disillusioned and withdrawn from the world. All play key roles in the novel.

The twin themes of disenchantment and the abandonment of authentic values feature strongly in the book. You might suppose that Couto has simply become disillusioned with the outcome of the liberation struggle, but his view is more subtle. In an interview published in *Istoé*, Brazil, during September 2007, he said that, as a member of Frelimo in opposition, he thought that 'the conquest of power would be the end of power – in the sense that everyone would have power' and quoted an un-named Frelimo poet: 'It is not enough that our cause is pure and just – purity and justice has to exist within us.' He added that many political leaders lacked this, even though he recognised that 'those in power have to enter a management logic where it is difficult to see where are the boundaries between the betrayal of principles and adapting to the real world.' This suggests a continuing struggle within Couto, which will likely continue to provide rich material for future novels from an original and authentic writer engaged in the quest for the literary construction of Mozambican identity.

Ester Scarpa
King's College London, and University of Campinas, Brazil
Alistair Clark
University of the West of England, Bristol

Doreen Baingana, *Tropical Fish*

Amherst, University of Massachusetts Press, 2005, pp. 148, $27.95
ISBN: 978-1-55849-477-0

Doreen Baingana is a young Ugandan writer who has already had some international recognition. She has been awarded a Washington Independent Writers' Fiction Prize, and the Commonwealth Writers' Prize for Best First Book (Africa Region). She has been recognised with a short fiction award from the Association of Writers and Writing Programme (AWP), and she has been short-listed for the Caine Prize.

Her collection of eight short stories, *Tropical Fish*, opens in Entebbe in the 1980s and moves to the USA. The stories give us insight into the lives of the three Mugisha sisters, Patti, Rosa, and Christine, born into a well-to-do home that 'falls apart'. Their father is an alcoholic who is eventually dismissed from his position as a senior accountant with Standard Chartered Bank. Their mother, a professional woman, manages to keep the home together and to see her daughters through secondary school and university. Against this background, we have the economic and social disintegration of Uganda under Amin and 'Obote II'.

Christine, the youngest child, is a keen observer of life; she has a vivid imagination and an enthusiasm for new experiences. However, she is easily bruised, so life becomes a series of disappointments. She fights back, both at home in Uganda and in the US. In the process, we get to know her best out of the three girls. In *Green Stones,* she is a child acting out her fantasies of adult life with her mother's jewellery – which we are later told is all fake, as fake as her father's commitment to his family. In *First Kiss,* we meet the fourteen-year-old Christine, jilted by her first date. In *Tropical Fish*, she is at Makarere and involved in an unsatisfactory dead-end relationship with an Englishman. When we next meet her, both she and the story are *Lost in Los Angeles*. African readers from whichever part of the continent will recognise their country people, so well described:

> They live the Southern California suburban life while saving money to build houses back home, educate their kids, make money, live well. What's so wrong with that?
>
> We are going back for good, eventually, but not anytime soon, oh no. (112)

In *Questions of Home*, Christine is 'back home', 29-years-old, but can she settle down to Ugandan life?

Patti is the eldest and we meet her in secondary school. *Hunger* is her story. In an attempt to tackle her father's disgrace, she seeks refuge in religion, and, to avoid facing life and its disappointments, she chooses not to leave the safety of home. She stays on to cultivate her mother's garden and keep her mother company.

Rose has two stories, *Passion* and *A Thank-You Note,* a story not previously published. In *Passion* we meet her as a sixth-former, bright, extrovert, frivolous and eager for life. Her budding sexual awareness is juxtaposed to her class having to analyse *King Lear* with a male teacher. In *A Thank-You Note* she has come to the realisation that 'Each one of us has to die alone' (86). She has AIDS and writes a letter to her boyfriend, possibly the person who infected her.

> I displayed my body once and men approved. I will do so again with burning scars, leaking sores, grey skin. This is all I have left: to die loudly, saying, Yes, I have AIDS. (88)

A Thank-You Note is a wonderfully crafted story and the most successful in the collection. It is here that we realise Baingana is a fine and sensitive writer.

Kari Dako
Department of English, University of Ghana

Olabisi Gwamna, *Dancing with Shadows & Other Stories*

Lanham: Hamilton, 2008, 89 pp.
ISBN-13 978-0-7618-3853-1

The back cover of *Dancing with Shadows and Other Stories* announces that the book has been written 'bearing in mind the generation of young Africans born to Africans in the United States', and that at the same time it aims at 'enhancing multicultural understanding' among an adult public interested in African studies. Reading Olabisi Gwamna's work, one understands that this dual target audience is not the result of an incoherent marketing strategy, but rather a reflection of the nature of the volume itself. Indeed, the book is a curious mixture of, on the one hand, children's stories, and on the other, fictional pieces too elaborate to be fully understood by young readers. This is emphasised by a perplexing evocation in one of the tales of 'Edward Said's discussion of the dilemma of the émigré'. (49)

While this lack of cohesion makes for a somewhat disorienting reading experience, the individual qualities of some of the stories should not be overlooked. For instance, among the narratives suitable for a young readership, 'The Teasing Sunset' features four girls who are sent to a farm to do chores, but are surprised by nightfall after choosing to delay their work to play. The story acts as a cautionary tale, but it also nostalgically captures the atmosphere of Nigerian village life and successfully depicts the potentially devastating consequences of its mischievous child protagonists' behaviour. In the more adult-oriented 'I Saw Her Coming Out of a Dark Hall', which has obvious autobiographical overtones, the writer provides a moving description of her fictional self's relationship with her mother.

The most compelling piece in the collection is arguably 'Signatures', which opens with the main character's reflection on the signing of her name and unfolds into a powerful and symbolically charged story. Slightly less convincing is the fact that two successive tales, 'The Boy Who Did Not Listen to His Mother' and 'Torn Pages', use the same narrative device: they both describe supernatural occurrences that are eventually revealed to be part of a protagonist's dream. Gwamna's writing also displays occasional stylistic weaknesses, and the book contains a puzzling number of typographical errors involving punctuation marks. These flaws, however, are counterbalanced by the author's fine sense of characterisation and occasional touches of humour. These contribute to making *Dancing with Shadows and Other Stories* an enjoyable read.

Daria Tunca
University of Liège, Belgium

Femi Euba, *Camwood at Crossroads*

Bloomington: Xlibris, 2007, 230 pp., hb. $28.79, pb. $18.69
ISBN 978-1-4257-1943-2

In *Camwood at Crossroads* the protagonist, Olumofin Falashe, tries to come to terms with the cultural conflicts inherent in being a modern, educated Nigerian. Not a great deal happens in the novel that, judging from the currency exchange rate, is set in the 1970s. The protagonist, who resides more-or-less permanently in the United States, revisits Nigeria on business. During the visit, he reminisces with a friend over their school days, and in another encounter, a meeting with his father, tries to establish a degree of emotional independence from the old man. Then Olumofin returns to the States to spend Thanksgiving with the family of his African-American fiancée.

Olumofin is torn by the contrasting demands made on him by Nigerian and by Western culture. He is uncomfortable in both, and the novel may be read as an extended rationalisation of the reasons he can never fully conform to either. His outlook is jaundiced. He is disgusted by corruption and exploitation in general; but within Nigeria these strike him very close to home as his father is the leader of a notorious cult. Olumofin, whose complicated inner life is revealed to us at length, constantly draws parallels between the flamboyant, syncretic religious movement invented by his father and the proselytising American Evangelical churches. These also have a place in the novel and initially appear to spring from more respectable origins.

Olumofin is a prickly character, hard to like. He views almost every social encounter as a manipulative jostling for position, in which he is anxious to come out on top. He resents casual demands on his attention from the people he meets by chance, scanning every word and gesture for either ignorance, evidence of his superiority, or status play – in which he engages immediately. It must be exhausting for him to be in such a permanent state of high alert! Perhaps this is the reason for his constant ruminating, his attempts to reduce experience to nicely ordered packets of logic. In fact, the narrative line is obscured by Olumofin's constant flashbacks, reveries and speculations. Not all of the latter are particularly acute: Olumofin's interminable philosophising can tend towards the banal: 'For if a body without a soul is like a woman without a body, what is the body of a woman then? Her soul? If a woman is merely her body, and that body is her soul, then a woman is her soul, a body which is nothing…' His attitude to whole groups of people – women, say, or African-Americans – is often patronising in the extreme. In fact, his attitude to anyone not of his own class and general background is more or less antagonistic.

Nevertheless by the end, the honesty, bordering on naiveté, that the protagonist brings to his remembrance of things past wins the reader over. Those passages of the book more concerned with simple storytelling are vivid, touching and puzzling. So much more is implied by the bare recital of events than by the author's commentary on them. The characters' interactions with each other reveal a great deal about their conflicted motives, their internalised assumptions; the processes of acculturation they are going through and their slow, painful growth towards maturity. Olumofin recalls his and his friends' first sexual adventures, the boys' bravado evaporating at the first threat of contact with real girls. He remembers the intoxicating intransigence of an admired schoolmate. He and his friend talk about their school days, mocking the assumed British mannerisms of an old teacher but never questioning their own set of acquired quirks. ('But seriously, old boy…' Lakija keeps saying.)

The language of the novel moves from heightened description of set-piece events – a third-person omniscient poet narrates here – to simple accounts of Olumofin's past told from his point of view, and to Olumofin's not quite stream of consciousness introspections. Euba uses the image of the crossroads throughout the novel to represent the fertile, problematic condition of Nigeria and also of the protagonist. He applies the image to the African-American family Olumofin will marry into. Olumofin feels an affinity with them, and is at pains to acknowledge the African substructure that give rise to some of their family traditions. The crossroads here represents a crucial moment of choice, full of potential, although things could go either way, towards creation or towards destruction. Eshu is explicitly involved in the narrative. For example, the transformation of Olumofin's father into a prophet takes place at a ritual site dedicated to the god.

Using this metaphor invokes the notion of Eshu as an unstoppable force, turbulent and unpredictably fruitful. Implicit throughout the novel is a notion of the transformative power of unpredictable mischief. In a second thread of imagery, cosmetic camwood powder is conflated with the powder used on divination boards to track the path of omens. This metaphor is less successful; sometimes it seems a little forced, whereas Eshu is embedded in the fabric of the story and seems to pop up sometimes in despite of the author, for instance, in the aftermath of his encounter with an air-stewardess.

Camwood at Crossroads is published by Xlibris, an internet print-on-demand press. This has both advantages and disadvantages: on the one hand it has enabled Euba to publish his novel, but on the other, the book could have done with the strict but fair hand of a sympathetic editor, to pick up some scattered typos and to rein in some of Euba's more abstruse speculations. An editor could also have advised on the conventions of translating African-American dialect into written text, a historically sensitive undertaking. Euba's rendering of pidgin is not half as contentious.

On the whole the novel is much more powerful when it has not been overly processed by the author's scholarship into something resembling an essay.

Folake Shoga
Independent Artist, Bristol

Toni Kan, *Nights of the Creaking Bed*

Abuja: Cassava Republic Press, 2008, 166 pp., N800
ISBN 9789784851817

Nights of the Creaking Bed is a collection of fourteen stories. Based in Abuja, the publisher Cassava Republic is dedicated to producing Nigerian literature for a Nigerian audience and may be found online at www.cassavarepublic.biz. Cassava Republic is making a great contribution towards providing a mature publishing environment for Nigerian authors and readers. The stories in this collection are not looking over their shoulders for validation from more developed countries, so to speak, and it is evident that Toni Kan feels no need to explain the Nigerian context, and no need to translate Nigerian manners into a form more easily understood by Western readers. The brisk, confident economy with which the stories are written is refreshing.

These stories are vivid. The author explores a range of social circumstances typical of Nigeria; the multitude of point-of-view characters given a voice to create an impression of Nigeria as a shimmering mosaic of ethnicities and backgrounds. Kan writes with a real concern for the dilemmas his characters have to face. He has a journalist's curiosity about the range of social problems facing his country people and the desperate tactics they deploy in order to survive. The inspiration of many of the stories may well have been news reports: a baby abandoned here, a kidnapping attempt there. Kan tries to imagine the circumstances that land his characters in their various predicaments.

The seriousness and honesty of Kan's writing, and an impetus towards realism in his style, makes me anxious to put my finger on something that, in many stories, is not quite working. In 'Buzz', an attempt at a *noir* detective story, the narrative is unconvincing because a collision between genres (gritty African social realism versus shadowy stylised *noir*), inescapable to the reader, is not taken on board. We read: 'Buzz searched through Next-door's pockets with one hand, keeping the other on his gun, his senses alert to the eyes in the crowd watching him.' Now that seems an implausibly passive Lagosian crowd to me.

Nigerian *Noir*, what would that look like? Some marvellous conflation of Nollywood and Hammett? Or would it look very like Cyprian Ekwensi's classic, *Jagua Nana*, a novel that combines a disillusioned, stylish, disreputable urban heroine with unlimited empathy for her choices, her motives, and her bad behaviour?

Comparison with Ekwensi illuminates the puzzle. For all his good intentions, Toni Kan doesn't quite inhabit his character's world. He hasn't got quite enough respect for his characters to grant them autonomy. He tries to see the world through their eyes but often doesn't pull it off. In 'Ahmed', Kan describes the title character's first journey out of his northern village to the megapolis, Lagos: 'He loved the gentle touch of the wind on his face. And he loved, most of all, the shimmering macadam and the mirages that loomed ahead, disappearing like hapless lakes as they approached.' Well, no they didn't: the character is sitting in the back of the lorry and the scenery should recede from him, not loom towards him. Ahmed has not fully come alive for the author – he isn't whispering in his author's ear, or Kan could not have made that mistake. Without that alchemy, Ahmed just cannot come alive for us. The austere and horrific description that ends the story confirms the author as a serious talent: yet since the protagonist has not been fully imagined – no other event has anything like the same intensity – callous as it may seem, we don't care.

The quality of the writing and the empathy and imagination shown by the writer mature within the anthology. I wouldn't be surprised if several years separate the best of these stories from the less engaging. Kan has sympathy with his characters, women and men, the striving and the fallen; but he has not yet as a writer managed to free himself from a moralising narrative convention common in Nigerian popular culture. Thus, every sexual adventure ends in disaster, especially for the woman involved, and every step out of line is a step over a precipice.

To adequately describe extravagance, strangeness and unpredictability IS realism in the Nigerian context. But Kan's relentless insistence on disaster – his accumulation of moralistic endings over the course of nearly fourteen stories – makes the situations described less plausible, not more so. A moment's reflection on real life would have reminded him that some sexual adventures end very well, thank you. In Nigeria, as in the rest of the world, I'm sure it's quite possible for women – even poor women – to have pleasant and productive love affairs. In Kan's portrayal there's always a catch, and it's either shame or death. I really don't buy the notion of woman as universal victim, and especially not from a country where one's mothers and aunts, not to mention sisters, girlfriends and wives, are as likely as not to be formidably self-determined people.

If Kan is going to be brave enough to write about sex from the female point of view, I'm sure it will not hurt his sales at all. But I do think, if he's going for realism, he ought to try and expand his view of how sexual encounters develop, and the range of feelings a woman might be going through at the time. One of the best stories in the collection, 'The Car They Borrowed', is also, in a way, the story with the biggest gap where emotional truth should be. What happens between the main couple is actually from a female point of view, unforgivable. The author displays no awareness that he might be missing something here, or that it might be productive when writing about relationships to pay attention to what is not said, and why not, and to how the muted person deals with their feelings. It is also important to understand that these things play out over time. Until Toni Kan attains this level of empathy his stories will be more didactic, and more superficial, than he probably intends.

The last story, 'Age of Iron', more tone poem than narrative, expresses the desperation, frustration and slide into apocalyptic visionary brooding Nigerians may recognise as a recurrent hazard of dwelling for any length of time on the problems of everyday life in their homeland. Perhaps it is this story that indicates Kan's creative motivation, a driven response to the contradictory imperatives of massive cultural change. This collection is a heartfelt reaction from a talented writer; he observes globalisation crashing into a set of vivid, sinuous lifestyles and creates new work from the pieces.

Folake Shoga
Independent Artist, Bristol

Elleke Boehmer, *Nile Baby*

Banbury, Accra: Ayebia Clarke, 2008, 265 pp., £8.99
ISBN 978-0-9555079-3-9

In September 2001 British newspapers reported the discovery of a human torso floating in the Thames. Police investigation indicated that it was part of the body of a four year-old African boy. Further forensic tests traced the torso to Nigeria. Although the precise identity of the child was never established, links were made between it and ritual practices of West Africa.

Nile Baby is a complex yet gripping story that delves into the spirituality of West African life. Written by a very compelling author, *Nile Baby* taps very heavily into a West African mythological belief in *ogbanje*, children who die before birth or whilst very young but return from their spirit world, sometimes several times over, to begin new cycles of life and death to their grieving mothers.

Told from the perspectives of two British teenage oddballs, Alice Brass Khan and Arnie Binns, *Nile Baby* relates how these two friends take away a human foetus from the laboratory of their school. Their initial aim is to use it as a practice piece for newly-learnt dissecting skills. In due course, however, they decide not to return the foetus but to 'liberate it'. However, when they are ready to set the foetus free in the waters of the Thames so that it can begin its journey back to Africa, it finds its own way of leaving.

Apart from 'The Beginning' and 'The Ending' of the book, where the sections are appropriately titled, *Nile Baby* is arranged into chapters that carry one or other of the teenagers' names. This is a very effective way of illustrating that the spiritual issue or experience of this story is complex and that it transcends colour difference as well as the gender divide. Alice recognises her own high African cheekbones in the bottled foetus. Yet, apart from the African woman, Katrina, who had given birth to and lost six children, it is her male, white friend Arnie who experiences the strongest spiritual connection with the foetus.

The central idea of the story, the interlacing of life and death, is flagged from the start with the citation from David Constantine's poem 'At the Time' and a quotation from the *Egyptian Book of the Dead* which preface the story. These inscribe the African belief of the living presence of the dead and the idea that the living dead are important and extremely influential in everyday life. Boehmer effectively and eloquently takes these concepts and interweaves them into a portrait of modern British life.

The problems caused by absent, particularly black, fathers, and by dysfunctional families are also incorporated with these complex concerns about spirituality as Boehmer courageously undertakes an exploration of contemporary Britain. The language she uses is simple yet effective, capturing the essence of West African as well as Caribbean expression and vividly carrying the nuances of African thought, fears and beliefs. The book catches the idioms of colloquial urban usage, particularly teenage talk, so that it reflects the British setting of the story. The language makes the images Boehmer paints both vivid and captivating so that, by the end of the book, the reader is left in no doubt that Boehmer is a powerful and valuable griot.

Elinettie Chabwera
Leeds University Centre for African Studies (LUCAS)

Stephen Simm. *Miss Kwa Kwa*

Johannesburg: Jacana Media, 2006, 213 pp. (R165.00)
ISBN 978-1-77009-260-0

A political satire that employs comedy to explore and offer insight into the gruesome realities of post-apartheid South Africa, *Miss Kwa Kwa* is a vivid, lively, readable book from a new writer determined to make a splash with his first novel. The author, Stephen Simm, who has six plays to his credit, has reworked a script he created with the help of actor Makgono Mamabolo and which premiered at the National Arts Festival in 2004. It was received with great acclaim and provided a vehicle through which its two creators poked fun at the 'rainbow' nation of South Africa. The whole spectrum of South African society – black, white, coloured, gay, heterosexual, greedy, open minded as well as the prejudiced – has now found its way from the stage into the pages of an exceedingly funny book that has significance beyond the society that provoked it..

Simm forces us to look at the realities of the post-apartheid state – the racism, greed, ambition and corruption – through the antics of Miss Kwa Kwa and others, such as Pieter Dippenaar and Leeyan. In the process, he challenges stereotypical portraits of South Africans, and demonstrates how anyone, black, white, male or female, can become trapped in a life of crime.

Miss Kwa Kwa captures the essence of urban South Africa, partly because of Simm's effective use of the journal technique that authenticates the book as the eponymous heroine's personal story. Miss Kwa Kwa's survival tactics throughout – but particularly in Johannesburg – succeeded in making me smile. I was, however, sometimes troubled by the glaring gender biases in the novel. I felt that Simm's women pertained to a generalised stereotyping of women's lives and I hope in any subsequent novels, he will avoid the pitfalls of stereotype. I hope he will strive to reflect the balance of women's lives in South Africa.

Elinettie Chabwera
Centre for African Studies (LUCAS), University of Leeds

Musa Idris Okpanachi, *The Eaters of the Living*

Lagos: Kraft, 2007, 111 pp., N300
ISBN: 978-978-039-195-9

Younger Nigerian writers continue to engage with misrule in Africa, their poetry responding to the crises the country faces as it emerges from years of military oppression and corruption. With *The Eaters of the Living*, a collection of some sixty poems, Musa Idris Okpanachi joins those angry at the plundering of a great nation: he is clearheaded about the writer's role as challenging misrule and the chaos it has produced.

There is much that is familiar about the way Okpanachi's poems howl at cannibalistic rulers, yet his rage grips and finds resonance. 'Code of Silence', for example, gives a picture of a society denied freedom of speech, because of a code that, the poet says, '[is] written across / Our lips / Hanging on our noses' (2–4). In a racy, wobbly style, the poet refers to the implements, the 'muzzles' (11) and 'bayonets' (12), used to intimidate those who speak out, to silence '[our] youths / Who dare face / The sun' (16–18). This poem's outspokenness is fused with righteous indignation to construct a powerful discourse against oppression. Okpanachi has other ways of making us think. In 'We Give You this Country', 'Manifesto', 'Circuits', 'A Prisoner in My Room', and 'Sail', he uses irony, hyperbole, sarcasm and satire. Reeking of revolution, these poems recall the fiery spirit that burns in the poetry of Niyi Osundare, Odia Ofeimun and Tanure Ojiade.

In 'Our Homestead', despite 'stammering' because of 'anger / And [being] hoarse from weeping' (20-21), the persona recounts the violence that leaves 'our houses / Overturned', and insists that he retains his 'stubborn hope' (24). This 'hope' enables him to take a truly revolutionary stance that comes through strongly in 'Where I Stand' in which the poet-persona boldly states

> Here I stand
> Pronouncing death
> To the thieves, the impostors
> The hangmen
> And the false gods. (74-78)

His firm resolution is reiterated in poems such as 'I am Not Tired', 'Rage of Age', 'Be Free', and the particularly energetic 'Let the Dawn Come'. In the last, the poet decides to speak on even though he has a 'whitlow on [his] tongue' (95).

Like many poets of his generation, Okpanachi uses animal imagery to suggest the depravity of the rulers turned cannibals. He compares the utter baseness, the audacious cruelty, and the beastly cravings of the oppressors to the behaviour of animals. In 'Sail', a poem woven around the suggestion that Nigeria is a ship, the progress of the state is threatened by 'sharks, crocodiles / Seals, dolphins / And sea brutes' (7-9). In 'Rage of Age' there are references to 'Vultures' (25) and 'Maggots' (38); in 'The Delicacies of Gods' to 'wolves' (1);

and, with greater subtlety, in 'I am Not Tired' to 'chameleons' (7).

Okpanachi's genial humour, suppressed through the sections of the volume considered so far, bursts out in a group of love and quasi-love poems that are presented as recollections of personal experiences. In them, the poet speaks of love in time of hardship, and of the endurance of what some may see as a transitory emotion. He makes use of the trite words that are often used to tickle fresh minds in love affairs. 'Lily' is a brief example:

You are the Lily
Radiant in a floral garden
You are the white pebble
On the bed of the stream
The honey dripping
In golden drops
From the eternal
Abode of the gods

Who would have thought our fire-spitting, ideology-wielding poet was capable of this rhapsody? But Nigerian poets, and Nigeria herself, seems able to contain such difference. This may be valuable because howling poetry may turn into ashes without burning the skins of the plunderers. If that happens, we need to hold on to the human values reflected in love poems.

Okpanachi's poetic voice is critical of leaders and vital to society. It both reminds us of the struggle and engages us in it. At one and the same time, it makes us contemplate the situation and urges to take action to improve it.

Sule E. Egya
Institute of Asian and African Studies, Humboldt University, Berlin